'This volume should be required reading for anyone in the academy who believes that religion and higher learning can be neatly defined and easily kept apart. Drawing on the European hermeneutical tradition and informed by postcolonial insights, Lewin deftly describes the real-life messiness of both faith and learning and eloquently charts the many ways these two dimensions of human existence unavoidably interact and overlap with each other.'

Douglas Jacobsen and Rhonda Hustedt Jacobsen, *authors of* No Longer Invisible: Religion in University Education (*OUP, 2012*)

'Our contemporary cultural milieu is much more complex than dogmatic secularism would have you believe. In this fascinating, important study, Lewin considers the educational significance of an emerging 'post-secular' reality. Drawing on sophisticated conversations in philosophy, sociology, and theology, this book begins a public conversation we need to have not just about 'religious' education but the importance of transcendence to the educational project as a whole. I hope it is widely read.'

James K.A. Smith, *Professor of Philosophy, Calvin College, and author of* How (Not) To Be Secular: Reading Charles Taylor

'An original, important and provocative consideration of religion and secularism in the postmodern.'

Ian Stronach, *Professor of Education, the University of Manchester, UK*

'The appearance of 'cracks in the secular' means that we all have to find more appropriate ways of honouring religious diversity in our common life together. Education needs some humbler philosopher kings; reading David's book would make for a critical contribution to their formation. I am glad that David has written this book, I recommend it particularly to other empirically inclined sociologists of education like myself. You can be sure that when I need to 'chill out' with the philosophers of education I will be re-reading the chapters of David's book.'

Dr. Beth Green *is Program Director, Cardus Education. Cardus is a social policy think tank dedicated to the renewal of North American Social Architecture.*

'Lewin treats religious traditions as potential resources for educators without attributing to them any automatic authority over teachers and students. He offers a path that avoids the limited perspectives of either religious confessionalism or secularist reductionism. His argument moves beyond the tired aggression, defensiveness and mutual suspicion often displayed by religious adherents and by secular humanists. He approaches education in fresh and fertile ways, critically and creatively retrieving and applying past insights that have largely been ignored or forgotten. In synthesising Teilhard de Chardin and Tillich, Eckhart and Heidegger, John Milbank and Rowan Williams, he opens up a cluster of related elements vital for deep and worthwhile learning and pedagogy, including attention, contemplation, search, sharing and union.'

John Sullivan, *Emeritus Professor, Liverpool Hope University & Visiting Professor (Theology and Education), Newman University, Birmingham, UK*

Educational Philosophy for a Post-secular Age

'An original, important and provocative consideration of religion and secularism in the postmodern.'

—**Ian Stronach**, Professor of Education at the University of Manchester.

'The appearance of 'cracks in the secular' means that we all have to find more appropriate ways of honouring religious diversity in our common life together. Education needs some humbler philosopher kings; reading David's book would make for a critical contribution to their formation. David and I disagree on a number of things, not least his taste in movies. I am not a fan of Bruce Lee films or *Spinal Tap* for example – both of which get a mention in his book. David is not a fan of my insistence on empirical data and I also suspect he would nod benignly at my faith in an authoritative revelation of love and truth in the person of Jesus Christ. Yet David and I agree absolutely that the alignment of education with secularism is a huge problem, we agree that context is, nearly, everything and that education entails submission, attention to practice and a call to unite knowing and being. David and I both vehemently deny that to be religious means to be uncritical and we also question whether to be critical should be the sole object of the liberal education project. I am glad that David has written this book, I recommend it particularly to other empirically inclined sociologists of education like myself. You can be sure that when I need to 'chill out' with the philosophers of education I will be re-reading the chapters of David's book.'

—**Beth Green**, Program Director at Cardus Education. Cardus is a social policy think tank dedicated to the renewal of North American Social Architecture.

Educational Philosophy for a Post-secular Age reinterprets post-secular insights for educational theory by recognising that the persistence of religion in contemporary life raises new questions about the place of religion in education. Two common assumptions are critically examined: first, that the better educated a society becomes, the more secular it becomes, and second, that religion can and should be separated from public education. For too long religion has had an uneasy relationship with education, being seen either as a foreign invader, a problem to be solved, or as a mechanism by which to reinforce particular religious, cultural or national identities. In order to move educational theory beyond the debates about indoctrination and competing rights between parents, children and nation states, the argument undercuts rationalist conceptions of religion and education that tend to frame the debates in terms of competing truth claims or worldviews.

Drawing on a diverse range of theological, philosophical and educational sources, this book demonstrates the continuing significance of the Christian mystical tradition to educational theory. It proposes an exploration of democratic education that brings together two apparently irreconcilable poles: the meaning of religion in education and contemporary life, and the need for a deliberative democratic process that is fit for the post-secular age. It argues that religious literacy can be served by democratic encounters in public religious education.

Educational Philosophy for a Post-secular Age will be of interest to researchers, academics and postgraduate students in the fields of the philosophy of education, philosophy of religion, education policy, politics, anthropology and cultural theory. It will particularly appeal to those, of both secular and religious persuasions, interested in the place of religion in education and public life.

David Lewin is Lecturer in Philosophy of Education at the University of Strathclyde, Glasgow, UK.

New Directions in the Philosophy of Education
Series Editors
Michael A. Peters, University of Waikato, New Zealand;
University of Illinois, USA
Gert Biesta, Brunel University, UK

This book series is devoted to the exploration of new directions in the philosophy of education. After the linguistic turn, the cultural turn and the historical turn, where might we go? Does the future promise a digital turn with a greater return to connectionism, biology and biopolitics based on new understandings of systems theory and knowledge ecologies? Does it foreshadow a genuinely alternative radical global turn based on a new openness and interconnectedness? Does it leave humanism behind or will it reengage with the question of the human in new and unprecedented ways? How should philosophy of education reflect new forces of globalization? How can it become less Anglo-centric and develop a greater sensitivity to other traditions, languages and forms of thinking and writing, including those that are not rooted in the canon of Western philosophy but in other traditions that share the 'love of wisdom' that characterizes the wide diversity within Western philosophy itself. Can this be done through a turn to intercultural philosophy? To indigenous forms of philosophy and philosophizing? Does it need a post-Wittgensteinian philosophy of education? A postpostmodern philosophy? Or should it perhaps leave the whole construction of 'post'-positions behind?

In addition to the question of the intellectual resources for the future of philosophy of education, what are the issues and concerns that philosophers of education should engage with? How should they position themselves? What is their specific contribution? What kind of intellectual and strategic alliances should they pursue? Should philosophy of education become more global, and if so, what would the shape of that be? Should it become more cosmopolitan or perhaps more decentred? Perhaps most importantly in the digital age, the time of the global knowledge economy that re-profiles education as privatized human capital and simultaneously in terms of an historic openness, is there a philosophy of education that grows out of education itself, out of the concerns for new forms of teaching, studying, learning and speaking that can provide comment on ethical and epistemological configurations of economics and politics of knowledge? Can and should this imply a reconnection with questions of democracy and justice?

This series comprises texts that explore, identify and articulate new directions in the philosophy of education. It aims to build bridges, both geographically and temporally: bridges across different traditions and practices and bridges towards a different future for philosophy of education.

In this series

For a full list of titles in this series, please visit www.routledge.com

Buber and Education
Dialogue as conflict resolution
W. John Morgan and Alexandre Guilherme

Henri Lefebvre and Education
Space, history, theory
Sue Middleton

Thomas Jefferson's Philosophy of Education
A utopian dream
M. Andrew Holowchak

Edusemiotics
Semiotic philosophy as educational foundation
Andrew Stables and Inna Semetsky

Childhood, Education and Philosophy
New ideas for an old relationship
Walter Kohan

Between Truth and Freedom
Rousseau and out contemporary political and educational culture
Kenneth Wain

Democratic Education and the Public Sphere
Towards John Dewey's theory of aesthetic experience
Masamichi Ueno

Social Justice and Educational Measurement
John Rawls, The History of Testing, and the Future of Education
Zachary Stein

Towards a Political Theory of the University
Public reason, democracy and higher education
Morgan White

Spinoza and Education
Freedom, understanding and empowerment
Johan Dahlbeck

Educational Philosophy for a Post-secular Age
David Lewin

Educational Philosophy for a Post-secular Age

David Lewin

LONDON AND NEW YORK

First published 2017
by Routledge
2 Park Square, Milton Park, Abingdon, Oxon OX14 4RN

and by Routledge
711 Third Avenue, New York, NY 10017

Routledge is an imprint of the Taylor & Francis Group, an informa business

© 2017 D. Lewin

The right of D. Lewin to be identified as author of this work has been asserted by him in accordance with sections 77 and 78 of the Copyright, Designs and Patents Act 1988.

All rights reserved. No part of this book may be reprinted or reproduced or utilised in any form or by any electronic, mechanical, or other means, now known or hereafter invented, including photocopying and recording, or in any information storage or retrieval system, without permission in writing from the publishers.

Trademark notice: Product or corporate names may be trademarks or registered trademarks, and are used only for identification and explanation without intent to infringe.

British Library Cataloguing in Publication Data
A catalogue record for this book is available from the British Library

Library of Congress Cataloging in Publication Data
Names: Lewin, David, (educator), author.
Title: Educational philosophy for a post-secular age / David Lewin.
Description: Abingdon, Oxon ; New York, NY : Routledge is an imprint of the Taylor & Francis Group, an Informa Business, [2017]
Identifiers: LCCN 2016021538 (print) | LCCN 2016037861 (ebook) | ISBN 9781138923669 (hbk : alk. paper) | ISBN 9781315684901 (ebk)
Subjects: LCSH: Church and education. | Democracy and education. | Postsecularism | Education—Philosophy.
Classification: LCC LC107 .L48 2017 (print) | LCC LC107 (ebook) | DDC 371.07—dc23
LC record available at https://lccn.loc.gov/2016021538

ISBN: 978-1-138-92366-9 (hbk)
ISBN: 978-1-315-68490-1 (ebk)

Typeset in Bembo
by Apex CoVantage, LLC

Printed and bound in Great Britain by
TJ International Ltd, Padstow, Cornwall

Contents

Series editor's preface	xii
Acknowledgements	xiv

1 Introduction   1

A eulogy for the secular? 1
Post-secular education 2
Education, education, education 5
"Once there was no 'secular'" 6
Overview of the book 8

PART I
Understanding the frame   13

2 Formations of the post-secular   15

Introduction 15
The end of secularization 16
Defining the post-secular 18
The end of progress 21
Refining the post-secular 24
A post-secular core? 27
Conclusion 30

3 Religion and belief in a post-secular age   36

Introduction 36
The privileging of beliefs and worldviews 36
Criticality versus credulity 38
Dimensions of religious life 40

x Contents

Christian and cultural liturgies 43
What kind of freedom? 46
The sky is not a cow 49
The propositional frame 51
Educational implications of the propositional frame 55
Conclusion 58

**4 'Only a god can save us': Heidegger's god
after metaphysics**   65

Introduction 65
Overcoming Western metaphysics 65
Thinking as releasement 68
Heidegger's way 70
Heidegger and poetry 73
The deconstruction of the willful self 75
Conclusion 80

**PART II
Experiments in reframing**   85

5 Submission   87

Introduction 87
Philosophical hermeneutics 87
Auto-ethnography: Tai Chi Chuan 91
Primary affirmation as submission 93
Theological affirmation and submission 97
Appreciating submission 100
Conclusion 102

6 Attention   106

Introduction 106
Beholding 107
Paying attention 108
The paradox of intention 110
Intended attention 114
Weil and Murdoch on attention 115
The freedom of seduction 119
Conclusion 121

Contents xi

7 Union

125

Introduction 125
Education without how: Rancière, education and mysticism 129
How in religion 133
The mysticism of Rancière 136
The institution: Discarding the boat and forgetting the finger 138
Conclusion 140

8 Deliberative religious cultures

143

Introduction 143
The hermeneutics of religious understanding 144
The sacred need not be sacred 147
Deliberative religious education 150
Some problems with deliberative culture 152
Conclusion 154

9 Conclusion

157

Index

162

Series editor's preface

When Immanuel Kant, in his preface to the first edition of his *Critique of Pure Reason* (Kant 1929, p.8)[1], declared that "our age is, in especial degree, the age of criticism" and that "to criticism everything must submit" he particularly singled out religion and law-giving as two areas that, although they "may seek to exempt themselves from it," actually should not do so, because "they then awaken just suspicion, and cannot claim the sincere respect which reason accords only to that which has been able to sustain the test of free and open examination."

In retrospect we might say that Kant provided the 'starting shot' for the philosophical *project* of secularisation, albeit that the *actual* secularisation of the Western world, as part of wider trajectories of modernisation, only took hold in the course of the twentieth century. Whereas some would claim that the process of secularisation is irreversible and that it is just a matter of time before it will have triumphed, others argue that the 'triumph' of secularisation has at least been interrupted and possibly reversed, and that our age can best be characterised as post-secular.

Rather than staying within the simple and simplistic opposition of the secular *versus* the religious, David Lewin provides a far more subtle reading of these developments in which the 'post-secular' does not signify a repudiation of secularisation but rather, as he puts it, a complication. In the first chapters of the book he shows that simple oppositions between, for example, the religious as being normative and the secular as being 'beyond' normativity, simply do not hold. The inherently normative nature of education, the fact that education is simply not possible without a sense of direction and discernment, thus means that the 'cut' between the secular and the religious is not as clear and as clean as some would want it to be.

He shows in a very eloquent manner how such expectations partly stem from a very particular, 'propositional' understanding of religion as a (cognitive) belief system, and how an understanding of religion and belief as performative helps to move beyond stale and, in a sense, false oppositions. In the second part of the book he makes clear, through an ingenious reading of the notions of submission, attention and union, that religious discourse and practice can actually enrich our understanding of the complexities of education rather than distort it.

If in the first part of the book Lewin shows why the opposition of the secular and the religious is less of an opposition than is sometimes assumed – particularly by those who see secularisation as a triumph over religion – the second part of the book brings this argument 'into play' in the context of understanding the complexities of education, leading to a subtle and insightful engagement with what matters and what should matter in education. This culminates, in chapter 8, in a powerful argument for keeping religion in the pubic deliberative sphere rather than relegating it to the private domain – an important insight, both for education and democratic politics.

If I were to summarise what David Lewin achieves in this important contribution to the discussion about religion and education in the context of questions about secularisation and the post-secular, I would say that he makes a very compelling case for the need for establishing a 'grown-up' relationship with religion and the religious – one that cuts through the idea that religion can only be understood and performed in dogmatic and authoritarian ways, and that also provides an effective critique of the idea that education can and ought to be a neutral, value-free space. In doing so he not only provides important intellectual resources for engaging with complex questions about education in post-secular times, but also provides orientation to those who are faced with the problems and paradoxes of what it means to educate under the social and societal conditions of our age.

Gert Biesta
Brunel University London
July 2016

Acknowledgements

It has been a privilege to be able to explore the relationship between religion and education as part of my professional activities. But in truth, the line between the professional and the personal has been difficult to draw. This book reflects my own professional transition from philosophy and religious studies, to philosophy of education and education studies. I have had a huge amount of support in making this transition and this book is a product of those varied influences. But the evident lack of religious literacy and the narrow focus of state-managed curricula around the world, in which meaningful religious education appears hard to justify, leads me to a certain pessimism with respect to our capacity to address the geopolitical tensions that contextualise the questions raised herein. Optimistic by disposition, I nevertheless believe that the state of religious literacy is partly a theoretical problem rather than an intractable feature of the modern world. This book aims to engage and extend these considerations.

I must express my gratitude to the Philosophy of Education Society of Great Britain for providing a large grant which supported a significant period of research leave in which the bulk of the book was written. I am also very grateful to Liverpool Hope University for its support of that research project and to the University of Strathclyde for providing me the space to complete this work. I also thank the students and staff from Brockwood Park School and Holy Cross College for the different ways in which they nourished my thinking during the formative years of this book.

I am grateful to the many students, colleagues and friends who have enriched the thinking in this book. In particular I would like to thank Anna Strhan, Claire Cassidy, John Sullivan and Marc and Maya Loon for their careful and critical readings of various chapters of the book in various stages of completion. The book is, I hope, much improved thanks to their insight. The manifold shortcomings remain my responsibility. Thanks to Bart McGettrick, Kenneth Newport, Phil Bamber, Beth Green, Cathal O'Siochru and the philosophers at Liverpool Hope University who have been an inspiration in all sorts of ways: Duane Williams, Steven Shakespeare, Patrice Haynes and Simon Podmore. Thanks also to the many philosophers of education who have supported my work over recent years, in particular, Sharon Todd, Paul Standish, Judith Suissa, Morgan White, Gert Biesta, Sharon Jessop, David Aldridge, Christine Dodding-ton, Richard Smith, Áine Mahon, Joris Vlieghe, David Torevell, David Lundie, Alis Oancea, Bob Davis, Richard Davies, Oren Ergas, Karsten Kenklies, Kevin Gary, Rohit Dhankar, Venu Narayan, Pete Katjar and many others who guided my thinking. Other formative friends and colleagues have continued to have an important influence on me, in particular, Joseph Milne, Todd Mei, Alex Chris-toyannopoulos, Fanny Forest, Valentin Gerlier, Lewis Owens, George Pattison, Bill Taylor, Francesca Sayer, Willem Zwart, Friedrich Grohe and the McGills.

Finally, this book is dedicated to my late father, Robert Ellerker Lewin, my mother, Henriette Caroline Victoria Lewin, and to Anuradha and Alexander. Without their support and love, this project would have been inconceivable.

* * *

Parts of this book have been published elsewhere as journal articles and I am very grateful to the journal publishers for permission to reproduce sections of those published pieces. Chapter 4 draws in part from: Lewin, D. (2015) "Heidegger East and West: Philosophy as Educative Contemplation" *Journal of Philosophy of Education*, 49: 2, 221–239. My thanks to John Wiley and Sons for permission to use material from this article. Chapter 5 draws in part from: Lewin, D. (2014) "The Leap of Learning" *Ethics and Education*, 9: 1, 113–126. My thanks to Taylor and Francis for permission to use material from this article. Chapter 6 draws some sections from Lewin, D. (2014) "Behold: Silence and Attention in Education" *Journal of Philosophy of Education*, 48: 3, 355–369. My thanks to John Wiley and Sons for permission to use material from this article.

Note

1 Kant, I. (1929[1781]). *Critique of pure reason*. Translated by Norman Kemp Smith. London: MacMillan and Co., Ltd.

Chapter 1

Introduction

A eulogy for the secular?

Is secularism dying? Is it time to believe again, to return, like prodigal children, to our religious roots, our spiritual home? Or is the idea of the end of secularism and the *return of religion* itself just a fleeting revival, within an ultimately certain trajectory: the death of belief. Brought up as a practising secularist by agnostic parents who had other things on their mind than religion, I found the community of a local Baptist church in outer suburban London offering a sense of belonging through a religious community framed by what seemed a potent vision of what human life could be. (I should confess that my interest in the church was enhanced by that fact that the Baptist Minister was the father of two important people in my life: my best friend at school, and his sister, with whom I had a brief but formative relationship). These teenage experiences remained important to me, and following a degree in theology I continued to think about the meaning of things and my place among them. Although my commitment to that church was not long-lasting (a not uncommon experience for students of theology!), an interest in *the religious* remained, a quality which, as I hope to show, can be meaningfully applied not just to religions conventionally conceived, but can cut across the sacred and the secular.[1] Through encounters with a variety of Eastern religious practices (training seriously in Tai Chi Chuan for many years), postgraduate studies in mysticism and religious experience, and working at Brockwood Park School, an alternative 'Krishnamurti' school, I developed a commitment to a rather amorphous and postmodern religiosity, which I can with hindsight reconstruct as an interest in the space between the secular and the confessional. Whether the post-secular is the best term for such a space remains to be seen.

Does any of this suggest that it is secularism rather than religion that is in terminal decline? From a European perspective, forms of non-belief (e.g., the 'no religion' category on public documents) are more characteristic of the emergent zeitgeist, though these categories are not identical with atheism (Lee 2015) and seem to stand somewhere between committed confessionalism and atheism. Just as there are many atheisms depending on which God or religion is being rejected (Turner 2002), so there are many secularisms depending on how the *prepositional* relations between religion and society are framed.[2] This leads to the recognition of multiple secularisms that the post-secular must somehow supersede, suggesting many possible formations of the post-secular.

The varied formations of the post-secular invite broad reflections about whether religion has something positive to contribute to culture. My general view, notwithstanding the manifest problems with institutional religion, is that tradition, insight and inspiration permeate the great religious cultures of the world. In the context of the rising tide of secularism in the twentieth century, it became unfashionable to acknowledge these riches, let alone draw explicitly from them. To say that the secular tide is turning may be something of a simplification, but framing this book in terms of the post-secular age is justified since it is widely recognized that religion is an "enduring and pervasive global cultural force" (Bowie 2012, 195). Not only could we draw upon religious traditions for insight and inspiration, but also, for better or worse, our cultural and educational structures are built upon them. While educationalists understandably focus on general literacy and numeracy, religious literacy takes on a particular significance here partly because the post-secular condition appears to leave young people somewhat spiritually perplexed, many finding that the logical conclusion from the presence of multiple modernities is something like the bland relativism that Allan Bloom (1987) lamented nearly 30 years ago, or, perhaps in reaction to such a vapid pluralism, reconstructing a revisionist religiosity that today is identified as extreme. Dinham and Francis (2015) suggest that religious education, in England certainly, does little to remedy this perplexed and polarized condition. The post-secular denotes how things have moved beyond this dichotomy, such that it is not a simple revaluation of our religious traditions, but a recognition of the multiple ways in which secularisms are felt, from benign, protected, liberal spaces of a softer secular public, to a kind of totalitarian disavowal of our historic religious setting (Berg-Sorensen 2013). This points to what sociologists of religion increasingly recognize as the fact that religious history is no longer read as a grand narrative either of secular decline, or of religious restoration.

Post-secular education

Although governments and educationalists around the world find various ways of negotiating the complex relations between religious life and education, it remains an unfortunate fact that "most democracies either ignore religious education or treat it very superficially" (Arthur et al. 2010, 5). This book is primarily concerned to explore the relations between religion and education in general, rather than with the curricula of religious education or the existence of religious schools. But issues around religious formation and education in schools are not separable from wider post-secular educational concerns, so it is worth making some preliminary remarks about the place of religion in schooling.

In the Western world, faith schooling can assume an evangelizing or conservatively religious function, as in some traditional Catholic schools and Muslim madrasas. But common in the UK, more particularly in England, is a 'weaker' form of faith schooling whose purposes are less evangelical, and in which soft religiosity informs the general ethos and, to some extent, the Religious Studies curriculum.[3] State funding is available to many faith schools in England though this state-funded faith school model is less common among secular states, notably the US and France, where a stricter division between religion and education is enforced. The politics of religion in England have shifted since the widely discussed 2003 interview in which UK Prime Minister Tony Blair's press secretary Alastair Campbell famously intervened, saying, "We don't do God." Campbell probably intervened for reasons that speak of a wider suspicion of the place of religion in public life, namely that an inevitable secularization will displace any public discussion of religion, and that this secularization is tied to the 'advanced' nature of Western liberal democracies. The kind of intellectualist neocolonial alignment of Western systems of governance with the triumph of reason over religious superstition has been regularly denounced over recent years and was probably ill judged even in 2003 when the post-secular had yet to be widely discussed. First of all, as Arthur et al. (2010) has shown, democracy is less in opposition to religion than is often assumed, and in fact, finds its roots in the development of particular forms of religiosity. Secondly, and more importantly for the present discussion, religion continues to form and inform public debate. In 2015, evidence of the fact that we do 'do God', in the UK at least, is demonstrated, for example, by the publication of the Woolf Report into religion and public life entitled "Living with Difference", which states that "governments and public services have a legitimate and indeed necessary interest in religion, even though they may insist . . . that they 'don't do God'" (Woolf Institute 2015, 14). Although religion remains influential, it should not enjoy 'special' status over the philosophical or aesthetic. Consistent with the 2010 UK Equality Act, I will not argue for any privileging of the religious over the secular, humanist or atheist, but will suggest that something recognizably *religious* is at play within much educational theory. As will become clear, the post-secular does not necessarily disavow secularism. Some readers will fail to see the need for the language of religion, a question that Chapter 3 will address. A short answer here is that religion is neither going away nor can be entirely separated from public life. Across Europe some alignment between church and state is the norm with the French case of separation being the European exception (Arthur et al. 2010, 16). Nevertheless, the commitment to separationism is often taken to be desirable, even where it is recognized that churches continue to exercise influence within the public lives of European citizens.

What a strict separationist view tends to overlook is that education has at least two key roles bearing upon religious life, one backward-facing, the other forward, or as Arendt (2006) would put it, between past and future. First, religious traditions bind us to the stories of our shared cultural heritage through

4 Introduction

educational processes and practices, bonds that are experienced with ambivalence, both as constraints as well as providing roots. Second, religious life, also entailing education, carries our histories and cultures into an uncertain future, a future that requires acts of human commitment embodying ultimate concerns. The Janus-faced nature of education and religion means, in other words, that education is bound by the traditions of the past and oriented towards transcendence through an uncertain future. By transcendence I have in mind something minimally defined, but sufficient to consider education at all worthwhile: what in the hands of the theologian Teilhard de Chardin (1959) might be called a *faith in the future*. While a theology of transcendence is not the only way to understand religious expression in a post-secular age, it is an important dimension that resonates with the purposes and practices of education. This transcendent dimension has been obscured by the complexities and insecurities of the postmodern, but the time has come to open up a renewed, post-critical dialogue: *towards shared transcendence*.

In the context of the political, religious and cultural turmoil since the events of 9/11 that have come to frame the post-secular, the notion of shared transcendence will sound naïvely idealistic and implausible. The world could scarcely be further from a shared vision of the good life than it is today given the increased ideological tensions and the evident failure of history to have ended with Western liberal democracy. There is precious little evidence of the possibility of shared transcendence, and the idea that post-secularism would be an appropriate context for developing the idea fares little better. Less controversial or naïve is the idea that the post-secular initiates a renewed sense of the responsibilities of educators to think about the political dimensions of modern life which should take more notice of diverse religious and cultural traditions. This has implications for the tidy division between public and private spheres that many conceptions of secularism espouse. It is important, of course, to remember that education is not just schooling but entails a wider conception of upbringing, formation and ongoing learning that makes this neat division between private and public untenable. If the efforts of Ivan Illich, Everett Reimer and others to de-school society – whereby the model of universal institutional public education is shown to be ineffective or even corrosive – were successful in softening the division between upbringing (which might be called informal education) and schooling (formal education), then the division between private and public spheres in education could not be so easily assumed. We will note how the secular division between private and public relies upon a kind of religious illiteracy, but the division also compartmentalizes our educational experience if we think only of education in the 'public' domain. Whatever home is, in these displaced and liquid times, it is the site of upbringing and formation that is thoroughly educational (in the sense of *Bildung*).[4] Because education occupies both private and public domains, and draws together tradition and transcendence, it is worth exploring whether education offers a way to imagine a shared transcendence.

Introduction 5

Education, education, education

In the chapters that follow I draw attention to the multiple modernities and narratives that throw the story of Western emancipation and enlightenment through education into sharp relief. My interests are specifically post-secular insofar as what I take to be a certain Western parochialism arises out of a secularization narrative that, from the perspective of global trends seems increasingly untenable. The educational significance of this secular perspective arises through a particularly problematic alignment of education with 'critique' and the assumptions of progress in which triumphalist reason displaces the pre-modern. In so many ways secular culture embodies a set of commitments that go unnoticed, and so I argue that the practices of secular culture are formative of identity and desire in ways that should be understood as educational. There are harmful dimensions to secular formation, inasmuch as secular culture adopts the ideologies and practices of neoliberalism. To interrupt the smooth flow of neoliberalism requires, I argue, some form of transcendence. I do not necessarily mean by this a conventional conception of God. Transcendence is again minimally defined as for example, a *feeling of absolute dependence* (as the theologian Friedrich Schleiermacher famously put it in the 1820s) or as *an awareness of what is missing*, to borrow the title of a recent publication about the relations between faith and reason by Jürgen Habermas (2010).[5] The argument of this book explores the role of transcendence in education partly by examining the ways in which education entails an attenuation and deconstruction of conventional ideas about selfhood and formation. This could ultimately be seen as a 'negation' of the self. What I call the post-secular *forms of negation* are not 'negative' in the undesirable sense, but might be acknowledged through what John Keats called a negative capability: understanding the uncertainties, doubts and limitations of existence, and maintaining an openness to mystery. While for some people, religions are there to provide answers to ultimate questions, I would suggest that actually religions offer spaces for reflection and opportunities to dwell in the mystery, rather than straightforward answers. The negative capability can be sensed, for example, in the curious uncertainty surrounding the etiology of attention in education. Who is in charge of attention, or can attention be managed? This kind of question is fundamentally anthropological, inviting us to interrogate some deeply held convictions about the tolerance and inclusivity found in modern public life. Towards the end of the book, I go on to argue for a reinterpretation of democratic education that takes account both of the widely divergent views of what education is for and the meaning of religion in contemporary life, while also arguing for a deliberative democratic process fit for the post-secular age. This deliberative culture is important if we are concerned to raise the question of the nature of the good life implied in the secular and religious forms of education. In his quest for a shared educational culture for a pluralist age, Neil Postman reflects on the necessity of gods, arguing that the loss of religion in modernity does not imply the loss of the ultimate

6 Introduction

concerns that the religions ostensibly address. Although Postman is prone to overstatement, he offers important insights that show how the secular public sphere does not remain neutral on the question of the purpose of existence, rather it inspires its own set of narratives:

> The question is not, does or doesn't public schooling create a public? The question is, what kind of public does it create? A conglomerate of self-indulgent consumers? Angry, soulless, directionless masses? Indifferent, confused citizens? Or a public imbued with confidence, a sense of purpose, a respect for learning, and tolerance? The answer to this question has nothing whatever to do with computers, with testing, with teaching accountability, with class size, and with the other details of managing schools. The right answer depends on two things alone: the existence of shared narratives and the capacity for such narratives to provide an inspired reason for schooling
>
> (Postman 1995, 18).

I do not suggest that we need gods or religion to avoid angry, soulless, directionless masses, but that secular and religious cultures embody values and commitments underpinned by narratives. So my own first religious experiences in the Baptist church were not, in fact, the first kinds of religious views or liturgies that formed me. My religious identity was not left unblemished, so to speak, by the atheist/agnosticism of family background even if, in my early years it was largely appropriated by the whims of consumerism, desire satisfaction and the pursuit of happiness. An important idea here is that there is, of course, no neutral formation. The idea of the neutral secular space neglects, I argue, the commitments entailed in any educational process, by seeking to establish education and religion as separate domains: public vs. private. The reader must keep in mind, though, that religion is not opposed to the secular: many Christians, for example, believe in the autonomy of the *saeculum* (the *saeculum* referring to the sort of worldly temporality that governs the secular world). In other words, many Christians and other religious people maintain strongly secularist views, requiring us to navigate a range of associations and connotations around the language of the (post)-secular. This will be discussed in following chapter, but for now I introduce John Milbank and Rowan Williams, who interpret secularism differently and therefore propose very different appropriations of the secular.

"Once there was no 'secular'"

With these words Milbank (1990, 9) begins his analysis of the limits of secular reason. While there may be something to his argument that secularism has come to frame the modern world, he seems to take this insight to an extreme conclusion. What is objectionable for Milbank and other 'radical orthodoxy' theologians[6] is that the secular privatization of the theological has simultaneously entailed a discrediting or denouncing of it. In this way the "alternative religion" (Shakespeare 2007, 9) of the secular order distorts the religious others and denies its own religiosity. Although Milbank and his cadre bring some insight to post-secular discourse, their desire to see reason consummated in the Anglican liturgy seems more *pre* than post-secular. It is Rowan Williams who steers the more balanced course between the secular and confessional.

"Call it what you like, but 'secular' does not quite capture where we are," recently declared former Archbishop of Canterbury Rowan Williams (2012, 2). One might imagine that Williams would be joyfully, smugly even, scribing a eulogy for the secular. But those familiar with the subtlety and seriousness of Williams' thinking would be less surprised to see him in fact plead that secularism "must not be allowed to fail" (2012, 11). Williams recognizes better than most the range of senses in which the term 'secular' is used, and understands that what he calls *procedural* forms of pluralist secularism are a world away from the more aggressive, intolerant, even totalitarian senses of secularism (what Williams calls programmatic secularism) that permit only one form of supposedly neutral public discourse. Williams offers as good a definition as any to get us started: "the non-secular is, foundationally, a willingness to see things or other persons as the objects of another sensibility than my own, perhaps also another sensibility than our own, whoever 'we' are, even if the 'we' is humanity itself" (2012, 13). The significance of the other perspective or sensibility will be vital to what follows, which I will consider in varied terms: transcendence, interruption, submission, being. Williams goes on to evoke the aesthetic imagination to exemplify varied perspectives and ways of seeing. That religion involves imagination as much as belief is a key idea that I will develop. Religions, then, offer varied forms of life that are hermeneutically charged, and aesthetically inspired.

Some of the assumptions that inform what will follow include: the belief that neither secularism nor religion are going away and so must (and certainly can) work together; that pluralism or multiculturalism is of general benefit to all; that a post-secular in which the "massive social and ideological project" of secularism "appears in retreat before resurgent religious bigotry" (2012, 11) is of grave concern today, and that some of our present social, cultural and religious tensions result from seeking a singular secular model that homogenizes, rather than encouraging an appreciation of the multiplicity of religious (and non-religious) expressions. Unlike Williams, I do not necessarily assume that access to those other perspectives and worldviews is key, not least, as Williams himself seems to acknowledge, because this would be an infinite task. Rather, my argument is more modest, entailing more negation than affirmation. It is a project of drawing attention to other modes of *being-in-the-world* and hoping thereby to dislodge the complacency of the current way of being that predominates in the Western world, and of showing that conviction (religious or otherwise) and critique, are not irreconcilable. This necessarily provisional statement of my guiding assumptions and my orientation will be elaborated in what follows.

Overview of the book

Part One involves the elaboration of the nature of secularism in the context of our view of religion more generally. The achievements of the secular age are not without cost. The secular is founded upon a particular framing of the religious, which itself has particular implications for debates within education and religion. The basic argument here is that religious literacy will not be served by allowing religion to be positioned by secular humanist or sociological perspectives, and the neat division of public and private – with religion being confined to the latter – arises from just that kind of positioning. For instance, this positioning reinforces the tendency, common in Anglo-American educational theory, to speak of education as though it is distinct from upbringing: as though upbringing takes place in the private sphere and education in the public sphere.

In Chapter 2, "Formations of the Post-Secular", I explore the range of ideas the post-secular evokes. Insofar as the post-secular disrupts the grand social theories from figures like Durkheim, Marx and Weber that secularization is part of social progress, I argue that the post-secular is a complication rather than a repudiation of secularization. Society is not simply progressing from religious to secular or irreligious; rather the secular is multifaceted, having a complex historical constitution. Like consumer capitalism and the neoliberal order, secularization is not the culmination and apex of modernity, still less the perfection of history and human reason, but a particular set of orderings or framings of the world with their own benefits and costs. The post-secular acknowledges the persistent presence of religious orderings of the world and contextualizes them within a wider discussion of geopolitics and culture. The implications of the post-secular for education are also explored, showing for example, that the public/private distinction, which makes little sense to many religious people around the world, cannot be maintained by constructing a value-free curriculum. The kinds of secularism that encourage pluralist debate are proposed as the best models for drawing insight from secularization. Chapter 3, "Religion and Belief" examines in more detail the reductive Western framing of religions in terms of doctrines, truth claims or worldviews. The notion that religions are kinds of belief systems has led educational philosophers to consider the competing rights and claims of parents, their children and society. These kinds of debate take place within what I call the 'propositional frame', a framing of religion that reveals the influence of positivist philosophy and Protestant voluntarism. Although important, these debates give a limited picture of the relations between religion and education, reinforcing the idea that belief is in tension with being critical and therefore with modern education. Through a discussion of religious and secular cultural liturgies, I show that forms of religious life cut across so-called secular culture, demonstrating the performative nature of belief. In Chapter 4 I examine Heidegger's attempts to overcome Western metaphysics in order to respond to the question raised at the end of Chapter 3: why have we tended to take such a reductive view of religion? This question invites an ontological investigation into the conditions of our thinking and being, something that forms the core of Heidegger's philosophy. Although Heidegger does hint at a turn to something that might be called mystical (if not straightforwardly religious), it is his analysis of the totalizing tendencies of what might be called technological thinking – a one-dimensional utilitarian framing of the world – that is the main concern of this chapter, since I argue its analysis of the world implies a post-secular condition. Having developed the idea of the propositional framing of religion and its impact on education, I move on to consider some religious ideas that are formative within educational thinking.

Part Two draws its structure from the three stages of prayer elaborated in some Christian traditions in which the religious subject firstly submits herself to God, and then is taken up in attention, quietude or silence of God, to finally experience union. This threefold pattern is to some extent an ironic device, since my argument is precisely that such schematic procedures, if they are to be employed, should be used with caution and are in certain respects antithetical to insight. However, many religious traditions employ these structures in a self-subverting way and so, implicitly or explicitly acknowledge that the structures should be taken with a pinch of salt. If only educational institutions were able to employ the hierarchical metaphors of progressive ascent and development without taking them too literally, we would be in a better position to challenge some of the hegemonies of modern education which come under the broad rubric of managerialism and performativity.

Chapter 5 seeks to rehabilitate a concept that seems rather scandalous to the modern autonomous subject, namely submission. Here I develop the epistemological argument that learning always entails a kind of primary affirmation of what one is seeking to learn. This is most obvious in the infant who mimics and thereby affirms what she sees. Drawing on the philosophical hermeneutics of Paul Ricoeur, I argue that an understanding of the role of a kind of pre-critical submission in all kinds of knowing and learning will help us to mediate the sharp cultural and educational opposition between being critical and being credulous. Attention is the subject of Chapter 6 where I argue that conventional views of managing attention through forms of coercion fail to appreciate the delicate nature of attention. I show how religious traditions and some educational philosophers offer rich accounts of attention which go beyond the rather narrow and utilitarian ideas currently popular among practitioners of mindfulness, for example. In Chapter 7 I draw together the discussions of submission and attention towards their spiritual culmination in the concept of union, an ambitious and rather unlikely concept for educational theorists to consider. The guiding paradox of the chapter is that mystical union generally presupposes that the religious subject is already enlightened or united with God, and simply has to *recognize* what already is. Drawing on figures like Rancière and Krishnamurti, I propose that education similarly must be able, from time to time, to denounce the progressive structures that it otherwise relies upon. One way into this is to

10 Introduction

see those structures metaphorically rather than literally. In a certain sense, as Rancière argues, equality between educator and student is already present, to be verified. The argument leads to an account of deliberative processes within religion, religious education and education more broadly, which I discuss in Chapter 8. Drawing on Biesta's account of deliberative democratic processes in education, I argue that religious views cannot be relegated to a private sphere not least because if placed there, they remain closed off from public deliberative culture. We have an unhelpful tendency to view religious commitments as inviolable, making them hostile to deliberative culture. But, in fact, most religious traditions have within them rich, albeit inconsistent, histories of hermeneutical complexity, demonstrating some capacity for a post-secular synthesis of deliberative and religious commitment. This is pluralist without being exclusivist, committed without being uncritical, educational without being paternalist.

This book is concerned that the ongoing presence of religion in modern life is too readily disregarded by educationalists who see it either as a foreign invader, a problem to be solved, or as a mechanism by which to reinforce particular religious, cultural or national identities. Every religion is differently inflected and enacted, and so the arguments developed here are broad, intended to destabilize some of the settled assumptions around the place of religion in education either for the separationists, or for those who regard education as a vehicle for religious formation. It is a book for those confessionally committed who feel that the modern age is too quick to marginalize the religious, but also for atheists or humanists impatient with the enduring influence of religion in public life. But those between the two will probably find the most to recognize here. As I endeavour to give form and name to the cracks between the secular and the confessional, every perspective brings some insight to a debate that can afford to exclude no one across the spectrum of belief (which should be read to include 'non-belief' of atheism). I hope that my efforts to speak to everyone do not result in each reading an apology for an other, and that what follows is more for everyone than for no one.

Notes

1 John Dewey (1986) was one of many philosophers to make the distinction between religions as historical and social entities which tend to entail metaphysical beliefs, from a distinctive religious quality that does not necessitate the institutional aspect of a particular historical tradition.

2 Anna Strhan has analyzed how secularism is differently related to (as she puts it, *instaured in*) certain Christianities. Her research focuses on the case of British evangelicalism to consider how secularism can be placed either 'against' (as antagonist) or 'with' (as partner) religious self-understanding (Strhan 2012).

3 See Pike (2010) for the distinction between strong and weak faith schools. Religious Studies in England is generally understood to take a non-confessional approach to religion in general in which many traditions (including secularism and humanism) might be studied. This is some way from the confessional orientation of traditional or evangelizing religious instruction. This book will only touch upon issues of religious education

Introduction 11

as a curricula subject, which, although hardly settled, are dealt with at length elsewhere (e.g., Conroy et. al, 2013; Aldridge 2015).

4 The term *Bildung*, roughly though inadequately translated as education/formation/upbringing, is important to Mollenhauer (2014) who provides a clear critique of this kind of compartmentalization of education and culture. *Bildung* was introduced into the German language by the medieval mystical theologian Meister Eckhart (1260–1328) and the term became established as a central concept within pedagogy among German theorists of the eighteenth century, continuing to be influential in the continental tradition today. Thus the notion that modern educational ideas have religious roots is vividly illustrated. My thanks to Karsten Kenklies for drawing my attention to this connection with Eckhart.

5 While Habermas' central concern is on what is missing within the debate between religious and secular citizens, the phrase captures a sense of the incompleteness of purely secular discourse.

6 Led by John Milbank and Catherine Pickstock, Radical Orthodoxy is a movement that originated within British theology that seeks to assert a renewed confidence of theology following the tumultuous contortions of the theology of the twentieth century in which theologians were often in retreat or apologists (see Shakespeare 2007 for a critical appraisal).

References

Aldridge, D. (2015). *A Hermeneutics of Religious Education*. London: Bloomsbury.

Arendt, H. (2006). *Between Past and Future: Eight Exercises in Political Thought*. London: Penguin.

Arthur, J., Gearon, L., & Sears, A. (2010). *Education, Politics and Religion: Reconciling the Civil and the Sacred in Education*. London: Routledge.

Berg-Sorensen, A. (ed.). (2013). *Contesting Secularism: Comparative Perspectives*. London: Routledge.

Bloom, A. (1987) *The Closing of the American Mind*. New York: Simon & Schuster.

Bowie, B. (2012). "Human Rights Education and the Post Secular Turn" *Journal of Beliefs & Values: Studies in Religion & Education*, 33: 2, 195–205.

Conroy, J., Lundie, D., Davis, R., Baumfield, V., Barnes, P., Gallagher, T., Lowden K., Bourque, N., Wenell, K. (2013). *Does Religious Education Work?* London: Bloomsbury.

Dewey, J. (1986). *Essays, a Common Faith: The Collected Works of John Dewey, 1882–1953*. Electronic edition. Retrieved from https://www.uio.no/studier/emner/uv/uv/UV9406/dewey-john-(1986).-essays-a-common-faith.pdf

Dinham, A., & Francis, M. (ed.). (2015). *Religious Literacy in Policy and Practice*. Bristol: Policy Press.

Habermas, J. (2010). *An Awareness of What Is Missing: Faith and Reason in a Post-Secular Age*. Cambridge: Polity Press.

Lee, L. (2015). *Recognizing the Non-Religious: Reimagining the Secular*. Oxford: Oxford University Press.

Milbank, J., (1990) *Theology and Social Theory: Beyond Secular Reason*. Oxford: Wiley-Blackwell.

Mollenhauer, K. (2014). *Forgotten Connections: On Culture and Upbringing*, N. Friesen, trans. London: Routledge.

Pike, M. (2010). "A Tale of Two Schools: Comparing and Contrasting Jacobus Fruytier Scholengemeenschap in the Netherlands and Bradford Christian School in England" *Journal of Beliefs & Values: Studies in Religion & Education*, 31: 2, 181–190.

12 Introduction

Postman, N. (1995). *The End of Education: Redefining the Value of School*. New York: Vintage Books.

Shakespeare, S. (2007). *Radical Orthodoxy: A Critical Introduction*. London: SPCK.

Strhan, A. (2012). "Latour, Prepositions and the Instauration of Secularism" *Political Theology*, 13: 2, 200–216.

Teilhard de Chardin, P. (1959). *The Future of Mankind*. New York: Harper and Row.

Turner, D. (2002). "How to be an Atheist" *New Blackfriars*, 83, 317–335.

Williams, R. (2012). *Faith in the Public Square*. London: Bloomsbury.

Woolf Institute. (2015). "Living with Difference: Community, Diversity and the Common Good" Report of the Commission on Religion and Belief in British Public Life.

Part I

Understanding the frame

Chapter 2

Formations of the post-secular

Introduction

In the run-up to Christmas 2015, the fresh breeze of secularism blew through a Kentucky school where, following complaints from some parents, a production of *A Charlie Brown Christmas* reportedly removed biblical references in order to comply with US federal laws designed to protect educational institutions from religious interference. As a state school superintendent confirmed "[t]he U.S. Supreme Court and the 6th Circuit are very clear that public school staff may not endorse any religion when acting in their official capacities and during school activities" (Reuters 2015). In the land of the free, Christmas plays cannot be explicitly religious, or at least must not contain biblical references so long as the state enforces this partition. Despite some secularist rhetoric, the porous nature of this partition has long been in evidence in the work of figures like Alexis de Tocqueville in the nineteenth century and Robert Bellah in the twentieth. Both offer accounts of how American civil religion is embodied in apparently secular symbols such as the presidency, the flag and the Pledge of Allegiance (see Bellah 1967). But why does the placement of the *Peanuts* symbols and brand not provoke similar reactions about indoctrination into forms of secularism or consumerism? Is it simply that Charlie Brown and his pals present no religious ordering of the world? One might imagine that the ensuing 'outrage' from parents and some media outlets (Fox News Insider 2015) can be justified as a post-secular response: religion is making a comeback, and public institutions had better adjust to this revisionist religiosity. I certainly hope that the post-secular is not reduced to a kind of reactionary agitation, partly because reported outrage is rarely a secure ground for meaningful dialogue, but also because the post-secular is more complex than any revivalism. Nevertheless, as I will go on to argue, the post-secular can be identified as a context in which the question of the relations between religion and education can, indeed must, be asked, and so these debates about the place of the Bible and festivals in publically funded institutions suggest that we cannot maintain the simplistic secular separationism that is present in the idealized secular republic.

16 Formations of the post-secular

What philosophical, ethical and pedagogical issues are raised by the new context of the post-secular? These questions form the main concern of this chapter. How we understand the term *secular* and what is intended by the prefix 'post' are by no means settled. Perhaps for this reason educational theorists have only recently begun to address the question of the post-secular.[1] In what follows I begin by exploring the varied conceptions of secularism and the post-secular, concluding that the post-secular complicates rather than overturns the so-called secularization thesis. The development of the science of social change in the nineteenth century, evident most clearly in Marx, Durkheim and Weber, told the story of progress culminating in the secular 'modern world'. The horrors of the twentieth century showed that something was amiss, though the rationalism and an associated skepticism have been hard to shake. My wider aim here is to draw attention to the increasing visibility of counter-narratives to the progressivist/rationalist view. In particular I take issue with the alignment of education with secularization and the assumptions of progress in which triumphalist reason displaces the premodern. One reason 'Western' education is sometimes regarded with suspicion, is its (often uncritical!) alignment with a conception of secular critique. I question the idea that to be modern is to be secular and critical, and therefore, by implication, to be religious means not yet fully critical, or modern. I do not mean to belittle the extraordinary achievements of modern education, or the general benefits – scientific, technological, social, etc. – of the modern world. Nor is there any excuse for the extreme antipathy towards the ideals of modern universal education expressed by extremist views (which I hesitate to call 'fundamentalist' still less 'religious' views), most obviously in the form of the Taliban or Boko Haram. But this polarized picture is too easily framed as an international conflict between modern, secular ideals, and crypto-religious ideologies that seem consigned to a life stuck in the past. The discourse of the post-secular provides an opportunity to mediate between these poles in ways that may not be obvious at first. This mediation is possible particularly through an exploration of the nature of religion and belief, a discussion that will be picked up in Chapter 3, where I question the idea that religion and belief are basically reducible to doctrines, truth claims or worldviews.

The end of secularization

Is Gianni Vattimo (2003, 29) right to say that the process of secularization ended around the close of the twentieth century? Detecting the waning influence of the secular, Steve Bruce presented a renewed case for secularization in Western societies, arguing that many of the strongest accounts of secularization across the social sciences (e.g., Marx, Weber, Durkheim and Freud) were being displaced by weaker, less thoroughgoing counter-secularization analyses that emerged towards the end of the twentieth century. Though descriptive of trends in post-Enlightenment Britain and across Europe, Bruce's affirmation of "a long-term decline in the power, popularity and prestige of religious beliefs and rituals" (Bruce 2002, 44) does not account for, and seems inconsistent with, developments and events across the globe. One year after Bruce's publication, the anthropologist Talal Asad announced the end of a certain picture of secularism as a progressive, liberal project in his book *Formations of the Secular*, stating that "[i]f anything is agreed upon, it is that a straightforward narrative of progress from the religious to the secular is no longer acceptable" (Asad 2003, 1). Asad, and those who have developed his lines of analysis, such as Saba Mahmood, José Casanova, William Connolly, Wendy Brown and many others (Scott and Hirschkind 2006), have enriched the terms of the debate around secularization. Nevertheless, the sense and contexts in which secularization has faltered remains an ongoing debate.

The turbulence across many parts of the world since the turn of the millennium (wars, revolutions, insurgencies and the like) has revealed a world of dizzying complexity where struggles do not result in identifiable victors and vanquished, but pervasive and perpetual conflicts cutting across political, cultural, religious and ethnic identities. Social, economic and environmental problems magnify – and perhaps have a decisive influence upon – these issues and differences. A widespread *fear of secularism* around the world is hard to disentangle from increased fundamentalism leading to the now commonplace observation that "secularism and fundamentalism feed off each other" (Williams 2012, 16).[2] A general fear of the 'other' is surely bound up with increasing religious fanaticism and fundamentalism that seem built into global tensions. While hard to explain, these fears cannot be dismissed as a temporary regression that swim against an inevitable tide of progressive enlightenment rationalism. Rowan Williams sees the instrumentalization of social relations as the characteristic and problematic effect of what he calls a *programmatic secularism*, which he defines as an intolerance of any religious expression within public life. The role of the public sphere is thereby reduced to the mediation of private interests. For Williams, social life cannot be reduced to the administration of more or less successful methods of maintaining public order and upholding private freedoms, but inevitably relies upon moral and social orders grounded in ultimate principles even if those orders are diverse and principles contested. The idea that these principles can be entirely eliminated from public life does, to some extent, feed some of the fears of those who feel excluded by this kind of minimalist, liberal public. From this point of view, religious revivalism and fundamentalism across the world cannot simply be explained away as temporary conservative reactions against aspects of modernity and postmodernity. The excesses of fanatical religiosity must be addressed carefully and with some sensitivity to context and recent postcolonial history if those excesses are to be mitigated or moderated.

Can the post-secular help us address these tensions? Post-secularism offers us an opportunity to engage with the contributions of our religious traditions without denying the achievements of modernity, partly because it resists and overturns the Eurocentric coalition between modernity and secularization

(Davie 2002). Asad's insight concerning the limitations of the secular invites us to introduce the concept of the post-secular, a term which Asad himself does not use in his book *Formations of the Secular* (2003), but one that has come to identify, among other developments, the so-called 'return of religion'.

What of this putative post-secular return of religion? Hasn't religion undergone a slow demise as churches fall into disuse, or are converted into upmarket residences? The Woolf Report provides a recent snapshot of the rise in numbers of people with non-religious beliefs and identities in the UK, from just under a third in 1983 to nearly 50% in 2015. The numbers who identify themselves as Anglican has slumped in the same period from 40% to 17% (Woolf Report 2015, 15). It is hard to argue against the idea that this decline suggests that religion should have less influence in educational affairs. John White (2004a) has long argued against the privileged place that religious education has enjoyed in the English curriculum.[3] But acknowledging the undue influence of religion in schools does not deny the urgent need for religious literacy (Dinham 2015). Religious literacy will help us move beyond debates about indoctrination and the competing claims of children, parents and state on matters of religion towards a more meaningful discussion of the values attached to religion and belief. So despite the decline of religion in Britain, philosophers, sociologists, anthropologists and theologians have all contributed to complicating the narrative of the general demise of religion. But I want to argue that understanding the post-secular takes on a particular significance in the present age because it encourages us to move beyond the normative debate about whether religion should or should not have a role in public education, to examine instead the ways religiosity (conceived more broadly than formal subscription to a set of doctrines) is inevitably involved in education. By this I mean that decisions about the ultimate purposes and values of an educational process are not optional, a point recently made by a Church of England report: "There is no such thing as neutral education. As soon as we begin to teach something to someone else, we are inevitably making value judgements about *what* we are teaching, *how* we are teaching it and *why* we are teaching it" (Church of England 2015). For certain readers less sanguine about any contribution of theology to educational theory, it will be of some regret that "the human sciences since the Age of Enlightenment have tried in vain to exorcise theology" (Bargatzky 1996). I want to maintain the language of *the religious* for reasons that will become clear, but which boil down to the simple idea that religion and education can be mutually supportive and illuminating (Sullivan 2012).

Defining the post-secular

In exploring the significance of the post-secular in modern philosophy and social theory for educational philosophy, I would like to provide an unambiguous definition of the key term *post-secular* that goes beyond the notion of a return, or what Williams (2012, 22) has called "restorationist religiosity". This

Formations of the post-secular 19

noble ambition is, however, fraught with difficulties. Like other similar terms (postmodern, poststructural), there are many conceptual issues and potential confusions with the framing of the post-secular. In a general sense the post-secular refers to the idea that modernity no longer entails an inevitable march towards secularism and the loss of faith. But already we are hinting at problematic conflations: of *secularism*, a term used to define a worldview in which religion is largely absent, with *secularization*, an historical process in which as societies 'progress' and modernize, religion loses its cultural and social significance (Casanova 2009). The latter process is itself easily related to the growth of atheism or humanism, but ought not to be identified with it. This failure to distinguish between a process and worldview makes it all too easy to overlook an arguably more fundamental distinction: namely the secular as the public domain which is free of the private interests of particular individuals and groups (which does not necessarily imply a loss of faith, but rather a privatization of it), and the secular as a broader process in which society is generally less religious. For this reason it could be argued that we are better off referring not to the space between the secular and the confessional, but between the secular and the theocratic because the secular does not oppose faith as such, but social institutions that incorporate religious commitments (Blair 2010, 23; Sullivan 2012, 185; Williams 2012, Chapter 2). Even though we should acknowledge that secularism, a general loss of faith, and a rise in atheism are by no means identical, there are many complex intersections and cross-pressures rendering a neat division between a secular public domain and a private religious sphere untenable. In practical terms this complexity is further exemplified by the fact that religious people can and do reasonably argue for a secular education environment.[4]

Not only is a neat division between private and public untenable, but it may also do violence to a range of marginal and not-so-marginal religious perspectives. This is partly because few religious traditions would accept the idea that religion can be entirely left out of public life, but also because the public sphere cannot be 'neutral' since, as Williams (2012, 13) puts it "evaluative discourse leaks out into the public sphere, sometimes in the moralizing rhetoric of political leaders, sometimes in the improvised rituals (of celebration or mourning or solidarity) that sporadically take over some part of the public territory." Once conceived as an inclusive principle of nondiscrimination, the privatization of religion, in fact, makes a nonsense of many central religious perspectives since "the very idea of deriving law from sacred texts is a repudiation of the public/private distinction" (Fox 2002, 22). There are good reasons why we have been so keen to embrace the idea that religion should be contained in the private sphere. It respects the commitments and values of citizens and releases shared dimensions of social life from the weight of those commitments. But as Asad suggests, there are equally good reasons why religion cannot be contained in this way, not least because religion is, by definition, a communal enterprise which could be seen to push against such containment. William Connolly (2006, 75) has neatly summarised Asad's critical perspective on the secular, a

20 Formations of the post-secular

perspective which presents the division between private and public as reflecting a partisan view of social and religious life:

1. Secularism is not merely the division between public and private realms that allows religious diversity to flourish in the latter. It can itself be a carrier of harsh exclusions. And it secretes a new definition of "religion" that conceals some of its most problematic practices from itself.
2. In creating its characteristic division between secular public space and religious private space, European secularism sought to shuffle ritual and discipline into the private realm. In doing so, however, it loses touch with the ways in which embodied practices of conduct help to constitute culture, including European culture.

Asad's analysis is broadly consistent with Williams' distinction between procedural and programmatic secularism. Procedural secularism takes a more pluralist attitude which disavows favour to any religious or non-religious group, while trying to maintain a broad representation for all (as, for example, in Indian public life), while programmatic secularism seeks to iron out any and every public manifestation of religious allegiance, with France often cited as the paradigmatic case (Williams 2012, 2).[5] So if the secular, as the neat division between private and public, cannot be maintained, we should avoid straightforwardly defining post-secularism as the reintegration of religion and public life since something recognisably religious has always formed part of our cultural identities. Thus, echoing Latour, the post-secular announces that we may never have been secular.

A more general sociological account of religion would have to acknowledge that across the world, societies are not becoming less religious. Even if it is the case that less people attend organized religious services, or that Britain's hidden majority choose to identify with the non-religious category, there is a pervasive interest in alternative religious categories and expressions (King 2009; Lee 2015; Woodhead and Catto 2012). But the view that traditional services are in decline seems only straightforwardly true of the European case. From the perspective of the academic community in London, for example, the ebbing tide of faith given famous expression 150 years ago in Matthew Arnold's poem "Dover Beach" appears to be a prescient intimation of the general trend of the twentieth century and beyond. Beyond British shores Christianity is, in fact, enjoying vigorous and continued growth: across much of Africa, particularly in Nigeria and South Sudan, but also in many other parts of the world, such as Norway, China and India, millions of people are joining or forming Christian churches and communities, not to speak of the growth of other religions, particularly Islam.[6] No doubt there are complex reasons for the wide growth in Christianity or Islam today, some of which might not appear conventionally religious, certainly not if we reduce religion to a commitment to propositional beliefs. There are, for example, perceived 'forms of capital' available to church communities, ways out of other forms of socio-cultural bondage as the Dalit (untouchable) Christians of India show. Add to this the complex interactions between ethnic and cultural identity in which religious expression, particularly in the context of increased migration, is an important part of religious identity and experience. Then there are the socio-political forces that have placed more pressure on relations between Christian, Muslim and other communities. In short, simple narratives of religious or cultural change – especially those narratives that see critical secularism replacing committed faith positions – are no longer tenable.

From the perspective of the nation state, the emergence of avowedly secular nations over recent centuries, in Turkey, Russia, the US, India and China, is far from linear. Gardom (2011) points out that each of these states, which when combined represent nearly half the world's population, is either struggling to maintain the separation of church and state, or is finding that religion has a range of complex influences on public life. Between Turkey and France the concept of laïcité (the separation of church and state) is instantiated in very different ways, revealing that the practices of secularism are certainly not uniform and become suffused with political interests and other social forces. The Russian government, for instance, appears to be both giving support to, and drawing support from, the Russian Orthodox Church presumably to reinforce national identity. A clear and singular account of the persistent presence of religious influence on public or political life is scarcely possible, and certainly not here held up as an ideal, but as a factor contributing to the complexities of the present post-secular condition.

This points to what Grace Davie (2002) calls the 'European exception,' whereby the conviction that modernization will inexorably bring about secularization is a Eurocentric prejudice. This goes to the heart of the parochialism that this book is addressing: to be modern is assumed to be secular, and so secularization and education become identified both by Europeans who call for a secular education system, and by many religious people around the world who identify 'European' educational processes as allied to problematic forces clothed in secularization. Hence one can wonder whether UNESCO's 'Education for all' agenda, which represents a rather narrow form of what it means to be educated (Black 2010; Nguyen 2010), might be antagonistic towards educational systems where the separation of religion and education would be entirely inconceivable.

The end of progress

There are other ways of defining and interpreting the turning of the secular tide. The rise of science and technology, the European wars of religion of the sixteenth and seventeenth centuries and the subsequent Westphalian treatises, the Enlightenment, modernity and postmodernity have all contributed to a sense that history is inexorably moving beyond the myths of our premodern forebears with their enchanted but incorrect worldviews, from primitive to progressive. It is hardly surprising that many of us have been seduced by the idea that human beings are coming of age, that reason is finally prevailing over superstition. And in the face of the developing empirical case against secularization as the loss of belief and practice, many secularists make a normative appeal for secularization that seems to take on a missionary, almost messianic quality. The religious mission has been replaced by secular/atheist zeal visible in the increasingly passé 'new' atheism of figures such as Richard Dawkins, Daniel Dennett and Sam Harris. It seems likely that the sharp tone within 'aggressive secularism' reflects a fear of resurgent religious bigotry, which itself seems more reactionary than substantive. If we are to escape this *reactionary circle*, then we will need a more nuanced and circumspect analysis that first of all would see through a naïve, rather Eurocentric, progressivism. As many post-secular theorists have argued, history has turned out to be more complicated than any neo-Hegelian narrative of *Geistesgeschichte* (roughly understood as cultural history in progressive development).[7] But, as the recent history of Christian theology suggests, this does not mean that traditions do not change and evolve.

Despite the impression of the Christian Church as a conservative ecclesiastical institution resistant to reform, Christian theologians have made significant efforts to reinterpret their tradition in light of modernity. In the twentieth century, for example, in the aftermath of the First World War, the progressive messianism of the nineteenth century was replaced by radical revisionist theologies of both the neo-orthodox schools of Karl Barth and the liberal theologies of figures like Paul Tillich and Rudolf Bultmann (see Bultmann 1984; Tillich 1964). In the 1960s the Second Vatican Council enacted significant modernizations within the Catholic Church (though for many this was, and remains, too little too late). A tradition's capacity for renewal seems to be in proportion to its capacity for survival. The postmodern condition does not mean that the commitments of the ecclesial institutions to truth have to be reinterpreted in relativist or aesthetic terms, in which 'truth' is no longer at stake. The liberal theologies of Tillich and Bultmann are not just "a reduction of the 'cognitive' claims of religion to 'merely' aesthetic claims" (Rorty 2003, 38) because, as Rorty argues, the anti-essentialism in postmodern philosophy and theology simply does not see the distinction between the cognitive and the aesthetic in tidy neo-Kantian terms. Without getting distracted by a discussion of the forms of truth (e.g., aesthetic) that postmodernism might allow, the point here is that modern theology has found a variety of ways to adapt to the modern and postmodern age, not simply by hiving off the religious to the private, aesthetic and experiential realm. This points, in other words, to the idea that the post-secular rejects the privileging of the cognitive over the aesthetic, since religion does not need to remain at the margins (which these days is where the aesthetic seems to reside). This could be of general interest to educators who might recognize a general privileging of the cognitive over the aesthetic in educational theory and practice. But this is not really my point. My interest is to challenge the cognitive or propositional nature of modern theory particularly as it applies to religion and the relation between religion and education. The other key aim of this book is to put into question the Western prejudice lurking beneath the surface of the secularization thesis. Western bias is as old as European history itself, but had a particular impact in shaping imperialist views of the Victorian era, which can be said to have culminated with Bronowski's Social Darwinist–inspired phrase *The Ladder of Creation*.[8] Anthropological views of culture have since evolved well beyond James Frazer's (2003) once influential view of humankind as the inevitable progression from magic through religious belief and onto scientific thought. But the Western European colonial conquest of other cultures remains a question with all sorts of proximate and ultimate causal explanations (see, for example, Jared Diamond 1997), most of which fail to call into question the idea that the victors are, by virtue of their victory, the most progressive form of culture, and the apex of evolution thus far.

Whether empirical or normative, our simplistic narratives of cultural progress seem to align with and reinforce conceptions of human development that structure ideas about education. I would argue that progressive and teleological thinking can make us blind to the variety and complexity of human identity and development since we become attached to a too linear conception of time and progress that is constantly reinforced by an ideology of 'development' and 'growth' (e.g., in political and economic terms). According to Vattimo (2003), two kinds of rationalism are mixed here: the belief that science has the exclusive claim to truth, and that history is the inevitable (dialectical) movement towards truth and with it emancipation for all. It is hard, therefore, to agree with Vattimo's apparent conclusion that in the post-secular age we have overcome these ideas, since the ghosts of scientific positivism and progressivism are very much active – they are the living dead – particularly within educational theory.

The complex history of late modernity presents real challenges for us attempting to understand the present educational culture. At least we should recognize that our traditions entail historical contingency, rendering linear narratives of progress rather suspect. Understanding something of the complexity and contingency of the present should expand the debate within educational philosophy towards a broader discussion of how our fundamental commitments and ultimate concerns figure within education today. This moves us beyond rather narrow considerations of curriculum issues around how to reconcile competing truth claims within religious education towards some universal reason, or how to express the rational civic core that all citizens must adhere to (in the UK expressed as the inculcation of 'fundamental British values'), or even how education can contribute to the prevention of religious extremism and 'radicalization'.

At stake here is what religion is for people today. The idea that religious life entails a choice to commit to a system of beliefs, truth claims or worldviews, is

24 Formations of the post-secular

itself a very particular, and rather unhelpful, one. As Wendy Brown (2013, 17) puts it:

> The conceit of religion as a matter of individual choice . . . is already a distinct (and distinctly Protestant) way of conceiving religion, one that is woefully inapt for Islam and, I might add, Judaism, which is why neither comports easily with the privatized individual religious subject presumed by the formulations of religion freedom and tolerance governing Euro-Atlantic modernity.

This conception of choice is related to a view of religion as a worldview, or set of truth claims, about which one makes that choice. We will see in the next chapter that this conception of religion as being about making choices between competing worldviews is generally unhelpful, since it contributes to a wide misunderstanding of the nature of commitment: as though only religious positions rely on commitments, while secular worldviews are reputedly based on firmer foundations of facts or reason. In fact, secular perspectives embody a range of commitments which are not necessarily visible at level of propositions or worldviews. The post-secular points to the recognition that the kinds of binaries that structure our thinking about religion – religious/secular, faith/reason, conviction/critique – are misleading, since the nature of religion is far more porous than the secularist account would acknowledge.

Refining the post-secular

There are many ways to frame the 'post' in post-secular, some of which indicate the shortcomings of secularism, while others are more affirmative. I hear the 'post' firstly in negative terms, drawing attention to 'negative' traditions within religious and philosophical schools. Oren Ergas (2015, 127) suggests that the post-secular "is not secular, nor is it exactly religious, or non-religious – certainly not in the familiar ways we have been accustomed to understand these terms."[9] That negativity has a wider theological context since post-secularism can indicate an inevitable recognition that human reason, cut off from faith, is insufficient, denying the transcendence at the heart (or ground) of the immanent world (Blond 1998, Introduction). For many philosophers the post-secular connotes a 'crisis of faith' within secularism itself (Habermas 2008), or "disenchantment with the very idea of disenchantment" (Vattimo 2003, 30). Perhaps visions of a re-enchanted world will seem unconvincing given the linear nature of modernity, but there seems to be an accumulation of reasons to acknowledge counter narratives to Weber's secularization thesis (Landy and Saler 2009). For philosophers of religion the post-secular can indicate a way out of the cul-de-sac of the identification of ontology and theology that Heidegger famously denounced as ontotheology (Thomson 2005; Lewin 2012), giving way to a religion after metaphysics (Wrathall 2003), or as Derrida put it, a "religion without religion" (Caputo 2002). For others the post-secular offers a renewed openness to questions of spirituality at a time when traditional institutional religions are being supplanted by wider, more porous interests in spirituality (Wexler 2007; King 2009). Then there are 'radical' theologians who see the term pointing to a new theological consummation in the ruins of the nihilism of postmodernity (Betz 2009, 3). Many political philosophers regard the post-secular as reflecting a general skepticism towards Western neocolonial tendencies, inviting a reassessment of the founding myths and assumptions of the Western-led international order of the present geopolitical economy (Christoyannopolous 2014). It is this 'international community,' and its unquestioned allegiance to the millennium goals (Education for all), that should bring this geopolitical context to the attention of educationalists. Still others would reject the very idea of the post-secular. A key insight of Charles Taylor's seminal study *A Secular Age* is that the secular is not best understood as simply the separation of private and public (what he calls secularity 1), or a decline in religious belief or practice (secularity 2), but the real significance of secularism arises at a deeper level in which a shift in the conditions of belief have made unbelief viable (secularity 3). Taylor's interpretation of secularization makes all this talk of the post-secular seem rather hollow (Taylor 2007).[10]

In many ways the post-secular finds its clearest expression within a sociological register, with the recognition that the assumed linkage between modernization and secularization can no longer be maintained (Habermas 2008, p. 17). In his influential paper "Notes on a Post-Secular Society", Habermas analyses the emergence of secularism, finding three apparently plausible considerations for its development. Although these three dimensions of secularism are no longer convincing (hence the post-secular), they invite consideration so as to better understand the roots of post-secularism. First is the idea that with the development of science and technology, theocentric worldviews are no longer tenable. A second consideration that Habermas discusses is the idea that post-industrial development of welfare and social security (he limits his definition to 'developed' nations) has led to less existential insecurity and therefore less psychological need to engage in religious practices to cope with the contingency and frailty of life. But it is the third sociological consideration that seems to be of greatest relevance to educational theory since secularization would involve the churches losing their control of various social subsystems, such as law, politics, public welfare, education and science. Here religious institutions "restrict themselves to their proper function of administering the means of salvation, turn existing religion into a private matter and in general lose public influence and relevance" (Habermas 2008, 17). But Habermas (2008, 21) goes on to say that what makes this a post-secular age is that religion in fact continues to have a public influence and relevance across those social subsystems and that "the secularistic certainty that religion will disappear worldwide in the course of modernization is losing ground." We see in this influential account the conflation discussed earlier between views of secularism as a neat separation of social spheres (private vs. public) with secularism as the disappearance of religion more generally. The terminology is intrinsically ambivalent but may also reflect the shifting view that Habermas adopts. The three phases of Habermas' engagement with religion – from the hostility of neo-Marxist critique, to a middle phase of supposing religion should only be private, to the more recent recognition of the necessity of religion in the public sphere – tracks the development of the nature of secular to the post-secular.

In the field of education theorists and practitioners must work within this conceptual fluidity in developing the different senses in which religion plays a part in the social organisation of public educational institutions. In other words, religion – in one sense or another – will inform public education, whether we like it or not. The procedural secularism as outlined by Rowan Williams, which declines preferential treatment to any particular religious body but does allow and encourage wide deliberations of those of all faiths and none, seems to be an important principle within a pluralist educational system. One must keep in mind the localized contexts of schools, something that religious educators in England and Wales are particularly aware of through the establishment of locally agreed syllabi for religious education. Although the focus of this book is not religious education as a curriculum subject, the sensitivities of those engaged in that debate can throw light upon the complex issues under discussion.[11] In addition the history of the involvement of the Christian church in public education in the UK adds a further layer of context to an already very complex picture.

Of course we cannot turn a blind eye to overzealous religious inculcation in educational institutions (public or private) in the name of liberalism or tolerance. But the idea that we can leave our religious attitudes at the school gates presupposes a particular conception of what it means to be religious that reinforces a parochialism, perhaps even imperialism, reflecting what could be called a Protestant view of what it means to be religious.[12] We cannot deny the formative dimensions of education, which means that seeing religious/worldview 'neutrality' as an educational ideal is problematic (Cooling 2010). It often entails a narrow and inadequate understanding of religion as the cognitive assent to truth claims, doctrines or worldviews. So any neat separation of religion and education should be resisted for both practical and theoretical reasons. From a practical point of view, it is vital that children and young people become religiously literate. From a theoretical perspective, an evaluative orientation to life is inevitable whether or not we engage explicitly in religious or non-religious views and discourses. This brings me to an important pedagogical distinction between directive and non-directive teaching.

Contrary to the common sense notion of teaching, it is not the job of educators to ensure cognitive assent to specific truth claims. I make this implausible claim because learning is better served by a non-directive pedagogy of inquiry than a more directive pedagogy of assent. A pedagogy of assent supposes that knowledge is constituted by a fixed set of facts and that education is assembling those facts in a coherent structure. Of course education cannot be entirely free of the process of absorbing or assenting to facts, but this rather flat model of learning fails to recognize the structure of learning as an interrogation of many ideas and assumptions that are already embedded in our being-in-the-world, ideas that must be *interrupted* by inquiry. The Socratic method of *elenchus* is the 'classical' form of this dialectical or 'inquiry-based' approach. Trevor Cooling (2010, 14) uses the example of a student asking about creationism in a science lesson, arguing that it might not be appropriate to simply dismiss it outright as unscientific. Cooling's point is that "grappling successfully with questions of meaning and significance contributes to developing into a healthy, balanced person and is a fundamentally important component of education." We will explore the epistemological issues in reference to scientific and religious knowing in due course. The shift from 'Religious Instruction' (often referred to as *catechesis* within Christian communities) to 'Religious Education' in the 1988 Education Reform Act in England and Wales, was in part intended to address the problem of indoctrination (Aldridge 2015): that any perception of indoctrinatory intent within confessional religious instruction was mitigated by an exposure to more than one religious tradition, thereby further ensuring that religious instruction could not simply entail a pedagogy of assent. A conception of pluralist or procedural secularism seems to offer a common language here, one that might be meaningfully captured by the term post-secular.

A post-secular core?

Having begun to measure the range of frequencies at which the interference of the post-secular can be detected, is there any conceptual core around which to gather? The short answer is no. I suggest that grand sociological secularization theories, which still echo through present-day discussions in educational theory, do not encourage an appreciation of the other. The theoretical underpinning of much nineteenth and twentieth century sociological theories, from Durkheim to Marx to Weber, that modernity adheres to secularization has encouraged a homogenized picture of world history, universal reason and progress that tends to place Western values at the apex of history. The political, sociological, philosophical and theological registers of the post-secular all hint at a concern that might be interpreted as an appreciation of other ways of knowing, being and educating which goes back to Williams' (2012, 13) definition of the non-secular as "a willingness to see things or other persons as the objects of another sensibility than my own." This appreciation is not too far from postmodern and post-colonial analyses of other cultures, all of which warn against the homogenizing imperialism of Enlightenment projects. A homogenizing imperialism has long been associated with Americanization of education as Bill Readings' (1995, 2) analysis of the modern university argues: "'Americanization' in its current form is a synonym for globalization, a synonym that recognizes that globalization is not a neutral process in which Washington and Dakar participate equally." But

28 Formations of the post-secular

this speaks of a broader Western (Euro-American) complacency which provides a wide context for understanding how education and religion are related.

The fact that social theory and philosophy have long debated the multiple modernities of the postmodern has not resulted in the elimination of the dominant discourses of power. That we regularly speak of the 'modern world', the 'technological age' and so on, suggests that we are forgetful of Western (secular) modernity's discursive grip, what Wade Davis calls our cultural myopia. That the Western liberal project, manifest in a highly urbanized and consumerist culture, seems to be the 'only game in town' scarcely needs to be stated. That this Western liberalism is bound up with conceptions of universal reason and progress that have supplanted local, indigenous communities appears equally unquestioned. Mass education in nineteenth-century Europe seems to have gone hand in hand with a colonialist reach of the civilizing power of Western European education. And *we* (UNESCO, the World Bank and the so-called 'International Community') now call for 'Education for All', whose noble intention is to bring the benefits of education "to every citizen in every society" (World Bank). We appear to have become inured to the one-dimensional nature of the cultural and educational imperialism at the heart of this project. In a series of articles and a powerful film (*Schooling the World*), Carol Black (2012) strongly argues that we have:

> In "developed" societies, we are so accustomed to centralized control over learning that it has become functionally invisible to us, and most people accept it as natural, inevitable, and consistent with the principles of freedom and democracy. We assume that this central authority, because it is associated with something that seems like an unequivocal good – "education" – must itself be fundamentally good, a sort of benevolent dictatorship of the intellect.

Just as Jacques Rancière (2006) has pointed to the contradiction inherent to installing democracy, Black argues that the installation of education for all negates the variety and complexity of indigenous education that has long existed across all aboriginal cultures and peoples. Black is surely overstating her case, romanticizing indigenous cultures and overdrawing the opposition between mass and indigenous forms of education. Moreover, there is a real danger here that the structural inequalities and injustices, around the education of women in particular, are overlooked without some intervention, or through some cultural sensitivity. Nevertheless, it is hard to refute something of the totalizing (if benevolent) intent of 'Education for all' and the near universal assumption that it represents an unequivocal good. Even if the 'Education for all' agenda is more complex and variegated than Black suggests, there still seems to be a creeping 'soft totalitarianism' here, that "there can be no rational argument about the sovereignty of the global market: consumerism and a kind of 'soft' totalitarianism go together" (Williams 2012, 71). Resisting a

Formations of the post-secular   29

view of modernity as the inexorable march of the disenchanted, industrialized and urbanized, the post-secular offers an opening to conceive of alternatives to a totalitarian identification of a modern, critical, educated citizen with secularization. Why not just postmodern? The possibility of multiple modernities is not simply the relativist and postmodern erosion of religious life, because these varied ways of being do, for the most part, entail an orientation that is, in some important (if difficult to define) sense, religious. It is a political, social and spiritual concern that we find alternatives to the neoliberal narratives of the future. But, to interpret Heidegger's enigmatic claim, it may be that *only a god can interrupt* the totalizing power of that narrative.[13]

The image and context of colonialist education is not as far from secularizing forces as one might imagine. Of course colonialism was initially motivated by more than economic and political interests, but by an evangelizing imperative that moved in a different direction to secularization. This is important in view of education since the missionary spirit of those colonial powers took great interest in schooling: the legacy of British colonialism is evident in the many elite schools in India today, which are Christian schools modeled on an image of Victorian English public schooling. Shouldn't we see secularization in opposition to colonialism? I would reply that many theorists of religion see the founding principles of secular society (the rise of science and progress) as historically embedded in Christian theological assumptions (Lewin 2013). The modern concept of progress is identified with Christian and Jewish conceptions of time and destiny.[14] Moreover, it is plausible to see modern secularism in terms of the mission of the West: that modern industrialized social life is to be exported to every part of the globe, and that we must save premodern, preindustrial cultures from themselves. Debates in political theory about whether the motives here are financial, ideological or religious, are ongoing, but in the context of what follows, the partition between secular and religious ideas is hard to uphold.[15]

Liberal democracy, aligned with consumer capitalism, is the manner of being-in-the-world that admits of no alternatives, and that therefore fails to recognize itself as just one mode of being. It entails, to use Heideggerian language, the oblivion of being. I am not wishing to deny the many benefits of the scientific revolution, the Enlightenment and modernity in general. One might observe that modernity is a victim of its own success in the sense that it has become so all encompassing, so totalizing or *enframing* (Heidegger 1977) that all other modes of being are all but invisible. Other ways of addressing environmental, social, political and spiritual problems are silenced. This is not, however, an attack on, or negation of, Western consumerist culture, technology, urbanization or secularism more broadly, but only an acknowledgment that this is not the only game in town and that we can longer suppose that it is. Wade Davis (2009, 19) has succinctly captured the cultural myopia in which Western modernity tends only to utilize or preserve the 'exotic other': "[t]he myriad of cultures of the world are not failed attempts at modernity, let

30 Formations of the post-secular

alone failed attempts to be us." It may be that an appreciation of other ways of being, including religious, spiritual, poetic, aesthetic, etc., of inhabiting a world which is more than the projection of the power of subjectivity, can be usefully described as post-secular. Or perhaps, with Williams (2012, 11), we are better off calling this a procedural secularism.[16]

Conclusion

We have seen that the post-secular age involves acknowledging the ongoing influence of religion on culture and on education particularly. Straightforward theories of secularization have to be reexamined in light of the enduring influence of religion. This means disabusing ourselves of the assumption that "to be secular means to be modern, and therefore by implication, to be religious means not yet fully modern" (Casanova 2010, 59). This assumption could be reframed for educators as follows: to be secular means to be critical, and therefore by implication, to be religious means not yet fully critical. The development of critical thinking must be uncoupled from assumptions around secularization since religions themselves are nourished by their own creative criticality. It is a great problem that today a dominant image of religious life is its antagonism to critique. Attacks on education by the Taliban in Pakistan or by Boko Haram in Nigeria, for example, are, of course, abhorrent. But understanding these fears as arising out of a misunderstanding of the relationship between criticality and credulity is an important step. In other words, we need a softening of the polarization between criticality and credulity, both for political and philosophical reasons. Politically, such a softening can ease tensions between polarized cultures around the world. Philosophically, it more accurately captures human knowing because critical engagement is always preceded by an affirmation. This is the hermeneutical condition, perhaps even the human condition (Aldridge 2015).

Mediating the polarization of religious and non-religious individuals and communities can help us acknowledge the shared interests and concerns that cut across human identities. This mediation should undercut certain unhelpful ideas that often appear in these debates, that, for example, non-religious people lack a moral compass, or people within a religious community all believe and behave in uniform ways. The site of the post-secular gives form to the fissures or cracks in the wall between the secular and the confessional. While many people may not be able to embrace the worldviews that modernity shows to be untenable, they often cannot ignore a certain religious sensibility or call made by the world, and so find themselves seeking out these cracks and fissures. As I will show in Chapter 3, philosophers might see this disposition and sensitivity as heralding a *religion after metaphysics*. Taylor calls this space a third way between orthodoxy and unbelief, a view that James Smith (2014, 64), quoting Taylor, neatly captures: "All sorts of people feel themselves caught; 'in the face of the opposition between orthodoxy and unbelief, many, and among them the best and most sensitive minds, were [and are] cross-pressured, looking

Formations of the post-secular   31

for a third way.'" After the putative death of God, the possibility of authentic religious life is an ongoing question, hence the rise in alternative forms of religion and interests in spirituality, but even fascination with the spiritual, appears to be coopted by the very secularist and consumerist forces that have denied the depth of the world (Williams 2012, 16). Of course these cracks will not concern all people in the world today (e.g., those who are securely religious or otherwise), but a significant number of people – those, for example, who consider themselves 'spiritual but not religious' – would, I think, appreciate the opportunity to explore a post-secular defined in terms not reducible to either pole of secular/confessional binary. Clearly then, the 'return of religion' in the post-secular must resist any simplistic notion of a return of traditional patterns of religious life. Post-secularism complicates rather than denies the secularization thesis.

Notes

1 Evidence of recent interest can be found by the publication in 2012 of a special issue entitled "Post-Secular Trends: Issues in Education and Faith" of the *Journal of Belief and Values: Studies in Religion and Education* (Bowie, Peterson and Revell 2012) and in 2014 *Critical Studies in Education* published a special issue entitled "Education in post-secular society" (Hotam and Wexler 2014).
2 This observation echoes a longstanding perception that the opposition between forms of capitalism and forms of socialism (Marcuse 1991), or indeed forms of religious fundamentalism (Žižek 2002), conceal a primary ideological unity.
3 In a journal correspondence with Andrew Wright following publication of John White's original article, both Wright (2005) and White (2004b) acknowledge that the popularity of a position might not in the end justify its inclusion within a curriculum (see Aldridge 2015, Chapter 6).
4 John Sullivan (2012, 183) states that a "major area of dispute between religious believers and those wanting a more secular social environment is education." Although Sullivan is broadly correct to say this, the statement implies a widely held assumption: that those wanting a secular public life are going to be hostile to religion, with the further implication that secularism is to be identified with unbelief. Although somewhat justifiable, the statement reflects the framing of the debate in terms that I find to be unhelpful, a point I shall develop in this chapter.
5 Harry Brighouse (2006, 83) appears to support a more pluralist, procedural type of secularism in education "[a] secular society would not be one in which religion was absent from the public sphere. It would be on in which religious cleavages did not coincide with cleavages in public debate, and in which religious and non-religious perspectives were advanced and evaluated in a spirit of mutual respect."
6 This is a complicated picture since birth rates and immigration impact the national growth rates of all religions. Nevertheless, China to take one example, has shown significant growth in recent years, as demonstrated in a recent article in the economist "Cracks in the atheist edifice" http://www.economist.com/news/briefing/21629218-rapid-spread-christianity-forcing-official-rethink-religion-cracks
7 This raises the question of whether Hegel's philosophy of history, and European Enlightenment philosophy more broadly, is irredeemably Eurocentric, colonialist and racist (Tibebu 2011).
8 Cecil Rhodes said, "We happen to be the best people in the world . . . and the more we inhabit the better it is for humanity" (Quoted by Davis 2009, 11–12).

32 Formations of the post-secular

9 Ergas (2015, 127) relates this to Eastern thought, a connection that I am very much in sympathy with: "Interestingly this very rhetoric undergirds Advaita Vedanta and Buddhism in many incidences with the Sanskrit words – neti, neti – not this, nor that, as indicating the nature of Brahman (ultimate reality) or the idea of non-self."

10 For Taylor, the 'post-secular' entails a narrow and inadequate conception of what it means to be secular. Taylor's "secularity 3" entails a shift not in belief as such, but in the conditions for belief. Hence there can be no post-secular in Taylor's sense of "secularity 3" (Warner, Vanantwerpen, and Calhoun 2013, p. 22).

11 Of course religious educators have a great deal to contribute to discussions within philosophy of education, particularly those pertaining to the role of religion in education (Aldridge 2015).

12 The use the term *Protestant* here is meant to be broadly inclusive of Protestant traditions that, in the wake of Luther, regard *sola fide*, by faith alone, to be the sole ground for salvation. This reliance on belief in a creedal formula becomes characteristic of Protestant sects (speaking rather loosely) that tend to flatten the richer Biblical hermeneutics to literal reading and acceptance by the will. Because human reason is treated with suspicion, being opposed to faith within this tradition, the door for more direct and literal readings to be accepted (or not) by faith is wedged open. Luther's development of the sola fide doctrine rests upon a distinction common in medieval theology between a theology of intellect (in the style of Dominican theology) and a theology of will (in the style of Franciscan theology). This distinction is sometimes referred to as between intellectualism and voluntarism, where voluntarism seeks to avoid the complex hermeneutical questions that attend commitment, rather suggesting that the purity of the will is paramount (See Dupré 1993).

13 In an interview for *Der Spiegel*, withheld from publication until after his death, Heidegger (1991) enigmatically stated that "Philosophy will not be able to effect an immediate transformation of the present condition of the world. This is not only true of philosophy, but of all merely human thought and endeavor. Only a god can save us. The sole possibility that is left for us is to prepare a sort of readiness, through thinking and poeticizing, for the appearance of the god or for the absence of the god in the time of foundering [*Untergang*] for in the face of the god who is absent, we founder." My intention with this reference is to indicate that an interruption to the prevailing liberal democratic order entails some radical reorientation that seems to require something 'transcendent'. Either that, or we will be visited by a global environmental catastrophe which will be impossible to ignore – an interruption of a different kind.

14 Debates on the continuity between Christian theology and secularization have their own history: "Blumenberg targets Löwith's argument that progress is the secularization of Hebrew and Christian beliefs and argues to the contrary that the modern age, including its belief in progress, grew out of a new secular self-affirmation of culture against the Christian tradition" (Buller 1996, 95).

15 John Hobson developed an influential theory of financial imperialism that has since been debated by figures such as Lenin, Arendt and Fieldhouse (see Fieldhouse 1961).

16 There are, of course, many religious figures who also argued for forms of state secularism: Mahatma Gandhi, Martin Luther King and, as we have noted, Rowan Williams.

References

Aldridge, D. (2015). *A Hermeneutics of Religious Education*. London: Bloomsbury.

Asad, T. (2003). *Formations of the Secular: Christianity, Islam, Modernity*. Stanford, CA: Stanford University Press.

Bargatzky, T. (1996). "Comments" to Sahlins, M. "The Sweetness of Sadness: The Native Anthropology of Western Cosmology" *Cultural Anthropology*, 37: 3, 395–428.

Bellah, R. (1967). "Civil Religion in America". *Journal of the American Academy of Arts and Sciences*, 96: 1, 1–21.

Betz, J. (2009). *After Enlightenment: The Post-Secular Vision of J. G. Hamann.* Oxford: Wiley-Blackwell.

Black, C. (2010). *Schooling the World: The White Man's Last Burden.* Retrieved from http://schoolingtheworld.org/film/

Black, C. (2012). "Occupy Your Brain: On Power, Knowledge, and the Re-Occupation of Common Sense" *Films for Action.* Retrieved from http://www.filmsforaction.org/news/occupy_your_brain_on_power_knowledge_and_the_reoccupation_of_common_sense/

Blair, A. (2010). *Church and Academy in Harmony.* Eugene, OR: Pickwick Publications.

Blond, P. (ed.). (1998). *Post-Secular Philosophy: Between Philosophy and Theology.* London: Routledge.

Bowie, P., & Revell, L. (2012). "Post-Secular Trends: Issues in Education and Faith," *Journal of Beliefs & Values: Studies in Religion & Education*, 33: 2, 139–141.

Brighouse, H. (2006). *On Education*, London: Routledge.

Brown, W. (2013). 'Introduction' in Asad et al. *Is Critique Secular? Blasphemy, Injury, and Free Speech.* 2nd rev. ed. New York: Fordham University Press, 7–19.

Bruce, S. (2002). *God Is Dead: Secularisation and the West.* Oxford: Wiley-Blackwell.

Buller, C. (1996). *The Unity of Nature and History in Pannenberg's Theology.* Lanham, MA: Rowman & Littlefield.

Bultmann. R. (1984). *New Testament and Mythology and Other Basic Writings.* Minneapolis: Fortress Press.

Caputo, J. (2002). *The Prayers and Tears of Jacques Derrida: Religion Without Religion.* Indiana: Indiana University Press.

Casanova, J. (2009). "The Secular and Secularism" *Social Research*, 76: 4, 1049–1066.

Casanova, J. (2010). "A Secular Age: Dawn or Twilight?" in Michael Warner, Jonathan Van Antwerpen, and Craig Calhoun (eds.) *Varieties of Secularism in a Secular Age.* Cambridge: Harvard University Press, 265–281.

Christoyannopolous, A. (2014). "The Golden Rule on the Green Stick: Leo Tolstoy's International Thought for a 'Postsecular' Age" in Luca Mavelli and Fabio Petito (eds.) *Towards a Postsecular International Politics: New Forms of Community, Identity, and Power.* London: Palgrave Macmillan, 81–102.

Church of England (2015). *The Fruits of the Spirit: A Church of England Discussion Paper on Character Education*, London: Church of England Education Office.

Connolly, W. (2006). "Europe a Minor Tradition" in D. Scott and C. Herschkind (eds.) *Powers of the Secular Modern: Talal Asad and His Interlocutors.* Stanford: Stanford University Press, 79–92.

Cooling, T. (2010). *Doing God in Education.* London: Theos.

Davie, G. (2002). *Europe: The Exceptional Case: Parameters of Faith in the Modern World.* London: Darton, Longman & Todd.

Davis, W. (2009). *The Wayfinders: Why Ancient Wisdom Matters in the Modern World.* Toronto: House of Anansi Press.

Diamond, J. (1997). *Guns, Germs and Steel: A Short History of Everybody for the Last 13,000 Years.* New York: Vintage Books.

Dinham, A. (2015). "Public Religion in an Age of Ambivalence: Recovering Religious Literacy after a Century of Secularism" in Leo Van Arragon & Lori Beaman (eds.) *Issues in Religion and Education: Whose Religion?* Leiden: Brill, 8–23.

Dupré, L. (1993). *Passage to Modernity: An Essay in the Hermeneutics of Culture.* New Haven: Yale University Press.

34 Formations of the post-secular

Ergas, O. (2015). "The Post-Secular Rhetoric of Contemplative Practice in the Curriculum" in P. Wexler and Y. Hotam (eds.) *New Social Foundations for Education: Education in Post-Secular Society*. New York: Peter Lang, 107–130.

Fieldhouse, D. (1961). "'Imperialism': An Historiographical Revision." *Economic History Review*, 14: 2, 187–209.

Fox, J. (2002). *Ethnoreligious Conflict in the Late Twentieth Century: A General Theory*. Oxford: Lexington Books.

Fox News Insider. (2015). Retrieved from http://insider.foxnews.com/2015/12/16/bill-oreilly-rips-school-district-removing-christmas-references-charlie-brown-christmas.

Frazer, J. (2003). *The Golden Bough*. Mineola, NY: Dover Books.

Gardom, J. (2011). "The Essay: End of Secularisation" *Varsity*. Retrieved from http://www.varsity.co.uk/opinion/3456

Habermas, J. (2008). "Notes on Post Secular Society" *New Perspectives Quarterly*, 25: 4, 17–29.

Heidegger, M. (1977). *The Question Concerning Technology and Other Essays*, trans. W. Lovitt. New York: Harper and Row.

Heidegger, M. (1991). "'Only a God Can Save Us': Der Spiegel's Interview with Martin Heidegger (1996)" in Richard Wolin (ed.) *The Heidegger Controversy: A Critical Reader*, London: MIT Press, 91–118.

Hotam, Y., & Wexler, P. (2014). "Education in Post-Secular Society" *Critical Studies in Education*, 55: 1, 1–7.

King, M. (2009). *Postsecularism: The Hidden Challenge to Extremism*. Cambridge: James Clarke and Co.

Landy, J., & Saler, M. (2009). *The Re-Enchantment of the World: Secular Magic in a Rational Age*. Stanford: Stanford University Press.

Lee, L. (2015). *Recognizing the Non-Religious: Reimagining the Secular*. Oxford: Oxford University Press.

Lewin, D. (2012). *Technology and the Philosophy of Religion*. Newcastle upon Tyne: Cambridge Scholars Press.

Lewin, D. (2013). "Technology" in Adams, Pattison, and Ward (eds.) *The Oxford Handbook of Theology and Modern European Thought*. Oxford: Oxford University Press, 435–454.

Marcuse, H. (1991). *One-Dimensional Man: Studies in Ideology of Advanced Industrial Society*. London: Routledge.

Nguyen, T. (2010). "Deconstructing Education for All: Discourse, Power and the Politics of Inclusion," *International Journal of Inclusive Education*, 14: 4, 341–355.

Rancière, J. (2006). *Hatred of Democracy*. London: Verso.

Readings, B. (1995). *The University in Ruins*. London: Harvard University Press.

Reuters. (2015). Retrieved from http://www.reuters.com/article/us-kentucky-charliebrown-idUSKBN0TZ2TP20151216

Rorty, R. (2003). "Anti-Clericalism and Atheism" in Mark Wrathall (ed.) *Religion After Metaphysics*. Cambridge: Cambridge University Press, 37–46.

Scott, D., & Hirschkind, C. (eds.). (2006). *Powers of the Secular Modern: Talal Asad and His Interlocutors*. Stanford: Stanford University Press.

Smith, J. (2014). *How (Not) to Be Secular: Reading Charles Taylor*. Michigan: Eerdmans.

Sullivan, J. (2012). "Religious Faith in Education: Enemy or Asset?" *Journal of Beliefs & Values: Studies in Religion & Education*. 33: 2, 183–193.

Taylor, C. (2007). *A Secular Age*. Cambridge: Harvard University Press.

Thomson, I. (2005). *Heidegger on Ontotheology: Technology and the Politics of Education*. Cambridge: Cambridge University Press.

Tibebu, T. (2011). *Hegel and the Third World: The Making of Eurocentrism in World History*. Syracuse, NY: Syracuse University Press.

Tillich, P. (1964). *Theology of Culture*. New York: Oxford University Press.

Vattimo, G. (2003). "After Onto-Theology: Philosophy between Science and Religion" in Mark Wrathall (ed.) *Religion After Metaphysics*. Cambridge: Cambridge University Press, 29–36.

Warner, M., VanAntwerpen, J., & Calhoun, C. (eds.). (2013). *Varieties of Secularism in a Secular Age*. Cambridge: Harvard University Press.

Wexler, P. (2007). *Mystical Interactions*. Los Angeles: Cherub Press.

White, J. (2004a). "Should Religious Education be a Compulsory School Subject?" *British Journal of Religious Education*, 26: 2, 152–164.

White, J. (2004b). "Reply to Andrew Wright" *British Journal of Religious Education*, 27: 1, 21–3.

Williams, R. (2012). *Faith in the Public Square*. London: Bloomsbury.

Woodhead, L., & Catto, R. (eds.). (2012). *Religion and Change in Modern Britain*. London: Routledge.

Woolf Institute. (2015). "Living with Difference: Community, Diversity and the Common Good" Report of the Commission on Religion and Belief in British Public Life.

World Bank. (2014). *Education for All*. Retrieved from http://www.worldbank.org/en/topic/education/brief/education-for-all

Wrathall, M. (ed.). (2003). *Religion After Metaphysics*. Cambridge: Cambridge University Press.

Wright, A. (2004). "The Justification of Compulsory Religious Education: A Response to Professor White" *British Journal of Religious Education*, 26: 2, 165–174.

Wright, A. (2005). "On the Intrinsic Value of Religious Education" *British Journal of Religious Education*, 27: 1, 165–174.

Žižek, S. (2002). *Welcome to the Desert of the Real*. London: Verso.

Chapter 3

Religion and belief in a post-secular age

Introduction

In the last chapter we considered some of the complexities evoked by the discourse of the post-secular. These complexities are derived, at least in part, from differing conceptions of what it means to be religious in the present age. We saw how the 'return of religion' shows some views of the relation between religion and education to be inadequate: religion is not just a temporary condition to be accounted for, a stage on the way of human progress towards secular rational enlightenment, but is an enriching feature of our world. This theme will be developed in the present chapter through an exploration of views of religion and belief that challenge the reduction of religion to doctrines and truth claims. I hope to show that the 'problem' of religion and education is not best understood as one of competing and irreconcilable worldviews. The post-secular announces a shift in the debates within religion and education away from questions around, for example, indoctrination versus autonomy, or relativism versus realism. The post-secular presents a fresh opportunity to reflect on the formative possibilities of education. So my aim could be considered as broadly postmodern: I will draw attention to multiple modernities and narratives that throw the story of Western emancipation and enlightenment into sharp relief. But my interests are specifically post-secular insofar as our Western parochialism arises out of an untenable secularization narrative. The educational significance of this secular perspective arises through a particularly problematic alignment of education with 'critique' and the assumptions of progress in which triumphalist reason displaces the premodern.

The privileging of beliefs and worldviews

In her editorial for a special virtual issue of the *Journal of Philosophy of Education* on "Religion and Education", Anna Strhan (2014) has offered a concise yet comprehensive overview of the diverse range of debates that have preoccupied discussions of the relations between religion and education over recent decades. What is striking about her account, and Strhan hints at this in the closing paragraph of the editorial, is how discussions within philosophy of education have presupposed that the *belief* dimension of religion is the core of religious life to the exclusion of almost everything else, that "the way in which religion has been theorised, in particular the focus on indoctrination, has privileged the equation of religion with belief."[1]

The privileging of belief is evident, for example, in Michael Hand's reply to Trevor Cooling's argument about the marginalization of religion within education (Cooling 2010). Here associating belief with the idea of a theory of the meaning of life, or a worldview, Hand (2012, 529) states:

> Theories of the meaning of life need not be religious, and a religion need not include a theory of the meaning of life. But, at least in the case of the major world religions, religious commitment typically does involve subscription to such a theory. It is appropriate to speak of a 'Christian worldview', for example, because the core Christian narrative of the creation, fall and redemption of humanity is plausibly construed as an account of the significance, origin and purpose of human existence.

This subscription to a theory of the meaning of life assumes that doctrines and beliefs can be interpreted as positions for which propositions can stand. Even more explicitly in reference to the propositional nature of religious beliefs, Hand (2015, 35) states that "[t]he differences between the followers of different religious and irreligious paths are fundamentally differences of belief: the followers assent to different propositions about what the world is like." As a philosopher of education, Hand's concern is the extent to which the relation between a worldview and education may be rationally justified.[2] Schools that promote worldviews considered epistemically controversial are a problem: "faith schools are objectionable because they attempt to secure children's assent to epistemically controversial propositions" (2012, 536). Hand's privileging of propositional belief and worldview in framing religion is, as Strhan suggests, typical within debates across educational philosophy. This chapter argues that this approach is problematic primarily because it significantly misrepresents the nature of religious life. Framed in this way, the kinds of debate we find are those to do with indoctrination or rights (e.g., of the rights of Catholic parents to bring up their children in the Catholic tradition), and this neither helps us understand religious life, nor the lived processes of education. The political problems of competing rights between children, parents and the state, tend to (though in principle do not need to) presuppose conceptions of religion and belief that this chapter is seeking to undercut: e.g., the competing rights of parents and their children to freedom of religion as witnessed by a recent major research project undertaken by the Spencer Foundation.[3] As I will go on to argue, notions of religious choice behind arguments around autonomy often reflect reductive and parochial conceptions of being religious.

I need to acknowledge the very real problem of accepting, asserting and teaching ideas "without due regard for relevant evidence and argument" (Callan 1985, 115). This identification of indoctrination with lack of evidence and reasoned argument has been discussed at length (e.g., Wilson 1972; Snook 1972; McLaughlin 1984; Gardner 1988), and it is not my intention to deny the significance of these debates. Rather I want to draw the debate in a different direction to show that evidence and argument are not the sole arbiters for religious life. For the most part people do not find their religious identity through the path of evidence and reasoning leading to a consistent and defensible worldview – a view characteristic of certain 'logocentric' traditions. Of course for many skeptics this is precisely the problem with religion. But I argue in fact that this does not mean that believers have blind faith, but rather that religious identity, as well as belief and faith, are not what we often take them to be. The educational assumption that criticality and credulity are opposed is derived, I suggest, from the ancient tension between reason and faith. If we can relieve that tension, then the opposition will not be so sharply drawn.

Framing religion in terms of truth claims or worldviews reduces complex forms of life entailing rich tapestries of meaning and practice to bare propositional truth claims. Religious truth claims then appear to be unsatisfying because they are either patently false or at best unfalsifiable. The modern scientific principle of falsifiability is presented as a key test that religious truth claims typically fail. Indeed, if religious claims cannot be assessed, then how can teaching them be justified? Critics suppose that something akin to a leap of faith within religious traditions makes religious claims unassailable and that therefore religion should be left out of education, especially where publically funded. The opposition between criticality and credulity is worth exploring in more detail since the demand for falsifiability only serves to reinforce the grip of the propositional framing of religion.

Criticality versus credulity

For many educationalists, the ultimate goal of education is less to do with inculcating specific facts or particular values than with developing a liberal and critical spirit of inquiry (Siegel 1988). This is not to suggest that certain facts and values are not essential dimensions of learning, but that what education should ultimately be about is a set of (critical) dispositions. Such critical and inquiring dispositions might be regarded as inconsistent with religious life, where religion is seen as involving the attenuation or negation of critical faculties in adopting a belief based on faith, scripture or tradition. This tension arises in part from regarding faith and believing as credulous activities in which our critical faculties are bracketed out or suspended. From this perspective, to believe might be seen as having confidence without evidence. Thus the modern scientist is not a 'believer'. She does not ground her worldview on any faith commitment, but rather on the bare facts as they present themselves. The simple dichotomy between facts and beliefs/values does not take us very far since education is always already motivated by a commitment of interest, engagement or value. The general model for critical thinking encouraged in modern education understands being critical as a process in which we become more objective in the formation of judgements. Grounded in positivism, this kind of objectivity is too often idealized as having no ground in commitment (or faith). I suggest that no such model of objectivity can exist because there is always a moment of commitment. As John Polkinghorne (1991, 7) has put it, "[n]o one of serious intent can escape the necessity of an intellectual bootstrap to raise himself above the earthbound state of unreflective experience."

If we could make clear-cut distinctions between the credulous believer and the incredulous critical inquirer, the world would be a simpler (though perhaps duller) place. In that simpler world belief and faith are the poor cousins of knowledge. Unable to compete with the evidential basis of factual knowledge, they appeal to gaps left by the incompleteness of factual paradigms. Faith is pressed into the cracks in the wall of our scientific worldview. This dichotomy between fact and value (or knowledge and belief) is not only untenable, but is predicated upon a propositional view of the world since both scientific facts and statements of faith are rendered in propositional form. The sharp logical positivism exemplified in the Vienna circle's attempts to make a science of philosophy, which sees propositions unambiguously tied to empirical references, a process in which the fact/value distinction is absolute. Although this thoroughgoing positivism is less influential today as it was in the twentieth century, the general desire to teach facts without due consideration to the world disclosed by those facts reflects the ongoing legacy of positivism and the fact/value dichotomy. A brief example will help to illustrate the point.

Scientific knowledge about the origins of the universe and the big bang can take us only so far, at which point the door is opened to narratives beyond science. Scientific talk of a singularity of infinite density where the known laws of physics do not apply sounds almost as mythological as some creation narratives requiring the suspension of the general understanding of matter, energy and so on. Science finds its descriptive limits: there always appears to be a moment 'prior' to that which is perceived by modern science, an unfalsifiable 'trace' that resists elimination. Positivists deny the significance of any such trace by claiming it is a temporary lack to be explained as observational methods are improved or more data is gathered, while religious people (speaking very generally) regard such a trace to be more a condition of existence and observation as such. Whether we believe that the question of radical origins is ontological in nature or simply requires more research investment is ultimately a question of commitment. I am tempted to say more research will always leave a trace, but I thereby betray my own commitment within this debate. The problem is that certain religious people, who might be called fundamentalists, will draw a significant theological extrapolation from this trace, prizing open this negative space and filling it with what William James (2012) once called "over-belief".

40 Religion and belief

Both scientific positivists and religious fundamentalists share an ontology here: that being can be reified into statements of truth. They have more in common than either would wish to admit. In recent decades many scientists and theologians have drawn correspondences between scientific and religious narratives in order to argue that theologians might not need to settle for a rather vulnerable 'god of the gaps' or even a more subtle 'trace of god'.[4] If theology sees itself as straightforwardly propositional, then it inevitably comes into conflict with new scientific discoveries. In other words, the conflict narrative between religion and science of recent centuries entails an assumption that religious truth is propositional. As theologians and philosophers of religion like Rudolf Bultmann and Paul Ricoeur have shown, the philosophical and religious traditions and practices are better understood as operating at different levels from descriptive science (i.e., symbolically). Bultmann's programme to demythologize the New Testament, for example, offers a hermeneutically nuanced recovery of the meaning of events that goes beyond the literal and historical (the propositional). Moreover, the idea of 'differing narratives' of creation (for example, in Genesis) hints at a more flexible and hermeneutically subtle space for dialogue since it recognizes that accounts of origins bear an interpretive and hermeneutical significance (LaCocque and Ricoeur 2003). In other words, the science and religion debates can help us to see beyond the rather stale fact/belief (or fact/value) dichotomy. Scientific models themselves rely upon interpretive structures that do not boil down to straightforward facts: even physicists are in the business of telling stories by generating models with a certain explanatory power. Postmodernism generally, where it has not yielded to dogmatic relativism, offers a sense of the value of different and intersecting narratives. Those narratives are not simply in logical agreement or disagreement, but are part of the fabric of understanding our multi-layered world.[5] This should take us beyond the 'teach the controversy' debates in the US where evolution and intelligent design are seen to be radically opposed. This debate is predicated on a hermeneutical failing.

I have suggested that religions are not best understood as worldviews and that therefore the idea that propositional claims about the universe will not, in a straightforward sense, disprove religious creation stories, for example. Of course the sciences can and do reveal, challenge and refine the 'over-belief' that religions entail. But religions have symbolic significance and operate at different levels. This might make them 'unfalsifiable' and to that extent they might be said to have no claim to propositional truth. Indeed, it is the notion that religions are constituted by religious statements which are propositional that I take issue with. So it is not simply that religious claims are unfalsifiable but that falsifiability is an inappropriate test of the meaning of religion. To develop this argument I turn to the many dimensions which religion entails.

Dimensions of religious life

Philosophy of religion has moved on since Ninian Smart identified seven dimensions of religion.[6] But the general message, that religions are much more than a set of beliefs or a worldview, seems hardly to have penetrated the popular mind, at least where secularizing influences shape understandings of religion, such as education. Even if it cannot be denied that doctrine is an essential aspect of religious understanding for many practitioners, it is only one dimension of religious life,[7] and so the debates about conflicting religious positions, or the problems around indoctrination can, as Keller (2002, 7) puts it, seem "extremely limiting if one is trying to make sense of religiousness in the contemporary world." Indeed feminist critics have suggested that the preoccupation with beliefs and truth conditions might only reflect a masculine framing of religion that performatively denies materiality (Jantzen 1998; Irigaray 2004; I'Anson and Jasper 2011). Smart was the first to tell the history of this propositional view: the religions of the book (Judaism, Christianity and Islam), being textually oriented since they share the Hebrew Bible, have encouraged Western scholars to interpret other religions through the doctrinal/propositional lens. The real legacy of this Western lens is the tendency to reduce religions to propositions, truth claims or worldviews. Educationalists continue to be preoccupied with how competing worldviews should be handled, or to what extent transmission of worldviews is justified. These debates would be framed differently were they addressing the foods eaten, clothes worn or languages spoken by different traditions. Bringing up a child as a vegetarian, the norm across much of the Indian subcontinent, would hardly be considered indoctrination. Rather than disavowing indoctrination, perhaps we should argue, as many philosophers of education have done, for a rehabilitation of the positive, and inevitable, role of indoctrination in upbringing (Tan 2004, 263). The suggestion that foods can have religious significance might sound reductive in a different way – that we teach religion through experience of 'saris and samosas' is often cited as trivializing other cultures – but Hindu cultures take food to be an extremely important aspect of religious identity and social bonds. It seems to be the presumption that beliefs or worldviews entail an intellectual or cognitive dimension, and that this dimension is the core of religious life, which makes requiring religious assent of the child 'indoctrination' in the pejorative sense.

In contrast to this, I draw attention to the idea that for many religious practitioners beliefs will be unreflectively adopted or simply part of a background context, and therefore less important than is often assumed. I do not wish to draw a sharp boundary between religious life and propositional belief, but the balance must be redressed. Many religious practices, in India and China for example (which might be categorized as 'Hindu' or 'Buddhist', though these terms are not uncontroversial among scholars of religion), may have ethical, experiential and material significance for the practitioners; but ask the practitioner about why they perform the rituals they do, and the answer might be suffused with symbolism, or more likely just unclear or irrelevant. There is scarcely a consistent and affirmative metaphysics or 'theory of the world' behind a *puja* in which prayer, song and ritual are performed to bless a newly purchased car on a suburban street in Bangalore, for example. The puja rituals are ostensibly to host, honour or worship one or more deities, but the rituals seem only tenuously related to doctrinal theology or worldview in Michael Hand's sense of the term. When considering the gods of the Hindu pantheon it is perhaps better to wonder at their significance, or to express devotion, than to argue for or against their existence. It could be argued, therefore, that Hindu devotional rituals offer practices rather than metaphysics: the Bhakti tradition is defined by its emphasis on devotion. For this reason, many Hindus can follow *dharma* (duty or law)[8] without dogma and many can, therefore, simultaneously follow Christ, for example.[9]

In contemporary India (and across the world) the picture of religious commitment is complex due in part to the forms of capital that those commitments confer, whether that is *caste capital*, or the economic and cultural advantages that some Dalit (untouchable) Hindus nowadays perceive within conversion to Christianity. Although complex, the basic message for my argument is that on the whole doctrines and worldviews play an insignificant role in defining religious identity. This distance from doctrine and worldview is not only characteristic of Hinduism, but forms a significant part of most religious lives, where we distinguish the traditions contained in writings from the religious lives of the 'faithful'.

Moving to the European tradition, it seems that Rousseau understood the moral and ritual aspects of religious identity. Despite his deep antipathy towards doctrinal religion (Arthur et al. 2010, 38), Rousseau (2003, 96) developed a concept of civil religion of which "the Sovereign should fix the articles, not exactly as religious dogmas, but as social sentiments without which a man cannot be a good citizen or a faithful subject." Civic identity is fostered through religious symbols and practices, ensuring that citizens acquire the social sentiments appropriate to social cohesion. Rousseau's efforts to define a nondenominational religion appear to support a view of religion less about the doctrinal than the ritual, moral and, of course, civic. Such civil religion has been widely discussed by sociologists like Robert Bellah and has even been ascribed to Durkheim's sociological analysis of society (Wallace 1977). One might contend that the concept of civil religion is functionally irreligious, but in fact with Rousseau not only is there a distinct tone of religious tolerance and inclusion (apart from the radical exclusion – by execution – of those who are unable to commit to this civil religion!), but also the interpretation of civil rituals, symbols and narratives as religious, broadens our concept of religion beyond only beliefs or worldviews in the narrow sense. Drawing on Rousseau, de Tocqueville, Dewey and others, James Arthur (2010, Chapter 2) shows that the roots of citizenship education and Republicanism more generally are not secular, but are substantially founded upon the European Christian tradition.

But surely this prioritization of the rituals and symbols over doctrines cannot be said of the doctrinal, creedal and dogmatic Christian religion itself, the largest religion of the world today? Although contemporary disputes between different Christian groups or between Christians and creationists, for example, do suggest a religious life more structured by beliefs and worldviews, Christianity is more diverse with different conceptions of itself, some of which legislate against viewing Christianity primarily as a belief system or worldview. We have already noted Strhan's research in which evangelical belief is enacted in ways that blurs the boundary between believing and practicing doctrine. As Strhan (2013, 235) puts it, "holding on to belief requires the habituation of acts of daily discipline, mutual support, and reflexive acknowledgement of times of uncertainty and struggle." The formative power of habituating practices is of particular interest to James Smith, who blurs the boundary between secular and religious by reference to cultural liturgies.

Christian and cultural liturgies

Smith's writings on 'liturgy' (which for Smith is roughly synonymous with worship) show that the propositional or worldview conception of religion does not do justice to the power and meaning of Christian liturgies.[10] Drawing together Christian theology, philosophy and educational theory, Smith's basic view is that Christian liturgy is first and foremost a set of formative practices. Those formative practices address us less at the cognitive level of worldviews than is often assumed. Religious liturgies are inherently educational insofar as those liturgical practices "whether 'sacred' or 'secular' – shape and constitute our identities by forming our most basic attunement to the world" (Smith 2009, 25). For Smith all kinds of identity are shaped through liturgical practices, whether or not they are explicitly 'religious'. Smith's point is that we generally do not recognize secular practices as formative liturgies that shape and transmit identity because we take the secular domain to be value-free. One consequence of Smith's argument is that "there is no such thing as a 'secular' education" (Smith 2009, 26) in the sense that all kinds of educational practice entail an orientation to the world which is imbued with something fundamental to religions everywhere: liturgical practices.

To illustrate the power of secular liturgies, Smith (2009, 18–22) presents the habit of visiting a shopping mall in which ritual performances structure the experience and shape the desires of the shoppers. It is the effective shaping of human desires that makes Smith's interest educational as much as theological. In the mall, as in Western culture more broadly, consumerism coheres around consumerist liturgies. Icons are visible here: celebrity advertising presents the good life that many of us aspire to, seeking not to convince us of the consistency or rationality of its ideals, but appealing to the imagination. The shoppers receive this vision of the good as

> ... a religious proclamation that does not traffic in abstracted ideals or rules or doctrines, but rather offers the imagination pictures and statues and moving images. While other religions are promising salvation through the thin, dry media of books and messages, this new global religion is offering

44　Religion and belief

embodied pictures of the redeemed that invite us to imagine ourselves in their shoes

(Smith 2009, 21).

From this point of view, the distinction between secular and sacred liturgy is not clear-cut. This suggests that our everyday practices enact a way of being-in-the-world which cannot be straightforwardly separated from religion.[11] The ways in which our everyday activities are liturgical suggest that those activities orient our desires. Indeed, that is the point of the shopping mall, that our desires are oriented towards the acquisition of more consumer goods. For Smith, Christian liturgy is, of course, oriented differently: towards God.

Smith's argument is reminiscent of that developed by the theologian Paul Tillich. Tillich (1964, 8) argued that faith is less about the intellectual or cognitive content of beliefs than with our ultimate concern, a concern which grasps us as much as we grasp it. Both Tillich and Smith see worship operating at a level that might be seen as part of our 'pre-understanding' or framing of the world (both thinkers owe an intellectual debt to Heidegger in this and other respects). The significance of this is that *liturgy* or *concern* happens whether we like it or not (rather like Heidegger's notion of care — *Sorge* — as the structure of Dasein's being-in-the-world). This disrupts the notion of religion as a choice or decision, as well as disrupting the propositional/worldview conception of religion since it is, in a sense, pre-cognitive. Like Smith, Tillich is skeptical of the voluntarist conception of religious life, which tends to frame religion in terms of making choices between competing worldviews. Tillich regarded other concerns (e.g., political, social or moral concerns, or indeed personal interests and consumerist concerns) as preliminary or provisional and understood that preliminary concerns could be — problematically — treated as ultimate. Tillich (1967, vol. 1, 13ff) applies the term *idolatry* to the elevation of a provisional concern to ultimate status. In other words, where we stake our lives on a successful career with financial rewards, then we effectively worship the provisional as though it were ultimate. Theologians like Tillich could no doubt read Smith's account of cultural liturgy more critically: as an account of idolatry. But it is the continuity between secular and religious concerns in Tillich and Smith that is important here.[12] Clearly then, religion is not just what we do on the Sabbath, or what we believe (or even what we say we believe) in propositional terms, our theory of the world. It is these things but a lot more that is less visible and less cognitive. Equally, the religious nature of a school, for example, is not easily defined as though it can be contained within a mission statement, or the confessions of faith by its staff or students.

The reader might be tempted to reply that the consequence of my argument is that since everyone is engaged in some kind of liturgy, then everyone is effectively religious — a pretty meaningless proposition! My provisional reply would be only that I am not interested in establishing a correct propositional claim about the nature of religious life and its connection to education. To say that everyone is religious, while not being straightforwardly true, offers some useful insight in certain contexts (where people do not recognize that any way of life is deeply value-laden), so it is less a general truth claim than a device. It is a useful Hindu device to suggest that we are all devoted to something, and that we had better become conscious of our devotional practices, rather than let the market form and dictate them. Hence ritual practices are there to bring attention and shape to our devotional lives. At a more subtle level, the reader should note that my argument speaks not only to issues around religious epistemology/ontology but inevitably raises general epistemological/ontological questions about commitment and belief in general. There is a shift here: from seeing religious commitments as propositional truth claims, to seeing commitments as practices, forming and formed by religious practices. We might call this *practicing doctrine*. This notion of practicing doctrine is interestingly reflected in Rowan Williams' (2012, 16) reservations about the reduction of religious life to a set of propositions:

> All the major historic faiths, even Islam, which is closest to the propositional model at first sight, assume in their classical forms an interaction between forms of self-imaging and self-interpreting, through prayer and action, and the formal language of belief; that language works not simply to describe an external reality, but to modify over time the way self and world are *sensed*.

In other words, the classical propositions and creeds of religious traditions are to be 'practiced' more than taken to be true (or false) propositions. There is, then, a philosophy of language built into this relation which rejects the correspondence view in which terms stand for objects. Language is performative more than propositional. This again affirms the point that this philosophy of religion also entails an examination of ontology and epistemology.

Smith's account engages more directly with the question of education. The point here is that the way liturgies are enacted has little to do with the adoption of a belief system, a set of truth claims or a worldview. This is why, employing the language of Charles Taylor, Smith (2009, 133) goes on to argue for the primacy of worship over worldview in the formation of human desire: "it might be more helpful to talk about a Christian social imaginary than to focus on a Christian worldview, given that the latter seems tinged with a lingering cognitivism." So for Smith the formation of desire shapes our being-in-the-world at a level that is *ontologically prior* to the decisions we make as religious or non-religious subjects. In one sense, our intentions precede our actions, but those intentions are themselves shaped by formative practices. At this point it becomes hard to prioritize intention, action and belief since they are all implicated in the motion of the hermeneutical circle of our being-in-the-world. But certainly our liturgical practices have an effect. Stated bluntly, all actions are liturgical, just as all liturgies are formative and educational. The question for Smith is this:

how are our varied liturgies forming us? What kind of being-in-the-world is developed in the liturgical practices of the present consumerist age?

What kind of freedom?

Both secular and religious liturgies contain within them a conception of the good life. The secular liturgy of the shopping mall inculcates a culture into lifestyle habits more perniciously than religious indoctrination. I say this because religious liturgies – on the whole – are explicitly framed as formative practices, whereas secular liturgies hide behind the veil of freedom: the indoctrination of secular liturgies employs the desires of apparently autonomous individuals who regard themselves as free to choose (between brands X and Y). Smith finds that the conceptions of freedom and autonomy embodied in consumerist liturgies conceal the enframed nature of the choices before us. How often do we see adverts for perfumes, for example, telling stories of breaking out of conventions and becoming 'free'? [13] Are we not enslaved by this kind of freedom? As Smith notes, our modern conceptions of liberty are more or less universal in their rejection of teleological conceptions of the good life. Traditions that attempt to shape desire towards the good life, for example, the Platonic or Christian traditions, are objectionable because they impose a heteronomous vision of the good life. The imposition of a heteronomous vision of the good is almost inconceivable today simply because it opposes the subject's autonomy which has become the *sine qua non* of modern subjectivity, the liberal 'ultimate concern'. The material benefits of modernity are profound, but perhaps the greatest achievement is that sense of individual liberty and choice over the kind of life one wishes to live. Indeed our education system today has this libertarian conception of autonomy as one of its founding principles (Gutmann 1982; Brighouse 2009). One could argue that it is precisely the goal of autonomy which distinguishes our modern education system from premodern initiation, inculcation or indoctrination, and thus transmission of belief contradicts autonomy (Siegel 1988). With the concept of autonomous freedom installed within our social imaginary certain problems and questions present themselves to educational theorists: the freedom of parents seem to be in competition with the rights of the child with respect to 'life choices'; the right of the state to impose a particular form of common schooling is in tension with the individual choices of parents and their children. These debates might then hinge upon the point at which the child's rationality, and thereby their autonomy, is sufficiently developed to challenge the authoritative rationality of the parents, or where the limits of state authority over individual freedoms lie. These examples seem, broadly speaking, to reflect a Hobbesian ontology in which the original condition of human subjects is to be in conflict. From the perspective of freedom as radical autonomy, a genuinely common good where interests can be shared, rather than sublimated or privatized for the sake of a social contract, is almost inconceivable. The modern liberal state is there to ensure a minimal negative

Religion and belief 47

liberty, in contrast to the notion of true civic liberty that Isaiah Berlin (2002) has famously traced back to Aristotle. This tension here between autonomy and the common good (too often interpreted heteronomously) has animated political philosophers for a generation. In the context of education theory James Arthur (2010) has provided a clear account of a *Republican* 'resolution', or at least the acknowledgment of this tension. Arthur's Republican idea of the common good is conceived deliberatively, allowing for sufficient autonomy and identity without the pure will of an autonomous subject.

Turning from a political to a theological response, the opposition between autonomy and heteronomy is fallacious since it presupposes that divine law and personal freedom are opposed. The general theological view, often regarded as paradoxical, sees personal freedom as only realized when aligned with divine law. Attempts to mediate this polarity are well known: e.g., St Augustine and the Pelagian controversy, Kant's paradox between individual autonomy and the moral law, or Tillich's (1967, vol 1, 185) attempts to demonstrate the continuity between freedom and destiny.[14] Smith's argument develops a similar account of freedom which questions the radical autonomy of the individual subject. He suggests that modern secular liturgies form within us this sense of freedom, making any other conception of freedom, such as that entailing the submission or attenuation of the self, hard to conceive. For Smith the educational dimension of the formation of desire within the theological traditions offers crucial resistance to this since God's law and his will puts in question "the desire for autonomy that is impressed upon us by secular liturgies" (2009, 176). The concepts of freedom and autonomy, imposed and reinforced by secular liturgies within the consumerist culture of late modernity, are not recognized as historically or culturally contingent inventions or constructions, built upon Kantian and Cartesian metaphysics, but are taken to be the human condition. In philosophical terms we are, as Sartre put it, *condemned to be free*, having no ultimate law but the nihilistic will of our own making.

Some accounts of philosophical and intellectual history seek to inform us of that context and educate us on the contingency of our view of subjective freedom.[15] But these narratives largely operate at the conceptual level, and one is left wondering how these narratives can compete with the secular liturgies that train and practice that condition of autonomous freedom. Certain traditions and practices (religious or not) offer 'counter-liturgies', some of which Smith is keen to draw attention to. Art can be one such counter-practice. Williams (2012, Chapter 1) argues that an aesthetic dimension can shake us free of the instrumentalism of secular public spaces. Indeed art can interrupt the smooth circulation of capital and desire satisfaction, but seems largely coopted by those very circulatory systems, where art collectors seem more like investors than beholders, and the public are framed as consumers of art as 'experiences'. Such concerns animated much of Heidegger's later work and his drawing upon the poets who speak the interruption of language itself. We will return to Heidegger's contribution in Chapter 4.

48 Religion and belief

Both Smith and Tillich offer an important contribution to a discussion of the post-secular. They understand that secular perspectives embody a range of commitments, concerns and liturgies which are not necessarily visible at level of propositions or worldviews. The post-secular points to the recognition that the kinds of binaries that structure our thinking about religion – religious/secular, faith/reason – are misleading since they are far more porous than the secularist account would have us believe. Smith's account of secular liturgies might also be understood as applying to broader contexts. As we saw in the last chapter, Carol Black's concerns around *Education for All* reveal how the idea of the 'international community' seems to be predicated on a secular liturgy which takes its imaginative reference points from notions of progress, development, improvement and growth. The secular worship of progress and our Eurocentric cultural bias seem to work with the consumerist culture in which the good life is measured almost exclusively in terms of material gain, growth and competitive advantage. The liturgies that frame our culture in one-dimensional consumerist terms are reinforced by a neocolonial ideology performed through the exclusion of anything that falls outside to the biases present within the international community[16] and enacted by policies such as *Education for All*.

Religion as 'belief systems' has become acceptable shorthand for religious life. With this shift we are also compelled to examine whether one belief system is 'better' than another: Which is more ethical? Which brings about greater happiness? Which is more 'plausible' or 'defensible'? We take competing positions, challenge opposed positions, defend assumed positions and become aware of our *positionality* in the process. But consideration of position is not neutral. It frames our thinking about the nature of religion and its place in education, and provides the context in which we seek to separate private religious practice from shared public life. That different worldviews need to be, in some sense respected or reconciled is one logical outcome, and the classroom is one place in which various forms of respect and reconciliation might be tested. Little wonder then, that educationalists often sharply distinguish religion from education, as in French laws of laïcité where the division between public and private in state education is robustly upheld. The seeds of laïcité were sown before the French Revolution in the naturalized theology of the French Enlightenment, which despite complex attitudes to religious authority was progressively drawing reason, knowledge and education away from the clutches of established churches. Other historical processes also play into this division between private and public. The establishment of state-funded schooling in the nineteenth and twentieth centuries across much of Europe cannot be understood apart from the Enlightenment legacy of the eighteenth century in which education was often aligned with the promotion of rationality and empiricism. It should be noted, though, that the view of the European Enlightenment as necessarily in opposition to religion, which my argument roughly presupposes, is a view that better characterizes some states and contexts more than others. Comparison of

Religion and belief 49

French and Scottish Enlightenment traditions, for example, shows very different attitudes to the place of religion in public life:

> Unlike their French counterparts, the great minds of the Scottish Enlightenment never saw Christianity as their mortal enemy – not even Hume, the self-proclaimed sceptic. For the clerical disciples of Hutcheson, Church and Enlightenment were natural allies, in much the same way as science and the humanities were not pitted against each other, but were two halves of the same intellectual enterprise
>
> (Herman 2003, 79).

While acknowledging this complexity, it is true to say that as the Age of Reason took hold, so did the philosophy of positivism, a view of the world in part shaped our current view of religion. We can, then, link the conception of religion as set of beliefs or propositional truth claims and the secular move to separate private and public.

The sky is not a cow

Echoing Taylor, I call the framing of religion in terms of doctrines and propositions the 'propositional frame.' The propositional frame works subliminally to structure our thinking about religion, presenting us with certain problems and questions about indoctrination and the rights of parents to raise children within particular religions. As a set of conceptual rules determining the nature of (religious) knowing, the propositional frame shares much with Foucault's (1970) conception of *épistème*, which itself has often been compared to Kuhn's notion of the paradigm (Piaget 1970, 132). Foucault's interest is primarily in the description of the shifting historical *épistème* than with explaining why those changes take place. Given the elusive nature of this conceptual framing, this is not surprising; still some effort to consider this shifting mindset is worthwhile.

Much of this work is undertaken by philosophers and theorists who are working within a Western 'culturally Christian' context in which the propositional view of religion is the norm. Despite the strength of James Smith's account, I would not deny that the history of Latin Christianity could plausibly be read as a history of belief and doctrine, where disputations, inquisitions and creedal formulations appear to take propositional form. But we have noted that there are other dimensions to religion beyond the propositional. I now turn to another religious studies scholar who took a more direct approach to challenging the propositional conception of religion.

Wilfred Cantwell Smith (1998, v) argues that the idea that believing is religiously important is a modern one, that "a great modern heresy of the church is the heresy of believing". Smith goes on to say that is it the 'anti-religious' thinkers who hold "even more doggedly than theologians that believing is what religious people primarily do." Smith (1998, 11) illustrates his point with the

50 Religion and belief

example of the ancient Egyptians, a highly sophisticated culture of people who believed that "the sky is a cow." With the benefits of modern science 'we now know' (as the saying goes) that the sky is not a cow. But were the Egyptians plain wrong? The question is not whether the Egyptians were right or wrong, but what they meant by this idea.

> I am seriously suggesting that the ancient Egyptians' apprehension of their environment evidenced in and made possible through such statements may well have been – however partially or poetically – of a reality that is indeed there. My guess is that they perceived something about the sky, about animals, about themselves, and about the relations among these, that Ayer and his friends have missed
>
> (1998, 14).

Smith is, of course, referencing the reductive dismissals by the logical positivists for which Ayer stands as totem. Smith (41ff) analyses a number of key terms: opinion, creed, faith and belief in order to develop a convincing case that the term *believing* does not, in fact, primarily refer to holding propositionalist opinions about states of affairs. To believe is related to the German *belieben* which, signifying love (German *Liebe*; Latin *libido*), means "to hold dear" or "to prize", evoking senses of loyalty and faithfulness (further indicating that 'faith' refers to a commitment of the heart rather than assenting without evidence). These linguistic associations are alive in present-day English. If the prime minister implores us to 'believe in Britain' as the election approaches, or a teacher encourages a student to believe in herself in advance of the exam, the usage of belief is, in Austin's terms, performative rather than representational. Similarly, speaking of a dog as a faithful friend does not tell us much about the dog's theological position. Thus to believe or to have faith, especially in their verbal forms, does not need to be equated with assenting to propositions about, for example, the existence of God. Wilfred Cantwell Smith, Charles Taylor, James Smith and Rowan Williams all share the desire to problematize the common sense idea that religious beliefs correspond with propositional truth claims. And if this propositional view of religion is a straw man within philosophy of religion, it is less so in philosophy of education.

My target here is the 'common sense' nature of certain views, not the idea that beliefs can be propositional per se. It would be disingenuous to suggest that there is nothing intellectual or cognitive at stake in debates between religious and other worldviews, that scientific discoveries had no substantial impact upon religious beliefs. But some theologians regard the modern discoveries of science as reawakening a sense of the real contribution that theology can make: not in competition with science, but by raising questions about the meaning of science as such.[17] My intention here is to question both the propositional framing of religion and the progressivism that underpins the rise of enlightened secularism. Both of these assumptions have problematic influences upon how

Religion and belief 51

we conceive of education today. It will be clear that I strongly take issue with the view of history as the inexorable rise of enlightened secularism; for this Whig history, which regards secularization as an inevitable outcome of modern science, industrialization and democratic state politics, needs to come to terms with many recent developments that we have already discussed, most notably, that religion is a pervasive and ongoing influence. This progressivism suits one narrative of modernity, the mainstay of twentieth-century sociological theories of secularization that Taylor has been particularly keen to denounce: namely the subtractive view. This subtractive view sees rationality replacing superstition, naturalistic explanations replacing theological or spiritual forces, and the world becoming progressively disenchanted following Weber's thesis.[18] In this account the removal of faith and the subsequent separation of church and state should lead to a "zone of absence" (Warner, VanAntwerpen, and Calhoun 2013, 8) in which neutral secular reason should be employed to structure social institutions in non-partisan terms. But as we saw with Talal Asad's account of the secular, this neutral zone turns out to privilege those for whom religious life has no meaning. Far from being neutral, such forms of secularism appear to some commentators to be doing violence to certain expressions of religious faith.[19] Taylor (2007, 525), on the other hand, tends to be more circumspect, defining secularism as something of a productive process, in contrast to a subtractive one. What is important for my argument is that the subtractive view which sees autonomous reason in terms of universal rationality and self-determination that is in tension with and able to subtract out religious commitments, has "sunk to the level of common sense" and so is part of the assumed backdrop of our worldview, or what Taylor calls, our "social imaginary" (Smith 2014, 26). This Whig history has informed the social imaginary of educational culture inasmuch as we tend to see the trajectory of human life in developmental terms, and this narrative forms part of the critical and emancipatory view of the child just as much as of the society. The influence of this developmental assumption and the progressivist narrative attached to it should be critically examined. But this can only happen when the presumed notion of what it means to be rational — itself part of the social imaginary — becomes questionable. In other words, only through bringing into question what has become common sense — progressivism and religion as proposition — can we begin to reimagine the proper role of religion in public life and in education specifically. Then perhaps we will not begin with the assumption that religion is a 'problem' for education (Strhan 2014).

The propositional frame

A number of threads have been laid out in this chapter which I now hope to weave together under the phrase 'the propositional frame.' Those familiar with Charles Taylor's work on secularism may note parallels here between his conception of the *immanent frame* and my account of the propositional framing of

52 Religion and belief

religion. The propositional frame should be seen as a *condition for seeing* facts and beliefs within positivist and propositional terms: our tendency to see beliefs and facts on the same ontological level suggests the invisible outline of the propositional frame, an ontology which structures the terms of the debate. Similarly, Taylor (2007, 542ff.) wants to show how the secular age brings with it the 'immanent frame' in which our being-in-the-world is self-sufficient and naturalized, not resting upon any transcendent source. Both involve *framing* because they structure the terms of the debate at a level that we are generally not conscious of. To live within Taylor's immanent frame does not mean our ideas or beliefs have necessarily shifted, but rather our presuppositions are reconfigured: the world we see no longer presupposes transcendence. Where once we saw pattern and intention, we may now see only chance and perhaps coincidence. Within the immanent frame, *coincidence*, to use that example, might simply be that: two contiguous and unrelated incidents which human sometimes project meaning onto. In our disenchanted age, many people are content to recognize coincidences as nothing more than this. A bad storm is unpleasant and inconvenient, but does not portend some divine interruption. This describes a shift in the range of interpretive options open to people, which is the decisive feature of Taylor's secular age. Taylor's insight is to see secularization not as the decline in church attendance or the rise of secular states and the progressive separation of Church and state (all of which is questioned by the 'return of religion'), but as a shift in less visible 'conditions of belief': the presuppositions that structure our encounter with the world. Taylor sees the fundamental condition that has changed from the Renaissance to the present, to be that belief in God is now one option among others, rather than the assumption. In short, atheism is possible, even the default, while belief must be admitted, confessed and justified. We live in an immanent frame and that means that choosing to believe in God is very much more explicit than it once was. Where premodern people may have asked questions about the meaning of a ritual, text, events and experiences, such questions would, argues Taylor, have taken place within the assumed presence of something ultimate, mysterious and transcendent. The question was less 'does God exist?' as much as 'what is the meaning of 'God'?' Since then, debates about God have often begun with justification for belief or unbelief. It is this conceptual backdrop that for Taylor has seen a decisive shift over the past five centuries.[20]

What I am calling the propositional frame, then, owes a conceptual debt to Taylor's thesis of the immanent frame: both structure how we engage with the world, the kinds of questions that occur to us, and what needs to be argued for – and therefore what can be taken for granted. So not only do we inhabit an immanent frame in which transcendence is no longer the assumed backdrop of existence, but we also inhabit a propositional frame in which we assume religion is constituted by beliefs and truth claims. These features of secularity, the immanent and propositional framing of the world, amplify the tensions between religion and modernity. Education, from the perspective of the immanent and propositional frames, can serve to emancipate students from religion by introducing them to critical thinking and to propositions that supplant the false beliefs of ages past.

The point here is to draw attention to the conceptual backdrop in which discussions around religion and education take place. As has been noted, theology has attempted to respond to scientific discoveries in a range of ways, sometimes appearing to offer a god of the gaps which is neither intellectually satisfying nor spiritually edifying. But what might be called the 'conflict narrative' between religion and science – seen paradigmatically in the Galileo affair – is extremely one-sided, if interpreted only in terms of the heroic efforts of objective and fair-minded scientists against the dogmatic and immovable institution of the church (see Brooke 1991; Barbour 2000). As with present conflicts in the Middle East, it is scarcely possible to untangle political maneuvering, economic interests, religious commitment and tribalism in the Galileo affair (Randles 1999). But even more significant than the political and historical complexities is that we tend to take the debates to be about what people believe explicitly and propositionally rather than examining the conditions of belief. We therefore tend to frame the conflict as one between the progressive and enlightened seekers after truth against the regressive and dogmatic religious authorities and institutions.

Within the propositional frame it is perfectly reasonable to suppose that religion boils down to acts of belief. For many people it is, in the end, one's beliefs that define one's religious life, a view that secularists and atheists are happy to assume since it accords well with the narrative of enlightened human reason supplanting superstition and falsifying beliefs. More telling perhaps is that many religious people also, particularly when pressed, interpret their own religious lives in terms structured by the propositional frame. Williams (2012, 15) points to the "secularization of a great deal of religious discourse" wherein religious people themselves assume the immanent and propositional frames. Williams (2012, 16) recognizes in this a reduction of religion to the propositional, saying that "[w]hen religious commitment is seen first as the acceptance of propositions which determine acceptable behavior – the kind of religiousness we tend now to call fundamentalist – something has happened to religious identity." The propositional frame structures both sides of the debate, providing a general backdrop within which discussions across religion and education are framed with a detrimental impact on mutual understanding. Christians are pressed to respond to evolutionists because they (both Christians and evolutionists) take for granted that the evidence of the Bible contradicts, or at best is in tension with, the claims of evolutionary biology. High school students of religion debate the justification that different religions offer for suffering (theodicy) or for the veracity of religious experiences and so forth, much of which supposes a view religion structured by the propositional frame.[21] The terms of these debates are seldom questioned. Webb Keane (2007) has shown that this propositional framing of religion is enacted in modern reformed evangelical Christian movements. Strhan (2013, 227) neatly summarizes the relation between propositional framing and formation of subjectivity: "Keane describes these Protestant practices as shaping subjects who located belief and agency in the self, creating the conditions for the emergence of the individualised, autonomous subject of the Enlightenment." This propositional framing is seldom critically examined outside of what is known as the lived religion approach (Strhan 2013, 225), and it is my contention that educational theory fails to take account of wider conceptions of religion drawn from developments within religious studies.

But how does this argument take account of certain concrete instances, for example, of Christians who believe in young earth creationism (that the world was created by God 4400 years ago according to a literal reading of the Biblical account). I do not wish to deny that such Bible-believing Christians are a significant part of the Christian community, nor that their beliefs are in tension with the facts laid before us by recent, and not so recent, scientific discoveries. The argument is that their religious experience, emerging out of the Protestant-reformed Christian tradition, is structured both by Taylor's immanent frame, as well as the propositional frame. The adherence to scriptural literalism reflects a 'logocentrism' at the heart of Western positivism and culture in which the logos (here understood as a narrow idea of reason, language and, by implication, propositional thinking) is regarded as the core dimension of human existence. So the religious traditions that rely more upon the 'word' of God – in particular the religions of the book (Judaism, Christianity and Islam, though even here, some schools within each of these traditions tend towards flatter more literal hermeneutics and others like the Jewish Midrash tradition have far richer hermeneutical traditions) are, unsurprisingly, more structured by this propositional frame. This hermeneutical consideration raises a vast debate that is beyond my scope (Vroom and Gort 1997). The point is that rather than seeing 'Christians', 'Muslims' or 'Hindus' en bloc, our conceptions of these religions need to take account of much greater religious and hermeneutical diversity. This requires intra-religious as well as inter-religious dialogue. Expanding our concept of religion to include elements beyond doctrine and proposition will, I think, open new paths of inquiry within the religion and education debate, just as it affords new readings of the relations between science and religion. It is not hard to see that the Bible, for example, is not a set of propositions to be taken at face value. It is well known that reading the Bible in different ways (what was once called the fourfold hermeneutic: literal, allegorical, moral and anagogical) demonstrates that there is more to the Bible than a belief system or a set of creeds. Similarly, Islam, which at first sight tends to the propositional and literal adherence to the word of the Qur'an, does also, in fact, rest upon wider textual and hermeneutical traditions (in particular the tafsir and Hadith). Those acquainted with religious traditions will be familiar with something of this hermeneutical depth, which does provoke the question of why more nuanced conceptions of religion have been largely absent from debates within educational philosophy, a question I will briefly address at the end of this chapter.

Educational implications of the propositional frame

If one believes that religions have an intrinsic and insatiable tendency to indoctrinate in order to reproduce (Copley 2005; Nasiretti 2009), or that it is logically impossible to impart religious belief without indoctrination (Hand 2002), then a neat dichotomy between facts and beliefs can be appealing. Where it is assumed that religious beliefs rely upon truth claims that are contested or debatable, the only correct term for imparting those beliefs to young people is *indoctrination*. Those who speak for aspects of religion in education reject the idea that religious education is essentially indoctrination by arguing that religious education leaves the ultimate decision to the student (Merry 2005). But even so, arguments that affirm the agency of the student still do not escape the propositional frame since the choices are presented at the cognitive level between competing claims to truth. The Woolf Report (Woolf Institute 2015, 13) devotes considerable attention to showing that "religion is not only a matter of personal deliberation, choice and commitment" pointing out that the terms "*cradle Catholic, ethnic Protestant* and *nominal Christian* refer to the ways in which a person's religious identity is not always a conscious choice on their part." Its balanced approach could be considered a model of procedural secularism for schools, making recommendations in which the nature of religion and belief as such become important questions:

> Education about religion and belief is essential because it is in schools and colleges that there is the best and earliest chance of breaking down ignorance and developing individuals who will be receptive of the other, and ask difficult questions without fear of offending. This is vital for the fruition of our vision for a fairer, more cohesive society
>
> (2015, 36).

Still, the report also states that a curriculum that does not contain elements of indoctrination would allow us to remove the current legal right to withdraw from religious education. This must prompt us to wonder what a curriculum free of some kind of indoctrination would possibly mean, and whether the authors, working from within the propositional frame, assume that a 'non-indoctrinatory' approach is plausible. Many teachers can and do distinguish indoctrinatory and deliberative approaches to education, but in one sense it is important to recognize that the goal of indoctrination-free education is derived from the propositional frame.

Although framing religion in terms of individual choice does, I suggest, tend to reflect a propositional conception of religion, it could be argued that the link here is not a necessary one. As we saw earlier, Hand (2015, 35) takes religious belief to concern the assent to propositions, but he also questions what he calls "direct doxastic voluntarism" (the view that we have direct control over our beliefs). Hand argues that although we normally cannot believe what we choose, there are occasions when we can. Most problematic here is not the issue of our inability to choose, but the binaries that Hand trades in: we believe and assent to some proposition or another. Our agency and subjectivity are not really in question, serving to make decisions and give reasons. Such conceptions work well with propositions that are intended to represent states of affairs (following Aristotle's law of non-contradiction). Hand's argument that beliefs are not generally choices we make only serves to reveal how his stance is framed by the propositional. Describing belief as a spectrum or sliding scale would seem a more natural counter to voluntarism, but Hand does not consider this because it would entail a partial break from the propositional frame.[22]

A more nuanced account of agency and decision in reference to belief can be found in Williams, who takes the argument a step further by suggesting that the privatization of religion that propositional belief reinforces is a parochial view of being religious. Such parochialism will provoke a political reaction:

> Islam is thus defined by liberal rhetoric into a version of individualized Christianity, a set of personal options for leisure time. To be thus defined, in stark tension with the grammar of the faith itself, naturally prompts a political resistance. Neither globally nor nationally have we yet fully understood these issues; some current discussion of 'faith schools' suggests a radical tone-deafness about all this, assuming that partnership between public institutions and religious communities is simply a subsiding of bigotry
> (2012, 19).

Although Williams provides a rather one-sided assessment of the 'faith schools' debates, he does indicate how the connections between the political tensions and theological reductions are expressed therein. The sensitivity of Williams' readings encourages a form of procedural secularism that avoids legal privilege to any specific religious position without denying the potentially positive contributions that these positions might make. As part of a pluralist procedural secularism, religious and non-religious views inform deliberative processes which are inclusive if not crudely representational (as we shall discuss in Chapter 8). This is the kind of mediation between private and public that is needed in the present age. None of this is meant to deny the student's or child's freedom in developing their own religious identity, but as James Smith noted, the notion of the freedom to choose cannot be taken for granted or adopted from the prevailing common sense view that the human identity is a fully autonomous subject.

Notions of voluntarism, most often associated with puritanical Protestantism and Kantian conceptions of will, tend to frame human autonomy as absolute. This absolutism, whether in Kantian or Protestant terms, sees religious decision-making in narrowly subjectivist terms. Consider, by contrast to this idealized conception of will, the emergent agency of young people in relation to the foods they eat, the clothes they wear, the language(s) they speak, and the traditions and rituals they undertake. Agency is not negated by formation any more than by character. Indeed, only through the formative negotiations of growth and life can agency and character be discovered, exercised and formed. We do not often find educational theorists debating the *ethics* of language transmission or diet formation. After all, children will eat something and will pick up language. But it is not immediately obvious why the transmission of religion is treated differently. When religion is understood through the propositional frame as a worldview, the question of indoctrination comes to the fore.

We began this chapter with reference to the debate between Cooling and Hand and return to it again to further illustrate the subliminal operation of the propositional frame. Of course Hand's propositional framing of religion does not necessitate an outright rejection of it: "[s]ome religious propositions are sufficiently well supported by evidence and argument as to merit serious consideration by reasonable people" (2003, 162). Although Hand's view of religion is rather more reductive than many others, if we expect Cooling to take a more nuanced view of the matter we might be disappointed. It is true that Cooling does not agree with Hand that education should be "shaped only by neutral, objective, secular thinking" (Cooling 2010, 24). At first glance Cooling might appear to support my argument since he is more supportive of the formative role for religion within education. Cooling (2010, 27) believes that education cannot be neutral since "beliefs, including religious beliefs, are integral to human knowing and therefore education." Cooling's analysis that all worldviews should be treated 'fairly' might be lent to a procedural secularism in which a range of perspectives, religious and non-religious, form and inform the debate. A clue to the problem with Cooling's analysis lies with his use of the term 'worldview'. For Cooling the question is not whether religion should be conceived in terms of worldviews, but whether the idea of an education that is 'worldview neutral' is coherent. Worldview neutral education is, according to Cooling, partisan, absorbing and reflecting the assumptions of a secular consumerist culture. On one level, Cooling's analysis is reminiscent of James Smith and his account of secular liturgies, but the difference is that Smith is explicit in problematizing the propositional conception of liturgy. Cooling, on the other hand, does not perceive or question the propositional framing of the debate itself. Both Cooling and Hand take different sides on an argument that does not question the nature of religion as belief in a set of doctrines or truth claims which amount to a worldview. One might say that Cooling and Hand share a metaphysical stance, an ontology, which I have argued is positivist, propositional and reductive. No wonder, then, that Cooling fails in the end to convincingly reply to Hand's (2012) criticisms since Cooling is playing the game by the rules of the secular reduction of religion to the propositional.

David Aldridge (2015, 180) convincingly shows that the real problem here is that neither Hand nor Cooling are prepared to address the ontological significance of seeing a theoretical and explicit worldview as derivative of a prior

58 Religion and belief

ontological intentionality. There is a wider discussion here that draws in Heidegger's conception of truth as an event of disclosure (*aletheia*) rather than as (propositional) correctness. For Aldridge, Andrew Wright's attempts to protect religious education from a thin pluralism that presupposes truth is not at stake, fails to recognize this difference: "[t]his is not truth understood epistemologically, as the assent to one or other theory, but ontologically, as the transformational disclosure of possibilities and an orientation in one's being towards the matter at hand" (Aldridge 2015, 186). This reference to Heidegger's conception of truth underscores what has been developed throughout this chapter: that religious truth is not best understood as a set of propositional statements. It is worth asking whether the propositional frame is straightforwardly equivalent to Heidegger's pre-understanding of being as it is formed in the present age (not that Heidegger's ontological considerations can ever be described as straightforward). From a Heideggerian point of view, our intentionality is not something we do or something we can entirely thematize. As constitutive of the being of Dasein, our intentionality precedes us – certainly preceding any cognitive intervention. The propositional frame moves in this direction, being neither something we do, nor something we can directly critically assess.

Conclusion

In this chapter I have explored the impact of the propositional framing of religion which I take to be characteristic of a secular reduction. Philosophers of religion have pointed out the Eurocentric bias within this notion of secularism and the propositional frame, an analysis that I have suggested should be extended to education. One view of the post-secular, then, would be to develop the opportunity to 'return to religion' in ways that go beyond reductive propositional framings – going beyond an understanding of religions as competing worldviews or belief-systems. Applied to education, we might explore how different symbolic systems offer rich narratives which make meaning, as recent work in edusemiotics appears to be doing (Stables 2005; Stables and Semetsky 2015). This might entail a cultural and aesthetic appreciation of alternative forms of religious life. A simple example is the exhibition of religious life and art at St Mungo's Museum in Glasgow. Here religious questions that cut across different traditions are raised within an ecumenical atmosphere (e.g., the meaning of angels or where the dead go). This is not a reduction of religion to the purely aesthetic, but offers a sense of the meaning and phenomenon of religion in a way that is sensitive to the complexity and significance of each. A more substantial examination of this question will be the idea of 'deliberative religiosity' in which religious perspectives come into meaningful contact with alternatives. These encounters would encourage a respect for other ways of being-in-the-world that are too often disregarded as primitive, premodern and uneducated. This may seem a little postmodern, poststructural and perhaps even relativistic, though I do not believe that it is therefore nihilistic or irreligious.[23]

The preceding discussion begs certain questions: If the propositional frame is indeed quite so reductive a view of religion, why has educational philosophy been allowed to take it for granted? How is it that more nuanced accounts of religion have not interrupted or informed these debates? One explanation is hinted at in the Cooling/Hand debate: that they share a metaphysics or ontology that precedes the content of the debate. The conception of being as straightforwardly represented through concepts – a representational or correspondence theory of truth – is a major target of Heidegger's philosophy. In the next chapter I will engage with Heidegger's philosophy to begin the larger ontological task implied here.

Notes

1 Strhan (2013) has elaborated the problem of interpreting religion through a Western Protestant lens which tends to be emphasised within evangelical Christianity. While this is a tendency that I will go on to discuss, Strhan also wishes to show that evangelical religiosity and belief is enacted through a range of lived practices, even if the discourse is one of propositional belief and truth claims. This is related to what I go on to refer to as practicing or doing doctrine.

2 Hand's concern here is to present two general conceptions of the term 'worldview', first as a theory of the world and/or meaning, and second, as a conceptual scheme that makes experience possible at all, such as Kant's categories. Hand is presenting neither as correct (though finds the former to be consistent with holding a religious worldview), but wants to show that these two senses are conflated by Cooling. My interest in this debate is to draw attention to a characteristic framing of the concept of worldview as a theory of things which Hand seems happier to attach to many religions (Hand 2012, 531). However, as will become clear, I do not believe these two conceptions of worldview can be kept distinct in the way Hand argues because our conceptual scheme forms what Taylor calls our social imaginary which itself has an impact, albeit at a subliminal level, on our general view of reality and what meanings we ascribe to things in the world. This is clear where Hand goes on to suggest that some agnostic people opt out of having a theory about the world – a worldview. This argument reinforces the voluntarism that I regard as problematic: religious people choose to take up a worldview while agnostics choose not to. If this is true at some theoretical level, it does not take us close to the phenomena of religious life for most people.

3 Further evidence of the ongoing currency of this approach can be found in a Spencer Foundation–funded project led by Adam Swift, Matthew Clayton and Andrew Mason (Politics and International Studies, University of Warwick, UK), who are interested in bridging the divide between "abstract philosophical principles and concrete policy recommendations in the area of religious schooling." The research involves "normative questions concerning the moral basis of the family, parents' rights to raise their children in accordance with their own beliefs and values, children's right to autonomy, and the state's interest in social cohesion and the creation of future citizens." (Spencer Foundation 2015)

4 There is much debate about whether Derrida's later work can be valuable resource for religious philosophy or whether it is radically atheistic (Baring and Gordon 2014).

5 Continental philosophy is more inclined to borrow from theology, philosophy of religion, fiction, poetry, myth, etc. (Vattimo 2003). Joshua Landy (2012) uses the phrase 'formative fiction' to speak of the non-propositional impact of literature (religious and otherwise) on helping us to become who we are.

6 Smart (1996) identifies seven dimensions of religion: the doctrinal, mythological, ethical, ritual, experiential, institutional and material.

7 It would also be a mistake to assume doctrine to only exist as regulative and propositional. The term 'doctrine' originally refers to *teaching*, which can be interpreted more as a process. Thus doctrines do not need to be reduced to propositions, but can act to give shape, rather than directly regulate belief (see Hunzinger 2003).

8 The concept of dharma is used by Hindus, Buddhists, Sikhs and Jains and is translated in various ways including to do one's duty, to be virtuous or the right way to live. That forms of the term cut across a range of religious traditions further reinforces my argument that religious identity is porous and flexible and does not rest upon specific, still less exclusive, propositional truth claims.

9 Of course 'Hinduism,' if it even exists as an identifiable religion about which there is some debate (Flood 1996, 16), is a diverse community of practitioners and practices. In particular the Bhakti traditions prioritise devotional aspects of religious practice. This is not to say that there is no metaphysics. The Bhakti tradition often identified with Shaivism in which the god Shiva is revered as the supreme being. My point is that even in modern Shaivism the metaphysics really seems to withdraw in significance.

10 Another good, though less explicitly educational, example of secular liturgies can be found in Wendy Doniger, professor of History of Religions at University of Chicago, comments that the ostensibly secular rituals of New Year's Eve, particularly making resolutions of change, share patterns with religious rituals (Green 2013). Those of us caught by consumerism are also more likely to celebrate Black Friday – a frenzied and ritualized high point of the consumer calendar – than Good Friday.

11 The spontaneous irruption of the French national anthem at moments of remembrance following the brutal attacks on public spaces in Paris on Friday 13 November 2015 illustrates well the idea of a secular state engaging in cultural liturgy. The irony that *La Marseillaise* carries within it a rather brutal chorus, "Let's water the fields with impure blood," underscores just how these kinds of liturgy are emotive and expressive rather than reflective of reasoned positions.

12 It is worth noting that Smith (2009, 87, n. 18) himself claims his position "has no truck" with Tillichian claims around ultimate concern for the reason that Tillich's ultimate reference point is not pluralist as Smith's position is.

13 BBC News recently reported that a Church of England advert featuring the Lord's Prayer could not be screened before the new *Star Wars* film. The president of the National Secular Society argued that the Church has no right "to foist its opinions upon a captive audience who have paid good money for a completely different experience" (Wyatt 2015) but thereby failed to see that his issue should apply to advertising generally. Whether the Church is well advised to use such an advertising media is another important debate.

14 In a similar vein, I have made my own attempt to mediate freedom and destiny within the philosophy of technology (Lewin 2006).

15 There are many examples. Much of Heidegger's work concerns human freedom and locates it within a history of metaphysics. But other similar approaches can be found in the work of MacIntyre (1981), Dupré (1993), Taylor (2007) and many others.

16 "We all know what is meant by the term 'international community', don't we? It's the west, of course, nothing more, nothing less. Using the term 'international community' is a way of dignifying the west, of globalising it, of making it sound more respectable, more neutral and high-faluting" (Jacques 2006).

17 The best exponent of a theology that synthesizes science and religion is that developed by the French priest and paleontologist Pierre Teilhard de Chardin.

18 The roots of this thesis are to be found in German Romanticism: Schiller, Goethe as well as Schopenhauer and Nietzsche.

Religion and belief 61

19 See Milbank (2010). Rowan Williams calls Milbank's thesis of an innate violence to secularism "a striking reversal of the received wisdom of modernity, for which religion is the inherently violent presence in culture" (Williams 2012, 15). Milbank's provocative thesis makes sense only in the sense that "it takes for granted contests of power as the basic form of social relation" (Williams 2012, 15).

20 Taylor's magisterial account of secularism has not been without criticism. Saba Mahmood has argued that Taylor's analysis reinforces and extends too narrow Euro-Atlantic Christian perspective (Mahmood 2013).

21 Strhan (2010) discusses the reductive nature of the Religious Studies GCSE examination process in England demonstrating the influence of what I have called the propositional frame when it comes to thinking about curricula.

22 David Aldridge has argued for the hermeneutical dimension to education to be taken more seriously, bringing Gadamer's conception of prejudice into view. In this context Aldridge (2015, 168) offers an analysis of the curriculum that is "not 'chosen' or 'decided' by the educator. We do not choose our prejudices. But this does not mean that curriculum is unrevisable." I find this account appealing since the agency of the teacher and the student is embedded in a mutual dialogue in which our choices are structured. We are, in other words, located between structure and agency. This is beyond the binary either/or in which we either have control of beliefs or do not. In reality it is somewhere in between, located in something like the grammatical 'middle voice' (Lewin 2011).

23 I am drawn to the understanding of relativism that allows that "things have the properties they have (e.g., beautiful, morally good, epistemically justified) not *simpliciter*, but only relative to a given framework of assessment (e.g., local cultural norms, individual standards), and correspondingly, that the truth of claims attributing these properties holds only once the relevant framework of assessment is specified or supplied" (Baghramian and Carter 2016).

References

Aldridge, D. (2015). *A Hermeneutics of Religious Education*. London: Bloomsbury.

Arthur, J., Gearon L., & Sears, A. (eds.). (2010). *Education, Politics and Religion: Reconciling the Civil and the Sacred in Education*. London: Routledge.

Baghramian, M., & Carter, J. A. (2016). "Relativism" in Edward N. Zalta (ed.) *The Stanford Encyclopedia of Philosophy* Retrieved from http://plato.stanford.edu/archives/spr2016/entries/relativism/

Barbour, I. (2000). *Religion and Science*. Norwich: SCM Press.

Baring, E., & Gordon, P. (2014). *The Trace of God: Derrida and Religion*. New York: Fordham University Press.

Berlin, I. (2002). *Liberty*. Oxford: Oxford University Press.

Brighouse, H. (2009). "Moral and Political Aims of Education" in Harvey Siegel (ed.) *The Oxford Handbook of Philosophy of Education*. Oxford: Oxford University Press, 35–51.

Brooke, J. (1991). *Science and Religion: Some Historical Perspectives*. Cambridge: Cambridge University Press.

Callan, E. (1985). "McLaughlin on Parental Rights" *Journal of Philosophy of Education*, 19, 111–118.

Cooling, T. (2010). *Doing God in Education*. London: Theos.

Copley, T. (2005) *Indoctrination, Education, and God*. London: SPCK.

Dupré, L. (1993). *Passage to Modernity: An Essay in the Hermeneutics of Culture*. New Haven: Yale University Press.

62 Religion and belief

Flood, G. (1996). *An Introduction to Hinduism*. Cambridge: Cambridge University Press.

Foucault, M. (1970). *The Order of Things*. New York: Pantheon Books.

Gardner, P. (1988). "Religious Upbringing and the Liberal Ideal of Religious Autonomy" *Journal of Philosophy of Education*, 22, 89–105.

Green, E. (2013). "Why Getting Drunk and Making Resolutions on New Year's Eve Are Profoundly Religious Acts" *The Atlantic*. Retrieved from http://www.theatlantic.com/international/archive/2013/12/why-getting-drunk-and-making-resolutions-on-new-years-are-profoundly-religious-acts/282744/

Gutmann, A. (1982). "What's the Use of Going to School?" in Amartya Sen and Bernard Williams (eds.) *Utilitarianism and Beyond*. Cambridge: Cambridge University Press, 261–278.

Hand, M. (2002). "Religious Upbringing Reconsidered" *Journal of Philosophy of Education*, 36, 545–557.

Hand, M. (2003). "Religious Education" in John White (ed.) *Rethinking the School Curriculum: Values, Aims and Purposes*. London: Routledge, 152–164.

Hand, M. (2012). "What's in a Worldview? On Trevor Cooling's Doing God in Education." *Oxford Review of Education*, 38: 5, 527–537.

Hand, M. (2015). "Religious Education and Religious Choice" *Journal of Beliefs & Values: Studies in Religion & Education*, 36: 1, 31–39.

Herman, A. (2003) *The Scottish Enlightenment: The Scots' Invention of the Modern World*. London: Fourth Estate.

Hunzinger, J. (2003). 'Postliberal Theology' in Kevin Vanhoozer (ed.) *The Cambridge Companion to Postmodern Theology*. Cambridge: Cambridge University Press, 42–57.

I'Anson, J., & Jasper, A. (2011). "Religion in Educational Spaces: Knowing, Knowing Well, and Knowing Differently." *Arts & Humanities in Higher Education*, 10, 295–313.

Irigaray, L. (2004). *Key Writings*. London: Continuum.

Jacques, M. (2006). "What the Hell is the International Community?" *The Guardian*, Thursday 24th August. Retrived from http://www.theguardian.com/commentisfree/2006/aug/24/whatthehellistheinternati

James, W. (2012). *The Varieties of Religious Experience: A Study in Human Nature*. Oxford: Oxford World's Classics.

Jantzen. G. (1998). *Becoming Divine: Towards a Feminist Philosophy of Religion*. Manchester: Manchester University Press.

Keane, W. (2007). Christian Moderns: Freedom and Fetish in the Mission Encounter. Berkeley, CA: University of California Press.

Keller, M. (2002). *The Hammer and the Flute: Women, Power, and Spirit Possession*. Baltimore: John Hopkins University Press.

LaCocque, A. and Ricoeur, P, (2003). *Thinking Biblically: Exegetical and Hermeneutical Studies* Chicago: University of Chicago Press.

Landy, J. (2012). *How to Do Things with Fictions*. Oxford: Oxford University Press.

Lewin, D. (2006). "Freedom and Destiny in the Philosophy of Technology" *New Blackfriars*, 87: 10, 515–533.

Lewin, D. (2011). "The Middle Voice in Eckhart and Modern Continental Philosophy," *Medieval Mystical Theology: The Journal of the Eckhart Society*, 20: 1, 28–46.

MacIntyre, A. (1981). *After Virtue: A Study in Moral Theory*. Indiana: University of Notre Dame Press.

Mahmood, S. (2013). "Can Secularism Be Otherwise?" in Warner, M. VanAntwerpen, J. Calhoun, C. (eds.) *Varieties of Secularism in a Secular Age*. Cambridge: Harvard University Press, 282–299.

McLaughlin, T. (1984). "Parental Rights and the Religious Upbringing of Children." *Journal of Philosophy of Education*, 18, 75–83

Merry, M. (2005). 'Cultural Coherence and the Schooling for Identity Maintenance'. *Journal of Philosophy of Education*, 38: 3, 477–497.

Milbank, J. (2010). "A Closer Walk on the Wild Side" in Warner, Vanantwerpen, and Calhoun (eds.) *Varieties of Secularism in a Secular Age*. Cambridge: Harvard University Press, 54–82.

Nasiretti, I. (2009). *Forced into Faith: How Religion Abuses Children's Rights*. New York: Prometheus Books.

Piaget, J. (1970). *Structuralism*. New York: Harper & Row.

Polkinghorne, J. (1991). *Reason and Rationality: The Relationship Between Science and Theology*. London: SPCK.

Randles, W. (1999). *The Unmaking of the Medieval Christian Cosmos: 1500–1760 from Solid Heavens to Boundless Aether*. Farnham: Ashgate.

Rousseau, J. J. (2003). *The Social Contract*, G. D. H. Cole, trans. London: Dover.

Siegel, H. (1988). *Education Reason: Rationality, Critical Thinking and Education*. London: Routledge.

Smart, N. (1996). *Dimensions of the Sacred: Anatomy of the World's Beliefs*. London: HarperCollins.

Smith, W. (1998). *Faith and Belief*. Princeton: Princeton University Press.

Smith, J. (2013). *Imagining the Kingdom: How Worship Works*. Grand Rapids, MI: Baker Academic.

Smith, J. (2014). *How (Not) to Be Secular: Reading Charles Taylor*. Michigan: Eerdmans.

Snook, I. A. (ed.). (1972). *Concepts of Indoctrination: Philosophical Essays*. London: Routledge.

Spencer Foundation. (2015). Retrieved from http://www.spencer.org/faith-schooling-principles-and-policies

Stables, A. (2005). *Living and Learning as Semiotic Engagement: A New Theory of Education*. Lewiston, NY: Lampeter: Edwin Mellen Press.

Stables A., & Semetsky, I. (2015). *Edusemiotics: Semiotic Philosophy as Educational Foundation*. London & New York: Routledge.

Strhan, A. (2010). "A Religious Education Otherwise? An Examination and Proposed Interruption of Current British Practice" *Journal of Philosophy of Education*, 44: 1, 23–44.

Strhan, A. (2013). "Practising the Space Between: Embodying Belief as an Evangelical Anglican Student" *Journal of Contemporary Religion*, 28: 2, 225–239.

Strhan, A. (2014). "Editorial: Education and the 'Problem' of Religion: A Special Virtual Issue" *Journal of Philosophy of Education*.

Tan, C., (2004) 'Michael Hand, Indoctrination, and the Inculcation of Belief, *Journal of the Philosophy of Education*, 38: 2, 257–267.

Taylor, C. (2007). *A Secular Age*. Cambridge: Harvard University Press.

Tillich, P. (1964). *Theology of Culture*. New York: Oxford University Press.

Tillich, P. (1967). *Systematic Theology. Vol. 1–3*. Chicago: The University of Chicago Press.

Vattimo, G. (2003) "After onto-theology: philosophy between science and religion" in Mark Wrathall, (ed.) *Religion After Metaphysics*. Cambridge: Cambridge University Press, 29–36.

Vroom, H., & Gort, J. (eds.). (1997). *Holy Scriptures in Judaism, Christianity and Islam: Hermeneutics, Values and Society*. Amsterdam: Rodopi.

Wallace, R. (1977). "Emile Durkheim and the Civil Religion Concept." *Review of Religious Research*, 18, 287–290.

Warner, M., VanAntwerpen, J., & Calhoun, C. (eds.). (2013). *Varieties of Secularism in a Secular Age*. Cambridge: Harvard University Press.

White, J. (2004a). "Should Religious Education be a Compulsory School Subject?" *British Journal of Religious Education*, 26: 2, 152–164.

Williams, R. (2012). *Faith in the Public Square*, London: Bloomsbury.

Wilson, J. (1972). "Indoctrination and Rationality" in I. A. Snook (ed.) *Concepts of Indoctrination: Philosophical Essays.* London: Routledge, 14–20.

Woolf Institute. (2015). 'Living with Difference: Community, Diversity and the Common Good' Report of the Commission on Religion and Belief in British Public Life.

Wyatt, C. (2015). *BBC News "Lord's Prayer Cinema ad snub 'bewilders' Church of England".* Retrieved from http://www.bbc.co.uk/news/uk-34891928

Chapter 4

'Only a god can save us': Heidegger's god after metaphysics

Introduction

I now turn to Heidegger's critique of Western thought in order to uncover his approach to philosophy and pedagogy. His critique involves a suspicion of the propositional framing of thinking – which is basically equivalent to he calls representational thinking – and indicates contemplative or meditative ways of thinking that give form to the spaces between the secular and the confessional. So his critiques of Western thought leave space for a recovery of religion and of thinking, after what he critically terms 'metaphysics' has come to an end. One important consequence of the end of metaphysics inaugurated by Heidegger could be "that the relation of philosophy with poetry is no longer conceived in antagonistic terms, or by the destruction of the boundary between metaphor and its 'proper meaning'" (Vattimo 2003, 31). This speaks to the reduction of language to propositions discussed in the preceding chapter. If we reject the propositional framing of language and discourse, then we can understand all language to be metaphorical, just as all being is hermeneutical. This does not require Heidegger to reject truth as such, but truth as metaphysics enframed by the standard representational guise (what Heidegger often characterizes as the correspondence theory of truth). Where the propositional logic of language can be understood as just one among many logics, the varied languages of poetry, myth and religion are given voice. An appreciation of multiple voices is an important implication of my understanding of the post-secular, placing Heidegger's post-metaphysical project within its range – though it might also be termed a kind of procedural secularism which is pluralist without being particularist. To be sure, Heidegger is not invoking a return to the mythical still less the mystical. But his critiques of metaphysics and the totalizing tendencies of modern technology deserve some serious attention within post-secular analyses.

Overcoming Western metaphysics

One finds a distinct skepticism towards the nature and direction of Western thought, particularly since Descartes, running through Heidegger's entire oeuvre.

The modern epistemological project in which truth is understood as obtaining a correct representation of the world is subject to relentless Heideggerian deconstruction because it presents modern science and technology as the dominant, if not exclusive, manner in which beings come to presence. Metaphysics reaches a natural death at the point when humanity has reached its zenith through universal technological mastery of the world, the fulfillment of Nietzsche's will to power (Heidegger 1977, 53–112). This becomes a problem, so Heidegger believes, because human beings have lost touch with the question of being and have become content to inhabit a world that yields to humanity's determinations. If humanity has any future, we must recognize the death of traditional metaphysics (evident in the Western – Platonic and Christian – tradition, as well as in modern science and technology) and we must learn what he calls 'thinking'. In order to reach an understanding of the kind of non-metaphysical thinking that Heidegger has in mind, we must say something more about metaphysics.

Heidegger's work is deeply rooted in the metaphysical traditions of Western thought, despite his critical stance and his efforts to secure a radical break from them. His chief influences were the ancient Greeks, the scholastic theological tradition, German idealism and phenomenology. Still, any consideration of his relationship to the history of Western thought should take account of the claim that his rejection of philosophy in favour of *thinking* is essentially an attempt to 'overcome' the tradition in which he finds himself. Does this central aim, the overcoming of metaphysics, in its attempt to go beyond the specifically Western tradition, suggest an encounter with Eastern thought? Although there are several reasons to think it could,[1] in the end Heidegger is suspicious of importing solutions to Western metaphysics from other traditions (e.g., Zen Buddhist or Hindu philosophy, for example). In the *Der Spiegel* interview of 1966, Heidegger famously claims that the transformation of the Western tradition cannot emerge "through the adoption of Zen Buddhism or other Eastern experiences of the world. Rethinking requires the help of the European tradition and a reappropriation of it. Thinking is transformed only by thinking that has the same origin and destiny" (Wolin 1993, 113). Here Heidegger is referring not only to the roots of Western metaphysics in ancient Greek thinking but also, and more obscurely, to the 'destiny' of Western thought. That destiny is bound up with the crisis of technological being and enframing (*Gestell*), in which the only way of being is to see the world in terms of resources (Heidegger 1977; Lewin 2012). For Heidegger, the crisis of technological enframing has its roots in the Socratic conception of being (as eternal idea: *eidos*) since this idea renders us incapable of remaining open to being. The problem seems connected with the desire for fixed conceptual or representational understandings which itself results from the identification of knowledge with a kind of abstract ideal. The threat here is philosophical (a failure to understand the world), existential (a failure to experience meaningful life), ecological (a failure to see the cosmos in terms other than utilitarian) and anthropological (a failure to become who we are as human beings).

But in arguing that we cannot simply import a solution to this Western crisis from the Orient, doesn't Heidegger rather foreclose the scope of revelation? Storey (2012, 115) argues that Heidegger's attempt at a 'retrieval' from within the Western tradition represents a reification of 'the West'. Furthermore, as Ma (2007, 7) points out, "[a]lmost all of Heidegger's oblique references to East-West dialogue appear in the context of a deep concern with the *Gestell* [enframing]." We could see enframing as encapsulating the problem faced by the West for which an encounter with the East might offer a solution. In an interview for *Der Spiegel* published posthumously at Heidegger's request, he states that ". . . only a god can save us" (Heidegger 1981), a phrase which suggests our impotence and invokes a *transcendent* agency (in the sense that it escapes technological enframing) as being capable of interrupting the direction of the West. On the face of it, this is a mysterious claim given Heidegger's critique of Western philosophy and theology as 'ontotheological', a critique of the tendency to conflate our conceptions of God (as the ground of being) and being itself. So this god can only save if it is not subject to ontotheology and must, therefore, be properly other, transcendent. Although it is plausible that this transcendent dimension would find its source in an Eastern tradition which does not belong to the Indo-European linguistic and cultural heritage, Heidegger is a hermeneutic philosopher who proceeds on the basis that our freedom is formed and structured by contextualised historicity (Heidegger 1996a; Lewin 2014a). He is, therefore, unwilling to sever the cord that attaches his thinking to the destiny of Western thought, even though, in his view, all other efforts to develop the metaphysical tradition − from Socrates up to and including Nietzsche, who for Heidegger precisely completes the Western tradition's movement towards nihilism − appear only to result in representational thinking, technological enframing and ultimately nihilism. But that representational problem is what makes importing solutions from the East so troubling: we will inevitably import the representation that conforms most completely to technological enframing. In other words, we will import only an image of the East and put it to use, a tendency evident in the appropriation of Eastern traditions to Western patterns of consumption and spiritual consciousness.

This direction of thinking and being has profound implications for education. Today we have become almost entirely inured to seeing education as the transmission and manipulation of more or less correct representations of the world. We have likewise taken for granted that education should be placed in service of global forces that seem to be incorporated into technological enframing. In other words, education is defined and justified in utilitarian terms. More worrying still, an international community (the 'we' of the totalizing world order) has determined that *Education for All* is an unequivocal good without critical interrogation of its own ontology. The intentions of UNESCO in their endeavours are not here in question. What is rather more questionable is that the conception of education instantiated within *Education for All* is not itself in question. Or to put it in Heidegger's (1968, 6) terms, "[m]ost thought-provoking in out

68 'Only a god can save us'

thought-provoking time is that we are still not thinking." The busyness of our age seems to Heidegger only evidence of the avoidance of thinking. Having an accurate and positive representation in the mind of the subject at hand is not thinking at all, but only a representational dominance over being.

The post-secular might be understood, then, as offering a way beyond the conceptual univocity of the metaphysical tradition without lapsing into relativism or nihilism. For Heidegger this is possible where thinking is open to being. One approach to Heidegger's understanding of *thought* is to see that it implies a kind of *releasement* (Gelassenheit) that invites comparison with contemplative traditions East and West.

Thinking as releasement

Perhaps more than anywhere else, it is in Heidegger's *Discourse on Thinking* that the idea of thinking as releasement is explored. The conceptual register of this terminology corresponds in tantalizing ways to ideas from contemplative traditions the world over, both East and West, from Shankara to Eckhart, from the Dalai Lama to Thomas Merton. But what are we to make of the strange juxtaposition between *thinking*, normally understood as referring to conceptions or considerations that take place in the mind, and *releasement*? We are perhaps more able to understand what *thinking* is not for Heidegger than to establish directly what *thinking* is. Thinking here has little to do with the kind of conceptual reasoning of the logician, or the internal narration that accompanies everyday life. Thinking is responsive, entailing an attention to being, which is why the question of thinking directly follows the question of being. The notion of *attention* is closely related.

Attention captures the sense of a kind of thinking that does not re-present to itself a mental picture, but abides in awareness. Heidegger employs different images to evoke an attentive relation between human being and being itself: from the early analysis of *Dasein*, through *Ereignis* (the 'event' of being), to the language of the forest clearing and of human beings as the shepherds of being. These images are indications of the opening of attention that discloses the world. I would suggest, then, that Heidegger's conception of thinking is almost indistinguishable from attention. That pedagogy should be concerned with the cultivation of attention is an important idea for a number of philosophers (such as William James and Simone Weil), a point we will develop in Chapter 6, and provides an interesting way of connecting Heidegger's discussion of thinking with education. The idea of attention also evokes a range of cross-cultural conceptions of awareness or contemplation, from Christian prayer to Buddhist meditation, and so offers a way to bring together a number of related ideas. But I would advise caution here. Heidegger's conception of releasement has a specific role in his wider philosophical concerns.

Heidegger's conception of releasement begins with the analysis of the history of Western metaphysics as the forgetting of being and the loss of true thought.

Modern humanity has isolated discursive reasoning or representational thought, characterized by modern science and philosophy (particularly in its analytic and positivist strains), as not only paradigmatic, but as the exclusive form of thought. This kind of calculative thinking has its place, but like a virulent virus, seeks to reproduce itself at the expense of all other forms of thinking. Taken on its own, calculative thinking is in danger of ascribing truth and reality only to that which can be defined and measured scientifically. As Caputo (1978, 264) puts it, "[w]e are rapidly coming to believe that the only form of truth is the truth which the mathematical sciences establish, and that such science is the only legitimate form of thinking." In the *Discourse on Thinking* Heidegger (1969, 47) says, "anyone can follow the path of meditative thinking in his own manner and within his own limits. Why? Because man is a thinking, that is, a meditating being." Is meditating here equivalent to attention, and can it legitimately be related to the contemplative traditions of the East? Is this thinking evocative of a contemplative, meditative or mystical state?

Caputo argues that since Heidegger steps back from philosophy and metaphysics, that thinking takes on more of a likeness to that which lies beyond philosophy, namely poetry and mysticism. In support of this claim Caputo draws on Heidegger's lecture course *The Principle of Reason*, in which Heidegger says "the most extreme sharpness and depth of thought belongs to genuine and great mysticism" (Caputo 1978, 6).[2] There does seem to be a close proximity between thinking and poetry, or perhaps it is more accurate to say that poetry offers a language and a form in which thinking can take place (see Heidegger 1968, p. 20). The poetic turn in Heidegger's later work, both in its encounter with the poetry of Hölderlin, Rilke and Trakl, and the somewhat poetic form that Heidegger's later work takes, draws attention to language that affords the opportunity to encounter language itself. But is this poetic turn a kind of mysticism of language? Heidegger is cautious about connecting his thinking with mysticism, explicitly denying that his thinking entails any kind of spiritual or mystical state or experience, always orienting the reader back to being: "experiencing (the experience of Being: thinking) is nothing mystical, not an act of illumination, but rather the entry into dwelling in Appropriation" (1972, 53). With the notable exception of Wittgenstein and the more recent 'theological turn' in phenomenology, which owes a great deal to the influence of Heidegger (see Janicaud 2000), skepticism towards the mystical, with its connotation of mystification and experientialism, has been commonplace across post-Enlightenment philosophy. In the realm of the post-secular, the mystical might seem like an appropriate opportunity to explore that which is beyond the secular and the confessional, and thereby to invite a new mysticism and spirituality to refresh the tired institutions of our religious traditions. But the broad criticism of importing Eastern philosophy can be applied here: importing the spiritual or mystical runs the great risk of repeating the metaphysical appropriation of the other in terms that suit our subjective determinations. In other words, we appropriate the mystical for our own self-interest. We construct, what Denys Turner (1999,

183) has called 'godlets': "[a]ny 'God' we could possibly love without detachment is not the true God badly loved, but not God at all, the mere godlet of our own invention." This concern that mysticism without detachment entails self-love seems highly pertinent to Heidegger's employment of the Eckhartian language of releasement, which precisely addresses itself to detachment as the ground of love. For Heidegger there is the problem that the Western theological tradition has had a tendency towards *ontotheology*, the identification of God as the ground of being and the ground of creatures. The danger here is that thinking gets entangled with representation, this time the representations of mystical experience. So while thinking is not easily defined, Heidegger wants us to see it in terms of appropriation: a mutual appropriation between human beings and the world, where attention unfolds into presence. Thinking does not take us away from being, as certain forms of meditative practice which call for the end of thought might suppose; rather, thinking is the ground and possibility of such practices. Hence Heidegger (1968) develops Parmenides' insight that thinking and being are the same. I now turn to Heidegger's way of writing, itself suggestive of a distinctive pedagogical strategy that has both rhetorical and substantive significance.

Heidegger's way

Heidegger's way of thinking suggests an openness to being which appropriates attention. Particularly in *What Is Called Thinking?* Heidegger draws attention to attention. There is as much performative as propositional significance to this since Heidegger is concerned with engaging the attention of the reader directly. By this I mean that reading Heidegger is a form of inquiry that can involve an *encounter* with the text. It is almost as if what is being said is less important than how it is being said. Does this mean we can get beyond *understanding* in the representational sense of the word (a clear picture which I could, for example, explain to another)? Approaching Heidegger's writing as a kind of *bearing witness* can be a useful strategy and resonates with his own development of 'formal indication', a device for showing rather than saying.[3] Those familiar with Heidegger's writings might read the sometimes paradoxical, strained, even contorted and catachrestic prose, as a barrier to meaning and perspicacity. Can this style be understood as performing language and performing attention? Can we go as far as to call reading Heidegger a contemplative act? Heidegger's abstruse style conceptually disarms the reader, demanding fresh attention to what may previously have appeared to be simple, or settled philosophical ideas.[4] George Steiner (1992, 11) remarks, "It is not "understanding" that Heidegger's discourse solicits primarily. It is an "experiencing", an acceptance of felt strangeness." This experiencing can be realised through the artful writing of the philosopher-poet:

> Heidegger's seemingly lapidary plainness, his use of short sentences – so contrastive with the German idealist philosophy from Kant to Schopenhauer –
> in effect masks a fiercely personal and intentionally 'delaying' or even

'blockading' idiom. We are to be slowed down, bewildered and barred in our reading so that we may be driven deep

(Steiner 1992, 8).

For the most part, our habits of reading and thinking precede us. We tend to read without care, and think what is given us to think through the structures of being that precede our existence. Thus Heidegger wants to break the spell of the *idle talk* that philosophy has fallen into. This requires, to some extent, a new idiom in which words are allowed to speak afresh, through which the strangeness of being can again be felt. If we are to bracket our critical voice in order to experience the strangeness of being, how are we to guard against a blind submission to the authority of the philosopher? As a reader of Heidegger, I think that the response to this is in the text itself.[5]

We might be tempted to seek a new idiom in the language of Eastern wisdom traditions. But this is only possible where those traditions are not appropriated by Western representational metaphysics, where we do not read Eastern traditions through the reductive lens of, for example, a 'belief system' or a 'worldview.'[6] It is the conquest of the other in terms of subjective representation that characterizes the culmination of Western metaphysics and is the danger of cross-cultural analysis. In his reading of Heidegger, Michael Peters (2002, 8) draws attention to the relation between subjectivity and representation where he says, "the world becoming a "view" and man becoming a *subjectum* is part and parcel of the same metaphysical process," a metaphysical process rooted in the conception of truth as representational accuracy. Peters goes on to quote from Heidegger's essay "The Age of the World Picture":

The fundamental event of the modern age is the conquest of the world as picture. The word 'picture' [*Bild*] now means the structured image [*Gebild*] that is the creature of man's producing which represents and sets before. In such producing, man contends for the position in which he can be that particular being who gives the measure and draws up the guidelines for everything that is

(Heidegger 1977, in Peters 2002, 8).

The temptation towards easy and lazy syncretism, the natural expression of representational thinking, is great, and often the result is not a true encounter, dialogue or reconciliation, but a projection of the known over the unknown where neither is illuminated. The mind that engages only in representational thinking struggles to dwell with the unknown, not having the patience of Keat's 'negative capability'.

It is not, of course, that the wisdom of the East is intrinsically lacking, but rather that our representation will always conceal more than it reveals. So for Heidegger the Western tradition from Plato up to and including Nietzsche has, in different ways, valorized representational thinking at the expense of the more contemplative modes that might correspond to attentive reading. This is the predicament of Western metaphysics that Heidegger is attempting to overcome. It is a metaphysical tradition that seeks to represent presence rather than let what is come into presence. In contrast to the modern conception of truth as correct correspondence between the representation and the world, Heidegger understands truth as *aletheia* (unconcealment); this entails the event of letting *what is* come into presence. As we shall see, this letting has particular significance for pedagogy since the educator depends upon the work of being to come into appearance; being itself has pedagogical initiative.

In the preface to Richardson's *Through Phenomenology to Thought*, Heidegger indicates that what holds for ontology generally also holds for efforts to make his philosophy accessible by way of secondary literature: "every effort to bring what has been thought closer to prevailing modes of (re)presentation must assimilate what-is-to-be-thought to those (re)presentations and thereby inevitably deform the matter" (Richardson 2003, viii). In other words, the secondary representation of thinking occludes the encounter. Instead of a second-hand representation, Heidegger is seeking a kind of unmediated experience predicated on a kind of attention. This conception of thinking suggests a philosophy of education that would question both teaching as an act of mediation between the world and the student (certainly questioning the kind of explanatory mediation that so bothers Rancière), and learning as the process by which the student acquires and refines a representation in the mind. In the end, the teacher must let the encounter between the student and the world take place by withdrawing. To teach is to draw attention to the world and then, in a sense, the learning is between the world and the student. It is not enough for the student to have a correct representation of the world that they bring, for example, to the exam hall. For Heidegger, education has to have an 'ontological' dimension in the sense that it must reach all the way down (Heidegger 1998; Thomson 2002).

But is this book not attempting to mediate Heidegger through a more or less correct representation? Am I bearing witness or painting a picture? The attentive reader may be aware of an ongoing dilemma: how do we read 'about' Heidegger without his ideas being represented and thereby deformed? Can 'drawing attention' bring academic discourse into the realm of a language that bears witness, that is, the poetic? Books and journal articles are not normally read in the way poetry is read (it is, perhaps, absurd to speak of one 'way' of reading poetry – or indeed academic books!). We are left wondering whether the academic discussion of Heidegger will inevitably fall into the kind of representational thinking that he consistently sought to overcome, the kind of dependency that sustains a thousand academic careers. But is this concern predicated on too stark a dichotomy? Are we in danger of opposing the poetic with the philosophical (or academic)? In *Parmenides*, for example, Heidegger himself suggests that *mythos* and *logos* should not be too readily placed in opposition (Heidegger 1992, 6). What do these tensions mean for pedagogy? Although these tensions are never fully resolved – indeed their presence can perform the creative function of continually drawing our attention back from the settled philosophical position – Heidegger's reflections on poetry are instructive.

Heidegger and poetry

Readers of Heidegger are sometimes drawn in to his pedagogical demonstrations of the process of thinking the difference between being and representation. More critical readers might be skeptical that anything much is being shown or said in his elusive pronouncements. Heidegger (1996b, 1) begins his remarks on Hölderlin's hymn *Der Ister* with the following words:

> We must first become attentive to this poetry. Once we have become attentive, we can then 'pay attention to,' that is, retain, some things that, at favourable moments, will perhaps let us 'attend to,' that is, have some intimation of what might be said in the word of this poet.

To discover what is said in the word of the poet seems to require a double-movement of attention, hence the circuitous, even paradoxical, manner in which attention is possible only after we have become attentive. An orientation of attentiveness (which is not directly controlled by the will) is the precondition of paying attention as an action of will. But it is more complicated than this. The orientation of attentiveness is indeed not entirely outside the domain of human willing since we can, of course, work upon our orientation by, for example, creating a space in which distractions are removed. Conversely, even this second moment of paying attention involves a 'letting' which undermines the notion of a clear agent engaged in straightforward action. The dynamics of the will are of huge significance to Heidegger and in relation to being might be said to characterize the core of his philosophical project (Davis 2007). The role of agency in relation to attention and education are also of critical importance and will be revisited soon in reference to subjectivity.

Heidegger goes on to reflect on the nature of interpreting poetry. Why is poetry in need of interpretation? Does interpretation help us behold the poetic word, or does it merely mediate and represent? Are we transported into the 'dwelling place' of the poetic, or is the poetic word structured, interpreted and domesticated into the digestible curricula and schemes of work appropriate to measurable educational outcomes? Does the positioning of the poem into an educational syllabus represent the enframing or imprisoning of the poetic word? Is this not the death of poetry? Heidegger is ambivalent about his own relationship (as teacher and philosopher) to the word of the poet: "At the risk of missing the truth of Hölderlin's poetry, the remarks merely provide a few markers, signs that call our attention, pauses for reflection" (Heidegger 1996b, 2). This is Heidegger's pedagogy: to be an accompaniment that draws attention through markers and signs, to open spaces for reflection. Any other more explicative move would not teach through a kind of bearing witness, but would represent and thereby deface or replace. Similar to Jacotot's emancipatory method in *The Ignorant Schoolmaster* (Rancière 1991), the task of teaching for Heidegger is not explication since that entails representational thinking. There is a patient, contemplative dimension to the relation to being that Heidegger's pedagogy evokes.

In attempting to understand how Heidegger can contribute to educational thinking we must also consider why it is that Heidegger relied primarily on the spoken word. The priority of dialogue goes some way to explain why most of his published writings were originally lecture courses and why he regards Socrates as the 'purest thinker in the West' (Heidegger 1968, 17). Since Plato's *Phaedrus*, speech has tended to be prioritised over writing for its ability to remain literally in dialogue. Notwithstanding the obvious irony that Plato passes down the dialogues in written form, writing is thought to fix the discourse to a particular representation, a process that is philosophically and pedagogically significant. Heidegger wished to 'let learning occur' not by giving his students a strong command of the facts, or considerations to be made, still less by establishing the correct interpretations of ideas or texts, but rather by showing a certain *way* of relating to the subject matter. For Heidegger (1968, 15) this requires the teacher to be "more teachable than the apprentices." Students of Heidegger reported a teacher engaged in precisely this kind of process of bearing witness and letting learning occur. Walter Biemel (1977, 7), one of Heidegger's students, writes:

> Those who know Martin Heidegger only through his published writings can hardly form an idea of his unique style of teaching. Even with beginners, he was able in no time to coax them into thinking, not just learning various views or reproducing what they had read, but entering into the movement of thinking. It seemed as if by some miracle the Socratic practice of address and rejoinder had come to life again.

This brings us again to the understanding of thinking as a kind of attention that leaves behind representations and in which being is let into its own nature. This is a thinking that can only occur at 'the end of philosophy'. In 1959 Heidegger (1973, 96) wrote, "(b)ut with the end of philosophy, thinking is not also at its end, but in transition to another beginning." Elsewhere Heidegger (1956, 52–53) says, "Heraclitus and Parmenides were not yet 'philosophers.' Why not? Because they were the greatest thinkers." Philosophy as it has come to be practiced in the modern West has little to do with thought. Part and parcel with the representational nature of Western philosophy is the reduction of thinking to a matter of reason, basically equivalent to Western 'rationality' or 'metaphysics'. Here philosophy is concerned to supply rational grounds or reasons and argumentation, and it is this effort to provide a 'rational account' that Heidegger contrasts with real thinking. Caputo (1978, 3–4) shows how Heidegger perceives the problematic nature of providing reasons:

> Many major philosophers in the past – Descartes, Kant, Fichte, Husserl, Wittgenstein – have called for 'reform' of philosophy and have laid claim to having finally discovered what philosophy truly is [. . .] They each proposed the definitive way to give an account (rationem reddere) of things in philosophy. But Heidegger's revolution is far more radical than any of these [. . .] Heidegger's call is a call to leave the domain of rational argumentation – the sphere of ratio – behind [. . .] Heidegger calls for a leap beyond the realm of giving reasons in order to take up a non-conceptual, non-discursive, non-representational kind of 'thinking' which is profoundly divided from any of the traditional varieties of philosophy.

Compare this disavowal of the conceptual and discursive, with, for example, the warnings expressed by the second/third-century Buddhist Nagarjuna about conceiving of truth in reified or conceptual terms. This is one well-known expression of suspicion towards conceptual reasoning and associated essentialism in Buddhist thought. Storey (2012, 122–127) has argued that Nagarjuna's negative dialectic is best suited to this non-conceptual register of Heidegger's later thought.

As we have seen, Heidegger's understanding of *thinking* should be distinguished from a range of ideas conventionally associated with the term (conceptualising, representation, calculative thought, providing rational grounds). Heidegger (1968, 8) wants us to "radically unlearn what thinking has been traditionally," and he wants to retain the term in part for etymological reasons; *Denken* shares an etymological root with *Danken* (to thank) (1968, 138 ff.). That thinking might entail an orientation of thankfulness encourages a realization that thinking is not something we simply determine through a matter of will but comes to us as something of a gift. After all, what *occurs* to us is often not directly up to us. This attenuation of agency brings us to consider the deconstruction of the willful self.

The deconstruction of the willful self

In previous chapters I have raised objections to interpreting religion in propositional terms. The idea of believing as a cognitive act has been questioned, as has the notion that religion is about holding beliefs or worldviews. Associated with this I have sought to challenge the idea that the religious practitioner makes choices about their religious views. None of this is to deny some cognitive dimension to religion but is concerned rather to rebalance a disproportionate interest in belief systems and worldviews particularly when it comes to debates about religious indoctrination. An important dimension of

76 'Only a god can save us'

the post-secular context for this debate has been to show that truth is less often conceived in univocal terms, and so other ways of conceiving religious truth become possible. After Heidegger this means reconceiving of a religion after metaphysics (Wrathall 2003). This is one approach to the post-secular: that with the metaphysical baggage of Western metaphysics cleared, new opportunities for being religious might be possible. But this is not something that human subjectivity can legislate or strategize. Therefore we have come to a consideration of subjectivity, agency and the will. In view of the eclectic account of religion that is perhaps appropriate to a post-confessional/post-secular context such as this, I will draw on Buddhist and Taoist sources here and there, justified by Heidegger's clear albeit circumspect interest in 'Eastern' thought.

We have seen that Heidegger's conception of thinking is fundamentally about responding to the call to attend to being, a way of being attentive that can be pedagogical. Heidegger's pedagogy can be characterized as a kind of gathering of attention that acts in a participative way to let being come into appearance. This raises questions of identity and agency since this responsiveness involves a self whose agency is not absolute. Elsewhere I explore the ways in which Heidegger's language evokes the linguistic form of the middle voice in which agency is neither fully active nor passive (Lewin 2011). In modern metaphysics this conception of the self, founded on Cartesian and Kantian philosophy, has been constituted as a stable ego identity: the ideal rational subject whose sovereign will is autonomous. Education has long regarded its goal as the formation of autonomous subjectivity. For Heidegger this subject is an expression of representational metaphysics since only a representation can confer the illusion of total power to the subject. The fact that this subject is linguistically subverted in Heidegger's later thought in particular offers an opportunity to relate Heidegger to the contemplative elements of Eastern traditions in the negative dialectics of Nagarjuna. The transcendence or negation of the substance both of being and of self is an important theme within the theology as well as the meditative practices of Buddhism and Daoism. In Daoist thinking, we see not so much a negation of substance and self as the fundamental nonduality of the self and Dao. This suggests a spiritual life that yields the power and dominance of the autonomous subject in favour of a harmonious immanence with the world. An important theme within Daoism is the way in which the will is in harmony with the world whereby action is effortless in *wu wei*. Despite the range and complexity of spiritual practices, there are broad themes that are consistent to do with a *realisation* (and the non-representational nature of this realisation is of critical importance) that the illusion of the individual and autonomous self must be attenuated or abandoned. Caputo sketches explicit parallels here between Zen Buddhism, Meister Eckhart and Heidegger:

> In Zen, when the self has become entirely egoless and will-less, it is admitted into 'satori.' In Heidegger, Dasein is admitted into the truth of Being, the 'event of appropriation.' Thus, to satori, the state of 'enlightenment,' we

relate the 'lighting' (lichten) process of the 'clearing' (Lichtung) which is made in Dasein for the event of truth. In and through this 'event,' Dasein enters into its own most essential being (Wesen), even as the soul enters into its innermost ground (Seelen-grund; Eckhart) and the self in Zen is awakened to its 'Buddha-nature' or 'self-nature'

(Caputo 1978, p. 214).

Like the contemplative traditions of Buddhism and Daoism, knowledge arises from (at least in part) a deconstruction of the self and the will. The refinement of human will is explored by Heidegger in many places, for example his "Conversation on a Country Path About Thinking" (1970), in which he presents a fictional dialogue on the nature of thinking, and indicates a turn to meditative rather than calculative thinking. The form of the conversation evokes an *aporia* in the reader which enacts the philosophical point. It can bring the reader to the kind of thinking and attention that I argued earlier was important to Heidegger's way. In other words, the conversation both shows and says. For many spiritual practices, the relation between the will, subjectivity and spiritual practice, entails a complexity and ambiguity that is shared by Heidegger's conception of thinking. For this reason, one of the first questions that occurs in the conversation is about the nature of the will: whether non-willing is a will to not will or an attempt to remain absolutely outside the domain of the will. There would seem to be the 'will' or desire to awaken releasement within oneself, and yet this very desire holds us back:

Scholar: So far as we can wean ourselves from willing, we contribute to the awakening of releasement.
Teacher: Say rather, keeping awake for releasement.
Scholar: Why not, to the awakening?
Teacher: Because on our own we do not awaken releasement in ourselves (1970, 60–61).

The strategy of negation here resonates with the teaching practices of the Zen master: "Like a Zen master, Heidegger does not tell us what to do, only what not to do. And in response to the natural question complaining of the resulting disorientation, he intensifies instead of relieving the disorientation, again like a Zen master" (Kreeft 1971, 535). This is one explanation for the aporia of the dialogue. But still we want to know who or what can awaken releasement in us? Beyond the aporetic, there is a logical problem which our general conception of agency forces on us: the binary logic that we are either active or passive. But Heidegger is pointing to the idea that agency is both present and absent. A higher acting, which is not activity, is required and is, therefore, beyond the distinction between activity and passivity. This acting has already been evoked as the Daoist conception of *wu wei*. Yet, a kind of releasement (not 'true' releasement) often remains within the domain of the will, if, for example, it attains to

78 'Only a god can save us'

a divine will. Although Heidegger adopts the term *Gelassenheit* from his reading of Eckhart (Hackett 2012, 687ff.), he seems to regard Eckhart's conception of releasement as still within the domain of this submission to divine will and so cannot fully assent to it (Heidegger 1969, 62).[7] In this conversation it is made clear that releasement cannot be represented to the mind, but it becomes less clear what the interlocutors can 'do' in order to learn a thinking that is releasement. So the teacher says: "We are to do nothing but wait" (Heidegger 1969, 62). And though they know not what they wait for, they must learn to wait if they are to learn thinking. Again the contemplative mood evoked in the dialogue is (to again use that Wittgensteinian characterization) both shown and said. For this reader Heidegger both brings the questions to presence and enacts the philosophical points. The interlocutors are hoping to learn what releasement means, though the agency of teaching and learning is similarly in question. Notwithstanding elements of something akin to Socratic conceit about who is teaching and who is learning in the dialogue, the reader is given a sense that the subjective agent cannot maintain a grip on the movement of the dialogue and must yield into the fluid movement.

The idea of attention likewise entails an attenuation of the will. We spoke earlier of Heidegger's evocation of poetry as a double-movement between the orientation of attentiveness that precedes and structures the possibility of the act of letting attention into itself. This shifting and ambiguous notion of agency has left Heidegger open to the charge that he equivocates on his philosophical (and political) commitments; that, for example, the destiny of technological thinking is paradoxically both determining us, and determined by us, leaving no clear statement of what is to be (or indeed can be) done (Heidegger 1977). We are brought to an *aporia*, left without a clear method of approach to the problems of our age. This problem cannot be dissociated from Heidegger's efforts to deconstruct the subject of Western metaphysics that found its apex in the Cartesian cogito and the Kantian autonomous will. This equivocation is not a failure but a feature of Heideggerian thinking. So I suggest the same equivocation would be detected were we to seek a stable Heideggerian *doctrine of attention*. Any such doctrine of attention would itself be prone to the representational metaphysics of the modern age. It is worth comparing for a moment the unequivocal confidence in the UNESCO mission of 'Education for all' as it is currently conceived, simply to draw attention to the contrasting power of the 'negative capability' of the aporia.

Could it be that the recent interest in mindfulness in education, in which mindfulness is employed for managing anxiety and behaviour to improve educational outcomes, depends on an unequivocal doctrine of attention? Such a doctrine might amount to a feeling of breath or the weight of one's body on the chair. I suggest that for Heidegger the current interest in mindfulness is in danger of concealing the 'essence' of attention, rather serving to reinforce the oblivion to being that needs to be overcome. This is because the representation of attention-management as a method to harness the contemplative power of the mind is a product of a technology of the self in which therapies support the management of the self within an enframed totality of control. It entails a representation of happiness and the good life that conceals the complex and circuitous nature of being-in-the-world and supposes that Dasein can be circumscribed and satisfied by a representation of happiness.

I have suggested that Heidegger's understanding of agency is not incidentally related to the nature of attention but centrally so. I have also argued that Heidegger's pedagogy, such as it is, invokes that understanding of agency. Heidegger's philosophical movement can be interpreted as an elaboration of the nature of attention, whether in terms of the care structure of Dasein's being-in-the-world (1996), of thinking as thanking (1968) and the meditative thinking of his *Discourse on Thinking* (1969), or man as the 'shepherd of Being' in the *Letter on Humanism* (1993); the complex double-movement of attention mirrors the complex double-nature of identity itself because attention is significantly constitutive of Dasein. The thereness of Dasein's being appears as the opening of being onto itself: i.e., as attention. We can take this further if we consider how language constitutes Being and human being. In a certain sense, all speech grants the world in terms of structuring our orientation to it, and so speech intimates the tripartite gathering of aletheia which involves Being, Dasein and mediation. This is because speech requires a speaker, a hearer and a world, and is therefore "the clearing-concealing advent of Being itself" (1993, 230). Speech too entails the transcendental condition for speaking, namely being, though Heidegger's philosophy of language is beyond my present scope.

From the perspective of the desire to locate Heidegger's thinking within a philosophical history it might seem natural to ask again, what does Heidegger mean by thinking? One reading of Heidegger could suggest that *attention* is the essence of thinking. But this answer elides the dynamic character of thinking as attention and, in fact, the tendency to want to project the 'thought' of Heidegger into clear formulations seems itself to emerge from a 'will to know' that, so Heidegger argues, places us in the state of inattention (or oblivion of being). The ready answer may have the ring of correctness to it, but that does not make it 'true' since it functions not to draw attention out but rather to stifle it. Only when human beings can "get beyond the 'willfulness' of Western metaphysics which is preoccupied with beings and the manipulation of beings" (Caputo 1978, 24) will the still voice of the truth of Being be heard. The task of thinking then is to "meditate upon Being as such, which metaphysics, despite all its talk about Being, is never able to think – except in terms of beings" (Caputo 1978, 24). In the attempt to overcome metaphysics, Heidegger has distinguished 'representational thinking' from 'essential thinking': representational thinking as the metaphysical method, and essential thinking as that which 'spends itself' on the truth of Being itself. In other words, the sciences and traditional philosophy, indeed metaphysics as a whole, involve a mode of 'representing' (*Vorstellen*) or 'manufacturing' (*Herstellen*) beings which necessarily conceals the truth of Being. To know the difference is one mark of the educated person: the person who has learnt to wait for being to show itself.

Conclusion

In this chapter I have tried to show that Heidegger's approach to doing philosophy is indicative of a philosophical and pedagogical view that has generally gone unrecognized. What dominates pedagogy today is the construction, transmission and refinement of mental representations. For Heidegger this is not thinking, and therefore should not be the foundation of education. Heidegger's method follows the Socratic endeavour of reducing students to *aporia* in which it is the representations that must be abandoned to the appropriation of being (Allen and Axiotis 2002, 16). The student must abandon all images if they are to let themselves be reduced to the *aporia* that is an essential moment in education. Thus, Heidegger's reconceptualization of thinking entails an equally radical and profound reconceptualization of education. A comparison with Eastern traditions does offer, I think, some opportunities to see this reconceptualization at work. This is because to learn from a Zen Buddhist master, for example, does not only entail a correct understanding of Zen doctrine – that we have associated with representational thinking – but also involves a more complete change of perspective that forms the ground of 'rational thought'. This total shift is ontological/epistemological (a distinction between the two is difficult to maintain here) and resonates with Heidegger's view of education.

It is clear, then, that the representational and propositional frames are related if not quite identical. A crude but recognizable characterization of the Zen Buddhist of Taoist traditions will often disavow any propositional conception of truth. The opening line of the Tao Te Ching, the central text of Taoism says precisely this: "The Tao that can be spoken is not the eternal Tao." Religions cannot be fundamentally propositional in a context where thinking cannot be simply representational. This will leave the reader wondering what he or she can take away from the argument if not some intellectual idea, some cognitive trophy to carry into some future endeavour. I hope this book resists such easy enframing, while not for that seeming a waste of time.

Notes

1 Heidegger's interest in Eastern thought was considerable and has enjoyed significant attention over recent decades (see for example: Caputo 1978; Parkes 1990; May 1996; Ma 2007). While the attempt to find such parallels can be fruitful, we must take care that the conclusions are not overdrawn. As Ma (2007, 15) tellingly points out, "[t]here seems to be a competition between scholars who ascribe greater similarities between Zen Buddhism and Heidegger and those who find more similarities between Daoism and Heidegger. In recent years, the latter have come to dominate." Heidegger himself was extremely skeptical of the value of drawing similarities in this way.

2 Familiarity with the original context, and the care with which Heidegger chooses his words will make Caputo's use of the quotation seem questionable. Heidegger precedes this quote with the words, "one is inclined to get the idea" (Heidegger 1996c, p. 36), suggesting in fact a quite different interpretation.

3 Dahlstrom (2013, 74) interprets the term as follows: "A formal indication is a way of pointing to existential phenomena, roughly fixing their preliminary senses and the

'Only a god can save us' 81

corresponding manner of retrieving those sense, while at the same time deflecting any 'uncritical lapse' into a conception that would foreclose pursuit of their genuine sense. Formal indications accordingly have a 'referring-prohibitive' function. Their 'fundamental sense' is based upon insight that, while any interpretation must emerge from our original access to phenomena, existential phenomena are not given to us directly. Hence, they need to be indicated but in a purely formal, revisable fashion. The sense of a concept as a formal indication is less a matter of content than a matter of enactment or performance." For Heidegger's own definition of formal indication: (2001, 16, 25, 40, 45).

4 What might be called Heidegger's method in much of his work is consistent: he begins with a characterization of the everyday sense of a term, or the conventional view of an idea (philosophy, technology, truth, language, art . . .), which is then deconstructed.

5 Heidegger (1968, 53) recognizes this tension where he quotes from one of Nietzsche's letters: "After you had discovered me, it was no trick to fine me: the difficulty now is to lose me . . .". As figures of authority within the history of philosophy, Nietzsche and Heidegger think on our behalf, which is a grave danger in any philosophical reading.

6 From Heidegger's point of view, no one holds a worldview, still less a belief system. Heidegger's essay "The Age of the World Picture" (1977, pp. 115–154) gives an indication of the predicament of the modern West, which regards cultures in terms of cultural representations. The point here has implications for any wider cross-cultural comparison. That we see other cultures in terms of worldviews demonstrates only that we have a representational conception of lived experience. It is worth quoting Heidegger (1977, 133–134) at length: "As soon as the world becomes picture, the position of man is conceived as a world-view. To be sure, the phrase 'world-view' is open to misunderstanding, as though it were merely a matter here of a passive contemplation of the world. For this reason, already in the nineteenth century it was emphasised with justification that 'worldview' also meant and even meant primarily 'view of life.' The fact that, despite this, the phrase 'worldview' asserts itself as the name for the position of man in the midst of all that is, is proof of how decisively the world became picture as soon as man brought his life as *subiectum* into precedence over other centres of relationship. This means: whatever is, is considered to be in being only to the degree and to the extent that it is taken into and referred back to this life, i.e. is lived out, and becomes life-experience. Just as unsuited to the Greek spirit as every humanism had to be, just so impossible was a medieval worldview, and just as absurd is a Catholic worldview. Just as necessarily and legitimately as everything must change into life-experience for modern man the more unlimitedly he takes charge of the shaping of his essence, just so certainly could the Greeks at the Olympian festivals never have had life-experiences."

7 Pöggeler (1990) argues that this understanding of Eckhart might apply to the pedagogical discourses where the traditional religious language still very much persists. But Eckhart as the non-dualist, where the ground of the soul and the Godhead are one, would seem to accord with a releasement beyond the domain of the will altogether. Caputo (1978, 180ff) suggests that Heidegger's misunderstanding of Eckhart's releasement results from the fact that Heidegger supposes Eckhart's releasement to be a willing to not will, and as such, to be an ethical and moral category.

References

Allen, V., & Axiotis, A. (2002). "Heidegger on the Art of Teaching" in M. A. Peters (ed.) *Heidegger, Education, and Modernity*. Lanham, MD: Rowman and Littlefield, 1–20.

Biemel, W. (1977). *Martin Heidegger*. J. L. Mehta trans. London: Routledge.

Caputo, J. (1978). *The Mystical Element in Heidegger's Thought*. New York: Fordham University Press.

Dahlstrom, D. (2013). *The Heidegger Dictionary*. London: Bloomsbury.

Davis, B. (2007). *Heidegger and the Will*. New York: State Univ of New York Press.

Hackett, J. (ed.). (2012). *A Companion to Eckhart*. Leiden, Brill.

Heidegger, M. (1956). *What Is Philosophy?* J. Wilde and W. Kluback, trans. New Haven, CT: College and University Press.

Heidegger, M. (1968). *What Is Called Thinking?* J. Gray, trans. New York: Harper and Row.

Heidegger, M. (1969). *Discourse on Thinking*, J. Anderson and E. Freund, trans. New York: Harper and Row.

Heidegger, M. (1972). *On Time and Being*, J. Stambaugh, trans. Chicago, IL: University of Chicago Press.

Heidegger, M. (1973). *The End of Philosophy*, J. Stambaugh, trans. New York: Harper and Row.

Heidegger, M. (1977). *The Question Concerning Technology and Other Essays*, W. Lovitt, trans. New York: Harper and Row.

Heidegger, M. (1981). "Nur noch ein Gott kann uns retten" *Der Spiegel* 30 (Mai, 1976): 193–219. Trans. by W. Richardson as "Only a God Can Save Us" in Thomas Sheehan (ed.) *Heidegger: The Man and the Thinker*, 45–67.

Heidegger, M. (1992). *Parmenides*, A. Schuwer and R. Rojcewicz, trans. Bloomington, IN: Indiana University Press.

Heidegger, M. (1993). *Basic Writings: Second Edition, Revised and Expanded*. New York: Harper-Collins.

Heidegger, M. (1996a). *Being and Time: A Translation of Sein and Zeit*, J. Stambaugh, trans. Albany, NY: SUNY Press.

Heidegger, M. (1996b). *Hölderlin's Hymn 'The Ister'*, W. McNeill and J. Davis, trans. Bloomington, IN: Indiana University Press.

Heidegger, M. (1996c). *The Principle of Reason*, R. Lilly, trans. Bloomington, IN: Indiana University Press.

Heidegger, M. (1998). "Plato's Doctrine of Truth" in W. McNeill (ed.) Cambridge: Cambridge University Press, 155–182.

Heidegger, M. (2001). *Phenomenological Interpretations of Aristotle: Initiations into Phenomenological Research*, R. Rojcewicz, trans. Bloomington: Indiana University Press.

Janicaud, D. (ed.). (2000). *Phenomenology and the 'Theological Turn': The French Debate*. New York: Fordham University Press.

Kreeft, P. (1971). "Zen in Heidegger's Gelassenheit" *International Philosophical Quarterly*, 11: 4, 521–545.

Lewin, D. (2011). "The Middle Voice in Eckhart and Modern Continental Philosophy," *Medieval Mystical Theology*, 20: 1, 28–46.

Lewin, D. (2012). *Technology and the Philosophy of Religion*. Newcastle Upon Tyne: Cambridge Scholars Publishing.

Lewin, D. (2014a). "The Leap of Learning," *Ethics and Education*, 9: 1, 113–126.

Ma, L. (2007). *Heidegger on East-West Dialogue: Anticipating the Event*. London: Routledge.

May, R. (1996). *Heidegger's Hidden Sources: East Asian Influences on his Work*, G. Parkes, trans. London: Routledge.

Parkes, G. (1990). *Heidegger and Asian Thought*. Honolulu: University of Hawaii Press.

Peters, M. A. (ed.). (2002). *Heidegger, Education, and Modernity*. Lanham, MD: Rowman and Littlefield.

Pöggeler, O. (1990). "West-East Dialogue: Heidegger and Lao-Tzu" in G. Parkes (ed.) *Heidegger and Asian Thought*. Honolulu: University of Hawaii Press, 47–78.

Rancière, J. (1991). *The Ignorant Schoolmaster: Five Lessons in Intellectual Emancipation*, K. Ross, trans. Stanford, CA: Stanford University Press.

Richardson, W. (2003). *Through Phenomenology to Thought*. New York: Fordham University Press.

Steiner, G. (1992). *Heidegger*, 2nd edn. London: Fontana Press.

Storey, D. (2012). "Zen in Heidegger's Way" *Journal of East-West Thought*, 2: 4, 113–137.

Thomson, I. (2002). "Heidegger on Ontological Education, or: How We Become What We Are," in M.A. Peters (ed.) *Heidegger, Education, and Modernity*. Lanham, MD: Rowman and Littlefield, 97–125.

Turner, D. (1999). *The Darkness of God: Negativity in Christian Mysticism*. Cambridge: Cambridge University Press.

Vattimo, G. (2003). "After Onto-Theology: Philosophy between Science and Religion" in M. Wrathall (ed.) *Religion After Metaphysics*. Cambridge: Cambridge University Press, 29–36.

Wolin, R. (ed.). (1993). *The Heidegger Controversy: A Critical Reader*. Cambridge, MA: MIT Press.

Wrathall, M. (ed.). (2003). *Religion After Metaphysics*. Cambridge: Cambridge University Press.

Part 2

Experiments in reframing

Chapter 5

Submission

Introduction

Where the post-secular blurs the boundary between the secular and religious, then religious ideas can cut across secular culture in interesting ways. The notion that education entails a moment of submission is such an idea. By submission I understand a range of ideas, from a certain modesty and humility, to a consideration or respect for authority (of the object of inquiry more than the teacher), to more radical forms of self-negation where education entails a change in the being of the student. Such ideas of self-submission cut across both religion and education. In this chapter I want to show that every movement of learning entails a kind of epistemological submission or affirmation that generally goes unnoticed and unthematized.[1] I will argue that one has to engage in a kind of pre-critical 'primary affirmation' in order to undertake the kind of learning necessary for a critical engagement with what one learns. That this is in contrast to the empirical tradition of the *tabula rasa* need not suggest an idealist/rationalist approach. Rather, following the Heideggerian theme developed thus far, this approach is best described as hermeneutical. I propose that any movement of learning is based upon an entry into a hermeneutical circle:[2] one finds oneself *always already* thrown into an interpretation which in some sense has to be temporarily affirmed or adopted in order to be either absorbed and integrated, or overcome and rejected. Speaking of the level at which we already begin within an affirmed pre-understanding or interpretation, the philosopher Paul Ricoeur (1967, 352) describes hermeneutics as proceeding "from a prior understanding of the very thing that it tries to understand by interpreting it." I intend to illustrate this principle through a constructive retrieval of an unfashionable pedagogical concept: *submission*. Consistent with my general approach thus far, I will draw on a range of traditions that contrast with the modern liberal Western perspective, in which the constructive role for submission has been almost entirely unthinkable.

Philosophical hermeneutics

Within the tradition of philosophical hermeneutics, the hermeneutical circle describes the interaction between the structure of our pre-understandings and our perception of things: our pre-understandings give rise to, or constitute our perceptions, while themselves undergoing reinterpretation following those perceptions.[3] Prior to this development within modern philosophy, hermeneutics arose to facilitate the complex process of scriptural interpretation. In this chapter, I will employ the insights of philosophical hermeneutics towards an interpretation of the structure of pedagogy. The significance of these insights for education are broad, though I would suggest at the outset that a proper understanding of affirmation within education can help us to resist the worst excesses of the efforts to secularize the modern curriculum. This is because no curriculum, no educational system, can be entirely free of commitment. A secular curriculum, as much as any, affirms a range of axiomatic principles for which there is no rational justification. In other words it is not a question of whether educators will make what I am calling a *primary affirmation*, but more a question of how that primary affirmation is instantiated. This, of course, resonates with the ideas developed in Chapter 3 whereby cultural liturgies are enacted that cut across the sacred/secular partition. The desire of secular liberalism to separate church and state clearly involves particular commitments about the appropriate role of the state, which, as we have seen, are far from uncontested. The notion that no educational system is without its pre-understandings is important not only to resist the caustic atheism and somewhat more tempered secularism that characterize recent cultural discourse,[4] but also to help us in assessing the appropriate contribution that any established tradition can make to education, and where that contribution should be seen as excessive or unfounded. To that end, I address in particular those seeking to understand the tensions between our embedded cultural traditions (whether that is framed in explicitly Christian, or more broadly liberal terms) on the one hand, and our responsibilities to educate informed, critical, engaged and autonomous citizens, on the other.

Returning to the structure of philosophical hermeneutics, I suggest that the process of interpretation/understanding that always precedes critical engagement, what Ricoeur (1967, 19) calls a first naïveté, requires a form of speculative engagement that places one in a relationship with the learning that is 'involved'.[5] For early Ricoeur, it is in the field of religious understanding that the movement from what he calls a pre-critical first naïveté to a post-critical second naïveté is particularly applicable, though this structure applies just as well to the process of understanding and pedagogy more generally, and so is worthy of elaboration. The narrative or hermeneutic arc here described can be applied to the young person as they appropriate, and are appropriated by, the world, as well as being applicable to a narrative of Western enlightenment history where progress passes through various complex stages. So how does this Ricoeurian device of the hermeneutic arc from pre-critical 'wager' to post-critical 'appropriation', which has been characterized as Ricoeur's "motley collection of academic apparatuses" (Stiver 2001, 65), throw light both of religion and education?

In *The Symbolism of Evil*, Ricoeur describes the first naïveté as the attitude in which religious truths are taken at simple face value. Ricoeur argues that the rational forces of modernity have made this simple relation to religious truth generally untenable, leading us to pass through a phase of critical distance, what he calls *distanciation*. But rather than simply ending up with a post-critical atheism, Ricoeur argues (1967, 349) that it is possible, and desirable, to move beyond this critical stage towards a post-critical *second* naïveté: "Beyond the desert of criticism, we wish to be called again." The details of how Ricoeur achieves this post-critical understanding are complex (1967; 1977). They relate to the more hermeneutically informed reinterpretations of tradition that many people experience: the narratives take on symbolic, anagogic, moral and aesthetic meaning (without necessarily negating the literal, though at least complicating what it might mean to be *literal*). Ricoeur's structure of understanding describes the *alreadyness* of primary affirmation as going through an inevitable phase of critique followed by an enriched and informed post-critical re-engagement with tradition. It is hardly surprising, then, that Ricoeur is known first and foremost as a hermeneutic philosopher. This general three-stage structure suggests a model for pedagogy that is fundamentally dialogical, though in the context of the post-secular, I want to draw particular attention to the primary affirmation that is the necessary precondition for any understanding at all. In his later writings, Ricoeur (1984) reconfigures the three-stage interpretive structure through his work on the unity of time and narrative in his "threefold mimesis" (Wallace 1996). Here Ricoeur employs a different, less theologically charged, language which allows the structure to be applied to literary (and educational) contexts more broadly. Ricoeur speaks of a first stage of prefiguration (mimesis 1), followed by configuration (mimesis 2) and finally refiguration (mimesis 3), or more obviously relevant to educationalists: (naïve) understanding, explanation, post-critical understanding. The literary turn in Ricoeur's later thinking encourages a clear identification of one's commitment as the prefigured 'pre-narrative' in which any understanding (as narrative) becomes possible. While this later expression is in many ways a broader 'literary' retelling of Ricoeur's earlier philosophical hermeneutics, I am keen to recall the more explicitly theological moment captured in the earlier work of *The Symbolism of Evil* partly out of an interest in the post-secular context.

More directly addressing the step of primary affirmation, Ricoeur describes the structure of the hermeneutical circle in the following terms: "The circle can be stated bluntly: 'We must understand in order to believe, but we must believe in order to understand.' The circle is not a vicious circle, still less a mortal one; it is a living and stimulating circle" (1967, 351). Unsurprisingly for Ricoeur, this statement clearly draws upon the theological idea of *faith seeking understanding* in which a step, or leap of faith is part of the process of engagement with something other (God).[6] As Kierkegaard saw (1980), the leap of faith cannot be organized or made rational. It must involve the total abandonment of what one understands to be the rules of the game such that it can be an authentic response

90 Submission

to an impossible question, or an infinite theological demand. Any response to a theological call is, in this sense, a wager.[7] We respond to a call made only in the hope, never the secure knowledge, that what we hear is not simply the product of our own pre-understanding. But that moment of pre-understanding cannot be undercut or avoided, leading to the inevitable criticism that Ricoeur makes true revelation impossible (because we cannot escape our own projections), a criticism that I will discuss in Chapter 8.

Nor is the pursuit of positivist or scientific knowledge able to avoid the leap of affirmation here defined. Philosophers of science have amply demonstrated the fallacy of the pursuit of objective scientific knowledge (Polanyi 1958; Feyerabend 1978). But this does not undermine the power of science; rather it shows the necessary structure in which scientific understanding develops, a structure which entails something akin to the primary affirmation. John Polkinghorne is explicit in his concern to relate the scientist's act of commitment to at least some basic consistency as a presupposition of any scientific research, with an apprehension of divine order in the cosmos: "The scientist commits himself to belief in the rationality of the world in order to discover what form that rationality takes" (1991, 6). But the implication of circularity is not intended to crush scientific progress, but to properly contextualize it, a context which demonstrates the affirmation of understanding: "No one of serious intent can escape the necessity of an intellectual bootstrap to raise himself above the earthbound state of unreflective experience" (1991, 7).

From a pedagogical perspective, the commitment, or leap, exists in the sense that in order to truly understand something beyond mere tautology, one has to enter into the appropriate orientation or perspective. A position is taken prior to any reflective or critical movement. This could be understood in terms of the hermeneutical orientation to a text: reading patiently and sympathetically or critically and analytically, or in terms of a more foundational epistemological problem of understanding in general. We might call this *the course of understanding* in so far as understanding is not simply arrived at following a direct encounter with some novel aspect of knowledge, but rather emerges over time, dialectically, through a course or process of primary affirmation, critical reflection and, finally, post-critical adoption and adaptation.[8] Acknowledging the limitations of the rather blunt analysis of world history in terms of the dated East/West binary (see Maxwell 2010, 1–32), I want to engage in some comparative analysis as a heuristic device to make a general point about the structure of pedagogy that, in the final analysis, does not depend upon the fine accuracy of the characterization itself. It could be said that this example itself plays the role of a first naïveté providing a platform for a critical engagement with the ideas I intend it to illustrate. And so, in the spirit of ethnographic inquiry, I present my own experience of learning and teaching of the Chinese martial art of Tai Chi Chuan in an autobiographical fashion, so that the structure of commitment, along with some of the consequent problems, can be clearly identified and elaborated. The underlying significance here is that structure of pedagogy in Eastern traditions is in stark contrast to the conventional view in more progressive approaches to education which generally assumes absolute autonomy to be the educational goal.

I want to preface this example with some reflections on the nature of Tai Chi Chuan as it has been appropriated in contemporary Western culture. Paul Bowman and Douglas Wile have written extensively about the appropriation of Chinese martial arts in Western cultures and the pedagogical insights to be drawn from those martial arts traditions (Bowman 2009; 2013; Wile 1996; 2014). Bowman examines the tensions that arise when these traditions and practices call for a kind of uncritical fidelity. He presents the example of Bruce Lee, an extraordinary figure within martial arts cinematic history, who chose to appropriate the tradition for his own untraditional approach to martial arts and martial arts pedagogy (Bowman 2013). There are many important lessons from Bowman's analysis of Lee.[9] But the central concern for now is to point out that any account of the 'real and authentic' Tai Chi Chuan, with the appropriate lineages justifying the authority of the master, must be called into question since the art itself developed its own narrative self-understanding, and to some extent the lineage histories that justify authority are recent inventions or at least rather selective readings of Chinese history (Bowman 2009; Wile 2014). As Bowman (2013, 18) summarises:

> Unfortunately . . . the tendency has been 'to treat the story of t'ai-chi ch'üan in an historical vacuum' (Wiles 1996, 4). T'ai-chi ch'üan, then, like all 'Chinese wisdom', up to and including Bruce Lee's, has been *Orientalised* and *allochronised*: constructed as ancient, timeless, unique, and decidedly other.

The general conception of Chinese wisdom and ancient 'authentic' practices is, pedagogically speaking, enormously significant, since attitudes to teaching an art with some lineage has, as I think the following narrative indicates, an impact on how that teaching is organized. With these caveats in mind, I hope the reader will indulge a less than perfectly critical perspective in the following pedagogical auto-ethnography.

Auto-ethnography: Tai Chi Chuan

When I first took up Tai Chi Chuan at the age of nineteen, I did not know what I was getting myself into. I thought it might be fun to do, good exercise and, knowing that the Master also taught Tai Chi as a serious martial art, I knew that I would learn some combat techniques. I was interested in the 'real' Tai Chi that existed before the translation and, as I saw it, reduction, into a general health art. Notwithstanding this interest in something *originary*, I began with an open mind, but with a sense that there were hidden depths to this ancient art. As the weeks of training rolled on, I become more interested and engaged.

The weeks became months, and the months, years, until, in the fullness of time I became a senior instructor running my own branches and training daily, sometimes for hours.

What began as an interest in health and martial arts, became so much more. I realized that *Tai Chi Chuan* represented a way of being that engaged the human body, mind and spirit on many levels. There was no way I could have understood the meaning of the art without spending a good deal of time engaged in daily practice. And the discipline of daily practice was not easy, but for reasons that are not entirely clear to me, I stuck at it. There is something of a paradox at the heart of this process. I sought some kind of engagement or fulfillment that I both did and did not recognize as present in the practice. I had some inkling that the discipline of daily practice was worthwhile, but there was no way that I could fully comprehend the meaning of what I was beginning to get into.

The point here is to draw attention to an epistemological structure as it arises in a number of contexts, a principle of pedagogy which I suggest is largely absent from current reflection on education. The structure has its roots in the Platonic epistemological principle of anamnesis in which our ability to recognize something understood as true, is dependent, on some level, on its prior existence within the soul. I have already suggested that this structure is best understood as hermeneutical, which, for the present purposes, could be seen as a reading of Platonic metaphysics. In the context of Tai Chi Chuan, this structure expressed itself in a sense that there was something to this art that I recognized despite the fact that I was unable to fully articulate the nature of the perception.

Perhaps I was simply enamored by the force of personality that my master exuded. Indeed it was inspiring to see my master's ability to maintain an inscrutable depth while also presenting a very pragmatic concern for his business as an instructor and practitioner. But throughout my training I was also torn. My master had certain ways of talking and behaving which seemed redolent of a lost age, from certain formalities within class, to strong expectations of commitment. Modern Londoners did not always adapt well to the structure and rigour that our master sought to uphold. Yet it was those very expectations that stimulated and energized those who held out to discover the meaning of Tai Chi Chuan in suburban London.

I recall a particular incident that, for me, captures something of the spirit of this commitment. It is such a minor incident that it scarcely seems worthy of discussion, but, paradoxically, the insignificance of the event adds to its significance.[10] Having been coming to classes for nearly a year, I had yet to speak directly to the master who primarily instructed senior students who in turn instructed the newer students such as myself – this hierarchy reflected the traditional approach. Then, for a reason that I do not recall, I was invited to speak with the master but had not given any thought to how I might address him. I was aware that students used the Cantonese/Mandarin honorific title *Sifu* to speak about the master, but I had not anticipated addressing him directly in this way. Being unsure, I nervously used his first name, at which point he gave me a look which demonstrably indicated the nature of the *faux pas*. My initial feeling was one of great embarrassment. This later gave way to a sense of confusion about the way in which Sifu allowed me to feel so dreadfully awkward without so much as a sign or word of relief. Reflecting on the incident that day, I considered that my interpretation of this event was, for me, a decision. I could choose to interpret the lack of sympathy with my discomfort which Sifu seemed to display as a failure of his part: a failure of his approach and/or character, an interpretation which might reinforce a general perception that Sifu was maintaining a hierarchy that suited his self-image. That masters of Chinese martial arts inculcate a sense of deference and with it a kind of authority and dependency is known, though often unacknowledged among practitioners (Bowman 2013). Of course that culture of dependency could be abusive in intent, or might be properly pedagogical by providing an opportunity to appropriate the self otherwise. In other words, I had an alternative to seeing Sifu as taking a traditional hierarchical self-image. I could resolve to see this event as an opportunity to look at my own relation to the world: that the situation enabled me to see just how fragile I was, just how overly sensitive my 'ego' was to such simple, everyday interactions. In choosing the latter interpretation, my embarrassment and shame became instructive, powerful even, rather than disabling or diminishing. This was the first of many interactions that I could interpret in different ways: often either as denigration or instruction. In affirming the latter interpretation, I was choosing to suspend the critical interpretation of my master in which my difficulties could be safely externalized. I was submitting myself to his approach since he was my teacher.[11] This example is offered as an illustration of what I call the *paradigm of submission* that, broadly speaking, is more characteristic of Eastern pedagogy[12] and expressed itself, in my experience, through the formalities of training as a student with a master.

I felt that many of the difficulties that other students had with the more traditional pedagogical style within the martial arts I was trained in (both fellow students but also students of mine) – the hierarchy, formality and a certain expectation of submission of personal will – could be understood in just the terms expressed above, as the opportunity to look at the movement of the self as the issue to consider. The temptation within Western thought to externalize the problem by assuming it to be a failure of the 'product' – the class or the instructors, was countered by a sense that most difficulties were actually the natural expression of the anxieties of self-identity, put under pressure both by the unfamiliar formalities, as well as the silence at the heart of the practice itself. A more general philosophical point seemed to be that submission became an opportunity to uncover the self rather than a negation of the self. So we arrive at a principle of the master/student relationship that I want to identify, namely submission.

Primary affirmation as submission

The real point here is that the student cannot ever fully anticipate the worth of the process they undertake until hindsight. Customer satisfaction scores

94 Submission

(e.g., the National Student Survey in the current of UK higher education) will only tell you so much. The tradition of the apprentice is required not simply to undertake a rigorous training process having fully understood what is at stake – what might be understood as a calculated exchange, where the student brings the cash and the teacher brings the knowledge. Rather the student is invited to submit to something that there is no way they can fully understand in advance, an irrational commitment that is not incidental within this pedagogy anymore than the leap of faith could be incidental for Kierkegaard. In Tai Chi Chuan I suspended the impression that my master was fallible or self-aggrandizing in order to proceed along a particular path. While, speaking objectively, my master may have been as susceptible to egoistic pretensions as anyone else, such an interpretation seemed to intrude upon deeper engagement. Interpreting the difficulties I was having with my training as a failure anywhere but within myself (e.g., with the master or the organization) was not going to help. Pride and self-regard had to be overcome but at the risk of submitting to a force that I did not have the capacity to fully assess. In this sense, the apprentice makes a leap of commitment in order to undertake the path of understanding. The student cannot know in advance whether the commitment they are making is worthwhile or not. There is, by definition, a vulnerability, risk or wager to be made by the student. And in Chinese martial arts, in particular Tai Chi, as well as in other Buddhist and Taoist traditions, the student must engage in extensive preparatory training culminating in a ritual initiation to demonstrate that they are worthy for what is known as 'inside the door' training, a level of technique and training that is reserved for those who show the greatest potential (Docherty 1997, 61–70). The reader who sees in this a rather questionable suspension of judgement should be reassured that judgement is not abandoned here. Rather, a commitment has always already preceded a thematic and reflective judgement. My story of Tai Chi is a little too crude, therefore, to capture the real point of the unthematic, hermeneutically embedded, nature of primary affirmation. And the interpretation of events that looks to the self for a response might miss the wider social and structural failings of institutions and societies that have framed particular events and practices in ways that may be less than fully inclusive.

It is important to note that *knowledge* is here not understood simply as a theoretical appreciation of a practice or state of affairs, but rather as lived understanding – that to know something is really meant to imply a unity of knowing and being. Perhaps the archetypal example would be that inferred from Plato's *Republic*, that in order to know justice one must attain to the virtue of justice, not simply to understand the principles of justice in theoretical form. One attains to justice because one understands, or perceives the nature of justice and desires the good. Similarly, one can read that Tai Chi has certain health benefits in any number of books, but only through rigorous practice can one really know the benefits of Tai Chi (Klein 1984; Docherty 1997; Sutton 1998). It is precisely this epistemological principle that plays the curious role in pedagogy that I want to highlight; for by definition, this real knowledge cannot be gained without engagement. But how does one know what to engage with prior to the illumination (or critical understanding) that follows? Historically this question has been easier to answer since there simply was not the range of traditions and teachings on offer. But our post-secular age is characterized by plurality, a spiritual opportunity that is pharmacological insofar as we are left to choose something that feels like it cannot be *chosen*: the nature and meaning of the good life. How are we today to pick through the range of traditions and ways of life seeking our allegiance (Karner and Aldridge 2004; Carrette and King 2005)? The problem of allegiance relates also to the possibility of exploitation.

A major problem with the pedagogical model that relies upon submission is the potential for manipulation and abuse. When it comes to the realm of spiritual pedagogy, within, for example, the 'Bhakti' devotional traditions in Hinduism, some of the key dangers of submission of the student to guru are reflected in Mary Garden's account (2005) of her experience on the guru trail during the 1970s:

> Eastern mysticism was new and exotic to Westerners, and we were in the vanguard as we traipsed from guru to guru, unable to see that we would have been better to give up on them altogether — at least until we had sorted ourselves out psychologically. But there had been no exposés or warnings of the damage that could be done to our minds and our bodies when we surrendered our critical thinking (and our hearts) to gurus. We were young and gullible, susceptible.

Nor is this kind of problem specific to Westerners who seek the ancient wisdom of the 'mystical lands' of the Orient. The Indian *gurukula* tradition, essentially a system of residential education in which a principal guru or sage teaches according to their own style within an ashram, makes demands upon any student whether they are Western or not. These days the gurukulas of India are generally confined to the ancient arts of classical music, Sanskrit, Yoga and other artistic and spiritual endeavors, a tradition in which, to this day students are expected to serve the guru and ashram in all sorts of ways, from cooking and cleaning to collecting alms. Submission is a principal component of the pedagogical process in which the appropriate orientation of the student provides the right context for sensitive reception of deeper knowledge. As Ozmon and Craver (2008) have noted, "the guru might encourage students to do things that seem meaningless and absurd to them but that lead to enlightenment. Thus, students must be able to place great confidence in their teacher." The more receptive the student, the greater the opportunity to learn, but also the greater the risk of abuse. Scandals surrounding certain Indian gurus have demonstrated some of the risks associated, with notable controversies surrounding 'Osho' Bhagwan Shree Rajneesh and Sathya Sai Baba (Milne 1987; Buncombe 2011). My present concern is less with the very real potential for abuse that

96 Submission

exists, than with the inevitable commitment that 'traditional' Oriental pedagogy entails. I regard this commitment as a hermeneutical disposition not confined to Eastern thought, but something that every student, to some extent, must take towards his or her subject of study. Indeed, it is this disposition of commitment, this primary affirmation, that both creates the possibility of abuse, but also sustains the engagement required to enter into a productive circle of understanding. The hermeneutical circle, in this case, is not simply an inhibiting structure to be escaped, but is equally a structure that facilitates and so is to be acknowledged as a space in which learning is possible. It is the pharmacological nature of the affirmation (just as prejudice is pharmacological for Gadamer), that it acts both as poison and cure, that seems to be an inescapable feature of pedagogy.

But, as has already been suggested, a problem of critical understanding inevitably occurs. On what basis can the student assess the quality or integrity of the guru? Why should a student enter into any specific form of commitment, when it is an irrational (perhaps arbitrary) decision that leads to their choice of Tai Chi Chuan, learning the piano, becoming a physicist, joining a monastic order, or whatever? This question is even more pertinent when the initial decision to enter into a commitment is made on behalf of the child by the parent. In the case of classical Indian music within a traditional gurukula, the student does not have complete access to the full depth of the artistic insight simply through hearing the performance of their guru. Only through extensive applied participation can the student fully understand and appreciate the music. From this point of view, knowing and being are indistinguishable. To be sure, the student can appreciate some aspects and depths present in the music (as through a glass darkly the truth can be perceived) and there may be an intuitive sense that the guru is the *real thing*. In the arts there is a certain aspect through performance which can be publically shared and thereby authority can be publically verified. But what of the spiritual guru whose insight is that much less expressive, and is only articulated in a depth of presence impossible to represent. The putative wisdom of Sri Ramana Maharshi cannot be just assumed by the novice who considers entry into the ashram. But where is the public demonstration of the guru's talents? Where are the diplomas? What credence can be given without the credentials? Reputation has a vital role to play, but this can also be manipulated. In spiritual matters, there seems to be much less room for maneuver within the hermeneutic circle, and so the vulnerabilities of the student seem that much more acute. But the problem of establishing the veracity of a teacher is not, of course, exclusive to Oriental traditions.

On the whole, the Western philosophical tradition no longer accommodates the authoritarian style of pedagogy characteristic of the Oriental world. Whether in the context of the Indian gurukula, the Zen Buddhist training explored in Eugen Herrigel's book *Zen in the Art of Archery*, or the tradition of fellowship that permeates the Chinese martial arts, the strong bond between teacher and student can appear rather peculiar or anachronistic to the uninitiated Westerner.

It can appear that the student is expected to submit too readily to the training regimen that is set out by the master. How can people be expected to put aside their critical faculty and enter into a commitment to some practice for which there is little rational account? But as I have argued, the expectation of a certain orientation or disposition is a prerequisite within the structure of understanding itself. The hermeneutical leap in Eastern thought could be seen simply as having been made explicit; the leap is externalized, formalized or ritualized. What purpose could this ritualization of affirmation serve? Is it conceivable that the ritualization of such a process is not the anomaly? Is it possible that the affirmative leap is lost to Western pedagogy because of the relatively recent shift towards an assumption of epistemological neutrality and the related rejection of all forms of authority? Furthermore is not our tendency to ignore commitment the anomaly? Since the scientific revolution, Western European culture has encouraged a humanism of dominance over nature.[13] Secularization has moved forward upon the wave of epistemological objectivity that regards any step of faith or unjustifiable commitment with great suspicion. Insofar as we regard ourselves as rational creatures, we anticipate eliminating any arbitrary commitments that might, in fact, be an essential part of the process of understanding. In Chapter 3 we explored examples of the ongoing quest for curriculum objectivity in the polarization of debates around the relevance of religious studies within modern education in which commentators demand objective criteria from which to (most often) reject the inclusion of religion. In general the modern scientist is not at home acknowledging the kind of primary affirmation I have discussed. But Western philosophers and theologians have not always been as metaphysically hesitant.

Theological affirmation and submission

For a book concerning the end of secularization, the Christian God might seem strangely absent. This can be justified by the underlabouring required before anything directly theological can (again) be spoken. Underlabouring, clearing the ground of extraneous conceptual overbelief, or glittering metaphysical constructions, although especially important in the present age, has always been a significant aspect of theology. Here we find a process of speaking about God which requires that we continually 'unsay' what is said, that we encounter a dazzling darkness.[14] The primary affirmation that we have discussed exists in shrouded darkness, resisting complete illumination. It is the paradoxical nature of hermeneutics that as soon as one grasps and thematises the object of inquiry, it is no longer embedded in lived experience: it is no longer what it is. That this bears some resemblance to mystical theology will I hope become clear – or at least less obscure. In *The Darkness of God*, Denys Turner explores the epistemological structure and process of primary affirmation as it exists in varied theological sources, from Plato's allegory of the cave, to the writings of Christian mystics such as

St Augustine and John of the Cross. A clear example of this paradoxical structure is expressed in a recurring theme of St. Augustine's *Confessions*. Early on Augustine asks "whether a man is first to pray for help . . . and whether he must know you before he can call you to his aid." Augustine (1961, 1) goes on to state the heart of the problem: "If he does not know you, how can he pray to you?" How can one commit to something without knowledge of that to which one commits? Someone who is lost may seek God in prayer, but that prayer may, in some way, be misguided or ill founded. For Augustine this problem is serious but not insurmountable. For God is not to be sought outside, but within, "eternally more intimate to me than I am to myself" (Turner 1995, 59). It is a divine seed within that draws the seeker to God. But the precise nature of this seed, which for Augustine is the source of all human longing, is not something that can be thematically defined or determined: it cannot be examined in the full light of the laboratory. As the source of human desire, God is both knowable and beyond knowledge. The dialectic of desire in Augustine draws upon a rich Neo-Platonic heritage in which the Good (or the One) remains, in some sense, at the apex of human understanding and activity. The condition of human desire is structured by the force of radiation of the Good, and it is our ability to respond to this force that, for Augustine, demonstrates the presence of divinity in humanity. Ultimately, for Augustine education cannot be dissociated from the process of coming to know God within. This example illustrates the Neo-Platonic epistemology that animates the Latin Christian tradition and has therefore been influential in the West. One can trace indications of an understanding of primary affirmation from Plato, through Plotinus and Proclus, Augustine, Bonaventure, Aquinas, Eckhart and even up to Descartes (Lewin 2011, 62–63). But a fuller study of this strand is beyond my present scope. We should at least recall James Smith's argument concerning the role of liturgy in the formation of human desire discussed in Chapter 3). The source of that desire may be divine, but that does not mean that desire cannot go wrong and be formed in ways that do not nourish the soul, a point that Augustine seems only too aware of in his *Confessions*.

As we saw earlier, from the Oriental perspective, the master-student relation is a complex and necessary one, said to encourage a detachment from the ego by way of surrender. The path of surrender to a master might seem a long way from modern Western schools, colleges and universities where often it is increasingly thought to be the job of the educator to adapt and commit to the needs of the learner, not the other way around. In these days of rising university fees, the consumer model is certainly not just a theoretical concern for the academy (Bok 2003; Palfreyman 2004). What Biesta (2006) calls *learnification*, a process whereby the consuming subject defines how and what is to be appropriated through learning experiences, is a crisis that is sweeping across much of educational culture and is displacing the essential dimension of teaching. We have moved a long way away from the tradition that once took for granted the providential nature of the world as the basis of education. For the premodern mind, education would begin with the affirmation of divine order and providence, a point to which I will return shortly.

There is a danger that the temporal distance of the Western theological tradition, and the cultural distance of Oriental thought and practice will render these observations irrelevant to the business of contemporary pedagogy. Indeed, anyone working within state education in the UK today can scarcely be unaware of the 'student-centred' paradigm that currently prevails. This orientation towards the needs, concerns and proclivities of the student no doubt has much to commend it: it appears to ensure a certain commitment to standards by teachers; it encourages an appropriate synthesis between engagement, entertainment and education, driven by the idea that students learn most effectively when they are engaged; and it is built upon a model of cooperation over coercion which in principle accords with modern sensibilities. This is some way from Indian gurukula tradition that would require months, even years of apparently menial application by the student to demonstrate their commitment, thereby ensuring that their interests in education are unsullied by utilitarian or individualistic interests. It is the starkness of the contrast between Eastern and Western pedagogy, even with the crude caricatures offered here that can prove instructive. The contrast can help us to glimpse some of our deeper assumptions about the freedom and individualism of our present context.

Western individualism in contrast to Eastern collectivism is a characteristic framing of the East/West binary, and though insufficient as a generalization, the problem of Western individualism is a meaningful one. Freedom is at the heart of our culture, individual creative expression the oil of the Western machine. This liberal spirit is understood to be built upon a broadly scientific rationalism which provides the context for the political science of Hobbesian social contract theory. Even Hobbes' social contract is predicated on an affirmation of life that is stated as a blunt law of nature. In other words, self-preservation is something like a primary affirmation "by which a man is forbidden to do that which is destructive of his life" (Hobbes 1975, Chapter XIV). Hobbes provided the narrative of political liberalism that secured the social only in terms of its protection against a pre-political and lawless state of natural isolation and violence (Dupré 1995, 129). Around the same time, Descartes was defining the apex of individualism as the capacity to think and thereby to be sure of self-existence at the inevitable expense of any secure knowledge of the world and other people. Whatever Descartes' intentions, the Cartesian legacy was a self-certain subject severed from passive objects that populate a dead universe. Prior to this, the Greek-Christian synthesis understood that a kind of divine intelligence inheres within the cosmos itself and is not solely resident within the minds of human beings.

Given the deep roots of Western individualism expressed today in a neo-liberal politics of absence, it may seem idealistic to hope that the post-secular can offer a new possibility of conceiving a public good that is both shared and

100 Submission

respectful of difference. It seems some kind of synthesis, some form of Williams' 'procedural secularism', might offer an opportunity here:

> religious convictions are granted a public hearing in debate; not necessarily one in which they are privileged or regarded as beyond criticism, but one in which they are attended to as representing the considered moral foundation of the choices and priorities of citizens. This is potentially a noisier and untidier situation than one where everyone agrees what will and will not 'count' as an intervention in public debate; but at least it does not seek to conceal or deny difference. And what makes this more than a free-for-all where the loudest voice wins the right to impose views is the shared recognition of law, that system of determining the limits of any individual's or group's freedom which represents the agreement in principle of all groups in a society to renounce violent struggle or assertion because of a basic trust that all voices are being heard in the process of 'brokering' harmony
> (Williams 2012, 27).

But this harmony will only be possible where all parties acknowledge the existence of the primary affirmation that individuals and communities see from, and we are able to question those affirmations in a spirit of mutual respect. In other words, we need to allow that people are always already engaged in more or less clear forms of submission within their own respective traditions and that such forms of submission are not absent from the so-called secular. The recurring theme here is the universal nature of concern (what we earlier called liturgy), of submission or of commitment that even a secular 'neutral zone' cannot free us from. Thus the procedural secularism that acknowledges the primary affirmations of cultures and traditions does not thereby disrespect those affirmations by claiming they have nothing to say to other people in the community.

Appreciating submission

I have indicated that learning is rooted in an embedded epistemology that is structured by a primary affirmation. The philosophical hermeneutics of Ricoeur (alongside Heidegger and Gadamer) provide a theoretical basis for understanding what could be called the *leap of learning*, a phrase that has a distinctly theological resonance, some of which I have drawn out. Beyond purely philosophical interest, are there any direct practical implications of this analysis?

In calling for some appreciation of the leap of learning, I am not arguing for a paradigm shift in educational theory from individual freedom to a more submissive attitude; still less am I recommending submission to the authority of a great teacher. But submission is a spectrum, attitude or orientation, rather than a clear-cut state or decision. An essential component of education is the spontaneous orientation of engagement in which attention is given. My claim in this chapter is that a form of submission is always already present, and therefore is essential to every form of understanding whether in the Indian traditional gurukula, the Tai Chi class in London, or the sometimes mundane context of school education. The simplest form of everyday submission is the act of listening and paying attention. In other words, attention is submission. In the following chapter I examine the nature of attention and explore how this faculty is not straightforwardly an aspect of human will. It is somewhat consistent with traditions of prayer and ritual to suggest that the relatively positive agency of submission is attenuated where attention takes over. More radically, the moment of total abandonment of the self (in union with God) could be conceived as an equal abandonment of the self, what Turner (1995, 139–140) refers to as an apophatic anthropology.

An interesting way to consider the relevance of everyday submission for educators today is to consider ways of acknowledging the affirmations made by students. One way to do this would be through a consideration of the gift of attention. The moment the student gives the teacher attention they take a risk, make a wager, albeit in a small way. Students could be encouraged to see that the gift of attention to a subject of study as just that, a gift. Recognition of the gift character of attention would not result in a miserly attitude in which the students measure out or barter their attention, as though conscious of a precious and scarce commodity in their purview. I note with some concern the increasing commodification of attention and the so-called attention economy (Stiegler 2010, 94). If anything, the culture of performativity and that of student satisfaction will encourage this privatization of attention. In this context students might see their own attention as a valuable commodity; after all, others do. Speaking generally, students would be better prepared to offer their attention if teachers did more to recognize and appreciate the gift of the student's attention without the performative undertone of the student as customer. This simple recognition, even if it is not ritualized in forms akin to the Eastern traditions we have touched upon, would assist students in recognizing their own place and responsibility. Yet the onus is on the educator to acknowledge the gift of attention, of affirmation, that begins the journey of education. The structures of modern education, from the use of aims and objectives in classes, to the transparency of the curriculum, can sometimes give the impression that educators must give a guarantee of success and engagement in advance of the process. These performative structures conceal the risks associated with the leap of learning, but the wager is an essential component of the process itself. The leap would not be the same if a harness supported us. But most seriously, there is a danger that performative structures contribute to a general concealment of this leap and its necessity.

Furthermore, it must be acknowledged that a moment of pure attention, whether listening to music, eating food or being with friends, is a form of giving up the self, of submission. The strange and the unfamiliar, in a word *the other*, offers an opportunity for giving of oneself, for what the philosopher of education Krishnamurti (Krishnamurti 1969) called 'freedom from the known'.

While we spend much of our lives engaged with the 'known', the movement of learning described by Krishnamurti is precisely understood as a freedom from the tired representations that constitute our daily experience of the world. For him it is only the quality of attention that makes education possible.

Conclusion

In this chapter I have argued that an understanding of the affirmation implicit in education, and in epistemology generally, allows us to dissolve the idol of objectivity that still haunts our conception of the modern curriculum. Eastern forms of traditional pedagogy present alternatives to the Western individualistic conception of liberal education. In the present climate where the notion of a 'neutral' relationship to learning underpins the broadly secular language of school curriculum development in the UK, the idea of submission could seem radical, scandalous or absurd. The post-secular context is therefore crucial in offering a space in which submission in education might be thinkable. My intention has been to demonstrate the implicit forms of submission that constitute the daily activities of educators and of students, whether or not they regard their activities in neutral terms. This view rests on the assumption that there is no neutral vantage point in education from which to teach the facts. I have presented these 'alternative pedagogies' in order to evoke the trace of commitment or the leap involved in undertaking any learning at all. Recognizing this commitment encourages us to value our rootedness in tradition while simultaneously calling for a critical engagement with the context of our tradition. It allows for what Ricoeur called 'Critique and Conviction' (Ricoeur 1998).

Notes

1 Although the chapter develops its argument around the idea of epistemological affirmation, and so seems to emphasise the cognitive dimension of human being, the argument could be equally developed for and applied to other forms of learning (e.g., aesthetic, spiritual, physical).

2 Although Martin Heidegger, Hans-Georg Gadamer and Paul Ricoeur are most associated with philosophical hermeneutics, Nietzsche specialists might seek to explain the hermeneutical approach set out here in terms of a Nietzschean philosophy of affirmation. Although I suspect such a connection may be fruitful, it lies beyond my present concerns.

3 This modern sense of hermeneutics develops largely in the wake of the philosophy of Martin Heidegger. As Karl Simms (2003, 39) has pointed out, Hans Georg Gadamer's book *Truth and Method* "represents the first attempt to develop a fully fledged 'hermeneutics' in the modern sense." But Ricoeur's more sustained treatment of hermeneutics is arguably at least as influential today.

4 Along with Alasdair MacIntyre, Ricoeur elaborated the religious significance of atheism by examining the theological significance of what he called the 'great' atheists: Freud, Marx and Nietzsche (MacIntyre and Ricoeur 1969). This kind of atheism offers a more substantial engagement with religious cultures than the passé new atheism espoused by certain secularists and humanists.

Submission 103

5 Heidegger's influential account of 'involved' relations with things is most consistently elaborated within *Being and Time* (Heidegger 1996). Ricoeur's hermeneutics owes a great deal to Heidegger's influence.

6 For St Anselm, who is most associated with the Christian dictum *faith seeking understanding* (fides quaerens intellectum), faith is understood more as an act of orientation or volition. In line with the thesis of a primary affirmation, Anselm (2001) understands this formula to indicate: "an active love of God seeking a deeper knowledge of God."

7 Ricoeur adopts the notion of the wager, made most famous by Blaise Pascal, to explore the nature of engaged hermeneutics: The wager is "that I shall have a better understanding of man, and of the bond between the being of man and the being of all beings if I follow the *indication* of symbolic thought. That wager then becomes the task of *verifying* my wager and saturating it, so to speak, with intelligibility. In return, the task transforms my wager: in betting *on* the significance of the symbolic world, I bet at the same time *that* my wager will be restored to me in power of reflection, in coherent discourse." (1967, 355)

8 Ricoeur calls this a 'long-route' to being via interpretive structures, in contrast to Heidegger's more direct route to fundamental ontology (see Kearney 2004, 22).

9 Bowman relates Bruce Lee's view of pedagogy to that of Jacques Rancière by arguing that both reject the stultifying regimes of traditional schooling, whether in martial arts or education more generally.

10 The idea of catching sight of the insignificant, emerges out of the hermeneutical insight that the structures of understanding in the 'involved' everyday experience, what Heidegger (1996) calls everydayness, are more illuminating than the *deworlded* knowledge elaborated out of the engaged context in terms of more grandiose theories of knowledge. In contrast to the account of my own experience, here are words that might otherwise characterize the depth of relation in more substantial terms: "Meeting one's Guru or Master is a Mystery. It is a date with destiny. Those who are lucky enough to stumble upon this seismic encounter may never be the same again. In that meeting one experiences, suddenly or gradually, an ecstatic release into the limitless singularity and depth of one's True Self." (Bampton 2009).

11 It should be noted that these interpretations/appropriations need not be mutually exclusive: the teacher can be interested in self-aggrandisement while the student can take away meaningful lessons about the self. But the focus and priority of concern might make these appropriations in tension with one another. In other words, the question is less which is the 'truth,' than which version of events was I deciding to take up?

12 This generalization might be justified in view of the broadly hierarchical pedagogical cultures of China, India and Japan. But this view may not actually account for the indigenous and 'authentic' forms of pedagogy that predate the influence of colonialism.

13 The infamous image of Francis Bacon advocating the 'torture of nature' may not be historically accurate (Pesic 1999), but the general notion that we have expected nature to yield knowledge is a fair characterization of modern scientific and technological practice.

14 The image of a dazzling darkness has been used repeatedly by theologians of the more mystical tradition (see Williams 1995; Turner 1996). The linguistic play between said and unsaid is central to Sells (1994).

References

Anselm. (2001). *Proslogion: With the Replies of Gaunilo and Anselm*. Indianapolis: Hackett.

Augustine. (1961). *Confessions*, R. S. Pine-Coffin, trans. Harmonsworth, Middlesex: Penguin Books.

Bampton, P. (2009). "American Guru Andrew Cohen & Allegations of Abuse" *Guru Talk*. Retrieved from http://www.guru-talk.com/2009/10/american-guru-andrew-cohen-allegations-of-abuse/

Biesta, G. (2006). *Beyond Learning: Democratic Education for a Human Future*. Colorado: Paradigm Publishers.

Bok, D. (2003). *Universities in the Marketplace: The Commercialization of Higher Education*. Princeton: Princeton University Press.

Bowman, P. (2009). "Aberrant Pedagogies: JR, QT and Bruce Lee." *Borderlands e Journal* 8: 2.

Bowman, P. (2013). *Beyond Bruce Lee: Chasing the Dragon through Film, Philosophy and Popular Culture*. New York: Wallflower Press.

Buncombe, A. (2011). Guru Sai Baba's Legacy: Death Threats and Scandal. *The Independent*, June 29.

Carrette, J. R., & R. King. (2005). *Selling Spirituality: The Silent Takeover of Religion*. London: Routledge.

Docherty, D. (1997). *Complete Tai Chi Chuan*. Marlborough, Wiltshire: Crowood Press.

Dupré, L. (1995). *Passage to Modernity*. New Haven: Yale University Press.

Feyerabend, P. (1978). *Against Method: Outline of an Anarchistic Theory of Knowledge*. London: Verso.

Garden, M. (2005). "The Potential for Abuse in the Guru-Disciple Relationship" *ICSA Newsletter*, 4.

Heidegger, M. (1996). *Being and Time: A Translation of Sein and Zeit*, J. Stambaugh, trans. Albany, NY: SUNY Press.

Hobbes, T. (1975). *Leviathan*. London: Dent.

Karner, C., & Aldridge, A. (2004). "Theorizing Religion in a Globalizing World." *International Journal of Politics, Culture, and Society*, 18: 1, 5–32.

Kearney, R. (2004). *On Paul Ricoeur: The Owl of Minerva*. Aldershot: Ashgate.

Kierkegaard, S. (1980). *The Concept of Anxiety: A Simple Psychologically Orienting Deliberation on the Dogmatic Issue of Hereditary Sin*, R. Thomte, trans. Princeton: Princeton University Press.

Klein, B. (1984). *Movements of Magic*. Wellingborough, Northamptonshire: The Aquarian Press.

Krishnamurti, J. (1969). *Freedom from the Known*. London: Gollancz.

Lewin, D. (2011). *Technology and the Philosophy of Religion*. Newcastle upon Tyne: Cambridge Scholars Press.

Macintyre, A., & Ricoeur, P. (1969). *The Religious Significance of Atheism*. New York: Columbia University Press.

Maxwell, A. (ed.). (2010). *The East-West Discourse: Symbolic Geography and Its Consequences*. Bern: Peter Lang Publishers.

Milne, H. (1987). *Bhagwan, The God that Failed*. London: Sphere Books.

Ozmon, H., & Craver S., (eds.). (2008). *Philosophical Foundations of Education*. Upper Saddle River, NJ: Pearson.

Palfreyman, D. (2004). *The Economics of Higher Education: Affordability and Access; Costing, Pricing and Accountability*. Oxford: OxCHEPS.

Pesic, P. (1999). "Wrestling with Proteus: Francis Bacon and the 'Torture' of Nature" *Isis* 90: 1, 81–94.

Polanyi, M. (1958). *Personal Knowledge: Towards a Post-Critical Philosophy*. London: Routledge.

Polkinghorne, J. (1991). *Reason and Rationality: The Relationship between Science and Theology*. London: SPCK.

Ricoeur, P. (1967). *The Symbolism of Evil*, E. Buchanan, trans. Boston: Beacon Press.

Ricoeur, P. (1977). *The Rule of Metaphor: Multi-Disciplinary Studies of the Creation of Meaning in Language*, Robert Czerney, trans. Toronto: University of Toronto Press.

Ricoeur, P. (1984). *Time and Narrative I*. Kathleen McLaughlin and David Pellauer, trans. Chicago: University of Chicago Press.

Ricoeur, P. (1998). *Critique and Conviction*. New York: Columbia University Press.

Sells, M. (1994). *Mystical Languages of Unsaying*. Chicago: University of Chicago Press.

Simms, K. (2003). *Paul Ricoeur*. New York: Routledge.

Stiegler, B. (2010). *Taking Care of the Youth and the Generations*. Stanford: Stanford University Press.

Stiver, D. (2001). *Theology After Ricoeur: New Directions in Hermeneutical Theology*. Kentucky: Westminster John Knox Press.

Sutton, N. (1998). *Applied Tai Chi Chuan*. London: A & C Black Ltd.

Turner, D. (1995). *The Darkness of God*. Cambridge: Cambridge University Press.

Wallace, M. (1996). *The Second Naivete*. Mercer University Press.

Wile, D. (1996). *Lost T'ai-chi Classics from the Late Ch'ing Dynasty*. New York: State University of New York Press.

Wile, D. (2014). "Asian Martial Arts in the Asian Studies Curriculum" *Journalism, Media and Cultural Studies*, 5, 1–60.

Williams, R. (1995). *A Ray of Darkness*. Lanham: Cowley Publications.

Williams, R. (2012). *Faith in the Public Square*. London: Bloomsbury.

Chapter 6

Attention

Introduction

It is natural to assume that educators are looking for the best ways to engage students and to capture their attention. But, as many teachers know, attention is an elusive faculty that does not always respond well to coercion. Coercion may demand concentration but that is not quite the same. In order to address the role and limits of attention in education, some theorists have sought to recover the significance of silence or mindfulness in education. In this chapter I argue that it is not enough to see silence as a useful tool for managing learning, or even as an end in itself. Where silence is pedagogically deployed, or simply enforced, educators seek the refinement of attention. Religious traditions have long been in the business of the formation of attention. As society has become increasingly secular, and corporate advertising has become the lingua franca of the new attention economy, the scarce resources of attention are in danger of exploitation, and educators are struggling to find their role within this crowded marketplace. Of course religions too have engaged in their fair share of such exploitation, but arguably in a somewhat more self-conscious way. By contrast it is the putative neutrality of the attention economy that obscures assumptions around agency and freedom of choice, leading us to complacently believe that we are free to attend to one thing or another, a complacency that advertisers rely on in their seductions.

In developing this argument I will invite attention to the problematic assumption that students are sovereign masters of their own attention. Because agency and identity are more complex and distributed than our conception of a liberal subject often supposes, the Cartesian and Kantian foundationalism that encourages optimism with respect to that agency should not be left intact. In this chapter I critically engage with these conceptions by drawing on a range of diverse sources, primarily modern Continental philosophy and Christian mystical theology. So between the submission of the previous chapter, and the union of the next, lies a moment where attention is curiously seized, neither only subject nor only object, but in the mediate gathering between the two.

Beholding

Behold: this may be the educator's essential word. Whatever else educators do, they draw the attention of students to things; they point out important aspects of the world that students should be aware of; they *bear witness*. The educator drags the student out of the cave of ignorance and, standing in the light of truth, gestures or speaks the essential word. Finally, the student must see for herself. To say *behold* is to recognize the autonomy of the other in the apprehension of being, and the autonomy of the world in the givenness of things. To say behold gathers the three dimensions of education: the teacher, the student and the world.

Although *Behold* is an archaic-sounding word, it is still used in a way that denotes giving regard to something, or holding it in view. It connotes being caught by something as though beheld by it. More often where we come across the word these days it can sound ornamental or rhetorical without much significance or 'cash-value'. But this impression is mistaken. Behold is related to the German *halten* to hold, originally meaning to keep, tend, watch over, or restrain. It calls us to attend, but also holds or even restrains that attention. Maggie Ross (2013, 30) calls it the "most important word in the Bible," where the chronicles of Scripture begin and end. As the translation of the Hebrew *hinneh*, behold is the first word God says to Adam and Eve after creating and blessing them. The Greek word *Idou*, often translated as behold, is the last word that the risen Christ speaks to his disciples ("...behold, I am with you always, even unto the end of the world. Amen." (Matthew 28: 20)).[1] Other biblical terms also have similar resonance and perform similar functions: 'lo', 'yea', 'see' and 'suddenly'.

Yet to behold is not to interpret, analyse or take into account. Rather it speaks at the point of world-disclosure: it can be said to speak the world. It is, as Ross (2013, 29–30) puts it "a liminal word; it signals the threshold of contemplation, where the self-conscious mind stops analysing and becomes attentively receptive, open in an ungrasping and self-emptying way to irruption from the deep mind." Is it possible that in beholding the world we can see things pre-conceptually, before they are represented as objects? Does the moment of beholding take place before educators get involved and start putting things in boxes? And is education not concerned more with the comprehension and explanation that follows apprehension or immersion? These questions reflect the epistemological tensions emerging in the nineteenth-century Continental hermeneutical tradition between primary phenomenological experience (*Erlebnis*) and secondary hermeneutical understanding (*Verstehen*). Hermeneutic phenomenology expended a good deal of energy resisting the idea of a pure transcendental phenomenology, which for Heidegger seemed redolent of a persistent Cartesian foundationalism that still haunted Husserl's phenomenology. For now such wider perspectives will have to remain on the horizon. But the extent to which education should be concerned with the *boundless present* prior to analytical and critical scrutiny remains a complex question. Perhaps schools, colleges and universities should do more to encourage quiet times, pauses, reflections and silences, to create spaces for attention and contemplation. Of course many schools structure silence and contemplation, some, like Quaker, Maharishi and Krishnamurti schools, in quite distinctive ways. Mindfulness in schools is becoming increasingly popular despite concerns around the secularized and decontextualized utility of its implementation (Hyland 2015). Helen Lees (2012) has provided a survey of the significance of silence in schools where she begins the important task of distinguishing forms of silence beyond simply the absence of noise. Lees argues for 'strong silence' as a positive force in education, as distinct from the forced negative silences that too often structure school experience. This is important work but could draw more upon the philosophical and theological traditions in which the phenomenology of silence is so richly developed.[2] To this end, I want to sketch out a relation between silence and attention in education. It has often been noted that silence is not just the absence of noise (Picard 1972; Caranfa 2004). But the notion that silence is constituted by attention — that it cannot exist without attention — is less often discussed (Krishnamurti 1996). The call for silence in schools might be helpfully recast in terms of a call to attention. But it is hardly surprising that it is not, since a call to attention is generally conflated with the teacher's vain repetition: pay attention!

Paying attention

'Pay attention': these words have become hollow prescriptions. In schools they invariably mean 'pay attention to this (or to me)'. Since attention is, one might say, the gift that keeps on giving, the problems for teachers arise when students do not direct attention sufficiently to the task at hand, often a technical, decontextualized, 'problem' to be solved within a prescribed and assessable scheme. These are not real problems, but representations of what real problems look like. Hence, as concerned John Dewey, students have the feeling that education is not living, but only a preparation for it. The difficulties in directing the attention of students are familiar to most teachers, but they suggest an overly simplistic conception of attention. In 1890, William James bemoaned the fact that philosophers had largely ignored the faculty of attention. James (1890, Chapter 11) encouraged the consideration of attention in education:

> the faculty of voluntarily bringing back a wandering attention, over and over again, is the very root of judgment, character, and will. No one is *compos sui* if he have it not. An education which should improve this faculty would be *the* education *par excellence*.

Simone Weil similarly argued that the central concern of pedagogy ought to be the training of attention. Today too much research assumes a clear conception of attention as a faculty that can be trained (Lotz et al. 2009), particularly where attention is identified with concentration or mindfulness. But this, as Masschelein and Simons (2013) have recently noted, is in danger of confusing attention with therapy. James (1890, Chapter 11) recognized that, although improving attention might be desirable, it is not necessarily practical:

> But it is easier to define this ideal [of improving attention] than to give practical directions for bringing it about. The only general pedagogic maxim bearing on attention is that the more interest the child has in advance in the subject, the better he will attend. Induct him therefore in such a way as to knit each new thing on to some acquisition already there; and if possible awaken curiosity, so that the new thing shall seem to come as an answer, or part of an answer, to a question pre-existing in his mind.

With a similar structure in mind, Dewey accounts for the distinctive aspects of agency in relation to attention by distinguishing involuntary attention (characteristic of children up to the age of seven) with voluntary attention (which is directed at some particular, often abstracted, end) and reflective attention (where the goal is not just an abstracted end, but is an answer to a particular question within the learner) (Dewey 1915, Chapter 7). This account of the development of education through stages offers some helpful distinctions, but does not ultimately answer the question of origins, the fundamental etiology, of curiosity or attention raised by James. More specifically, James indicates the problem that there are no methods to bring about curiosity or attention, and that this practical problem is not easily solved. The practical issue is surely related to the theoretical problem of radical origins. These practical and theoretical considerations are often obscured by the assumption that attention is the *sine qua non* of education and key to attainment. These days if educational theory considers the wider role of attention in education, it tends to be concerned with deficits of attention and the attendant problems of diagnosis and treatment.

In contrast to the ambiguities about the etiology of attention just outlined, this 'deficit model' of attention assumes an unverifiable norm: that, for the most part, students are able to direct, control and manage attention. As such, attention is the tacit ground of education, something we assume to be available, if not always present. From this perspective it seems self-evident that teachers are able to command students to pay attention. But I want to complicate this view by indicating that, rather like beholding, attention is not something to be demanded, still less coerced. It is more like a gift freely given. The student can offer the teacher their attention, but even here something paradoxical seems to be going on. Even the student cannot simply command attention as a general commands an army. The gift of attention turns out to be a gift both to the student (as giver) and the teacher (as receiver), in which both are beneficiaries. One might call this a virtuous circle. An attentive audience, for example, makes a performer that much more attentive which in turn rewards the attention both of the audience and the performer. Many teachers will recognize this of teaching: that the attentiveness of the students and educators has some broad (though not always predictable, even quite mysterious) correlation.

The student who *pays attention* is offering a gift to the teacher while also, at least to some extent, being given that moment itself. This is somewhat different to the concentration or trained mindfulness that is sometimes associated with attention. More specifically, this raises questions of identity: who is in control and who is responsible? Very often the question of identity is problematically structured by a polarized conception of agency: too often passivity and activity are regarded in opposition. I have argued that the obsolete linguistic mode of the middle voice reflects a mode of being which falls between activity and passivity, and that this mode of being has been unable to resist the sedimentation of the modern subject (Lewin 2011). Our modern conception of subjectivity assumes an unequivocal agency. The anthropology developed by Heidegger (whether as early *Dasein* or later conceptions as the clearing of Being) reflects the grammatical cleavage of the middle voice by locating Being and human being in the space between activity and passivity (see Davis 2007). Heidegger's contribution to the hermeneutic project is in part his conception of 'revealing' (Heidegger 1977) or 'disclosive looking' (Rojcewicz 2006) in which agency is not to be found at the polar regions of identity, but rather in the mediate gathering of the middle voice. This has left him open to the criticism that he equivocates on his philosophical (and political) commitments; that, for example, the destiny of technological thinking is paradoxically both determining us, and determined by us, leaving no clear statement of what is to be (or indeed can be) done (Heidegger 1977). Heidegger's understanding of agency is not incidentally related to the question of attention. His entire philosophical project can be interpreted as an elaboration of the nature of attention, whether in terms of care as the structure of *Dasein* (1996), thinking as thanking (1968) and the meditative thinking of his *Discourse on Thinking* (1969), or man as the 'shepherd of Being' (1993); the complexity of attention mirrors the complexity of identity itself because attention is significantly constitutive of *Dasein*. We could take this further if we consider how language is also constitutive of the world of Being and human being. In a certain sense, all speech grants the world and intimates the tripartite gathering of the beholding. This is because all speech requires a speaker, a hearer, and a world, and is therefore the "clearing-concealing advent of Being itself" (Heidegger 1993, 230). Speech too entails a transcendental condition, namely being. This path into Heidegger's thinking locates the question of attention within mainstream philosophical discourse. Nevertheless, it is the religious traditions that offer an equally rich account of the dynamics of attention to which I now turn.

The paradox of intention

The *paradox of intention*, as Marvin Shaw (2010) calls it, describes this complex situation rather more simply: that we may reach a goal by giving up the attempt to reach it or, conversely, that we may be prevented from reaching a goal by our intentional efforts to achieve it. Religions the world over warn of the propensity on the part of the novice to become preoccupied with the observance of ritual, which can be the very thing that prevents the attention that is central to ritual itself. The text, doctrine, practice or teacher provide assistance on the way but, as Buddhists have it, once the river has been crossed, do not carry the boat with you. Similarly, Christian theologians are often ambivalent about structured religious practices. Meister Eckhart, to take one example, extols the pilgrim:

> Leave place, leave time
> Avoid even image!
> Go forth without a way
> On the narrow path,
> Then you will find the desert track
> (Quoted in McGinn 2001, 114).

Here the track that the novice walks along becomes an aspect of projected will that must be subverted. But to 'do' this, to set upon this *via negativa* is always in tension with itself. This subversion of will can, on some readings, engage attention, since all aspects of self must be abandoned to what presents itself in total darkness. That this might entail the pure attention of a timeless moment, an escape from the temporal into the eternal is an attractive yet problematic idea. A typical reading of Eckhart as fundamentally Neo-Platonic would see the negation of time and history in Eckhart's *via negativa*. But does this interpretation not see Eckhart as a rather dualistic figure, reading in Eckhart a valorisation of the eternal over/against the temporal? There are subtler readings of Eckhart in which the non-dual relation between the temporal and eternal does not appear to imply such a straightforward Neo-Platonic negation of temporality.[3] This non-dual reading of Eckhart has a significance for education that may not be immediately obvious. Although a fuller discussion of this connection will have to wait until the next chapter, consider the ways in which the ideal and the pragmatic interact: curricula and subjects are important heuristic devices for structuring an understanding of our complex world, but there is a danger of becoming a slave to them, and so they are interpreted and adapted to context. The experience of being asked by a student whether Marx is a philosopher or a sociologist is enough to illustrate the point that intellectual framings must be subverted from time to time.

Furthermore, the idea that attention is an ahistorical faculty to be directed at will seems to negate the lived nature of temporality, certainly as we find in the phenomenological hermeneutics of Heidegger and Ricoeur. The divergence of progressive educational traditions from traditional formal pedagogy, for example, could be identified with the recognition of the complexity of will and attention. This is because progressive educators, as we have already noted with Dewey, highlight the spontaneous, organic, or 'non-directive' forms of learning, where the goals, as well as the agency, of the educational processes are less than clear. Progressive educators tend to emphasise the facilitative role of the teacher in contrast to a more directive approach associated with traditional pedagogy. From a progressive point of view, directing attention is not a straightforward intentional act that we can employ to the disciplined appropriation of the facts, or a cognitive tool at our disposal. Rather, genuine attention involves a submission of the self to the other which cannot be simply structured or enforced.

The philosopher Jiddu Krishnamurti, who explicitly and publically disavowed any association or affiliation with a school of thought or tradition within either philosophy or education, speaks from a broadly progressive educational perspective. There are no paths, ways, or hows, when it comes to the matter of attention, since attention is pure act, and truth is a "pathless land" (1996, 257). For Krishnamurti, the desire to focus attention is peculiarly susceptible to the delusions of intention, a cognitive kind of Nietzsche's will to power. What we think we are harnessing when we 'focus the mind' can itself be a representational or conceptual construction that inhibits the freedom of total attention. Of course, this difficulty pertains to practices of meditation more generally. We project our intention to achieve a goal which results not in the goal itself, but in the image or projection of the idealized goal. The danger here is that a preoccupation with methods, practices or even goals and aims, inadvertently displaces or extinguishes the 'flame of attention'. Krishnamurti (1963, 102) has much to say about the significance of attention in education:

> Learning in the true sense of the word is possible only in that state of attention, in which there is no outer or inner compulsion. . . . It is attention that allows silence to come upon the mind, which is the opening of the door to creation . . . How is the state of attention to be brought about? It cannot be cultivated through persuasion, comparison, reward or punishment, all of which are forms of coercion. The elimination of fear is the beginning of attention. Fear must exist as long as there is an urge to be or to become, which is the pursuit of success, with all its frustrations and tortuous contradictions. You can teach concentration, but attention cannot be taught just as you cannot possibly teach freedom from fear; but we can begin to discover the causes that produce fear, and in understanding these causes there is the elimination of fear. So attention arises spontaneously when around the student there is an atmosphere of well-being, when he has the feeling of being secure, of being at ease, and is aware of the disinterested action that comes with love.

In my experience Krishnamurti schools endeavour to create this atmosphere of well-being in which students can feel at ease by doing what they can to eliminate the fears often associated with education.[4] But here Krishnamurti seems to set up a structure in which attention leads to silence, a silence which then opens up to creation (we must be careful not to fall into the temptation to construct a system out of an approach that is very clearly antagonistic to the pervasive tendency to structure what can only be beheld). This is interesting to educators because the process of engaging the attention is ultimately concerned not with silence for its own sake, but contact with, and contemplation of, the *other*. If we can speak of the goal of attention, then surely it must be related to the idea of being taken up by what Krishnamurti here calls *creation*. Perhaps Krishnamurti intends something like the hermeneutic structure of disclosive looking or world-disclosure that is, as I argued earlier, an expression of beholding.

There is a common sense view of this attention in which awareness is fully present to itself in an ahistorical and groundless way. In speaking of 'behold', it is tempting to think of attention as a kind of ground zero, a Cartesian or Archimedean point from which the world emanates. This disclosure is in danger of being framed as some sort of ahistorical singularity. The task of meditation can then be pursuit of an absolute timeless now. Krishnamurti's focus on the 'choiceless awareness' of pure attention which is associated with what he has called the 'ending of time' (1985) and 'total freedom' (1996), might appear to arise out of just such a naïve ahistorical attitude in which all conditioning falls away and we see not shadows or reflections (Krishnamurti often speaks of how our conditioning leads us to see only images), but we behold what is. We might ask how Krishnamurti's conception of attention avoids the naïveté of assuming we should escape our historicality. In essence his concern is to be attentive to human conditioning, itself thereby achieving something of a freedom in relation to it, rather than seeking to escape from conditioning itself, but this delicate issue is beyond my present scope.[5]

I am suggesting that Krishnamurti's view of attention is consistent in certain respects with those who, like Heidegger, seek to move us away from a 'natural attitude' that sees attention in foundational terms (I use foundational here to echo the tradition of Cartesian foundationalism that might seek the cogito in a moment of pure attention where the self, and nothing but the self, is evident to itself). The tradition of phenomenological hermeneutics, most directly associated with Heidegger and Gadamer, offers a range of different but related conceptions of attention as always already constituted and formed through social and psychological contexts. Such accounts of being-in-the-world are explicitly engaged with the temporality and historicity of existence. The hermeneutic tradition seeks to restore the significance of historical existence to phenomenology. More recently, Bernard Stiegler (2010, 18) has wanted to include our technological apparatus into the constitution of attention suggesting that the short route to self-awareness (by way of some self-certifying Cartesian foundationalism) is misconceived.[6] This range of issues underscores the fundamental significance of attention as a topic that has received surprisingly scant consideration within philosophy of education.

The main difficulty that we have come across thus far is that there is a problem with suggesting that the will can directly command attention. The continental philosophical tradition will be helpful in developing a conception of

114 Attention

will that overcomes some of the difficulties of the idea of teaching attention. First I want to turn to some other ways in which educators draw attention to attention beyond the deficit model.

Intended attention

Recent interest in mindfulness, positive though it may be in many ways, seems in danger of falling into the trap of imagining that attention is within the purview of human will. Over recent years, forms of mindfulness have become increasingly appealing to educators with a range of curricular interventions (e.g., MINDUP, CARE, '.b' curriculum) and research (e.g., Oxford Mindfulness Centre; Centre for Mindfulness Research and Practice, Bangor University). Probably in part because the movement of mindfulness generally presents itself as religiously and ideologically neutral, it has been the natural partner for broadly secular, public institutions like schools (Ergas 2015). Perhaps mindfulness is believed to remedy the social ills that were once more widely treated (or suppressed) by institutional religions. But the range of differing techniques, philosophies, and attitudes that are placed under the banner of mindfulness should give us pause before we start planning attentional interventions. Forms of meditative practice have a range of utilitarian justifications: they are said to contribute to social-emotional learning (Davidson et al. 2012), foster self-knowledge (Lin, Oxford, and Brantmeier 2013), cultivate resilience (Greenberg and Harris 2012), treat ADHD (Carboni et al. 2013), and help teachers resist burnout (Jennings et al. 2011). But the sense that a specific mindfulness practice can be employed to address individual and social ills, or that it might enhance creativity or generally provide a sense of fulfillment, should be regarded as suspiciously reductive (Picard 1972, 2–3). There is something about the delicate nature of attention that yields to intrinsic reward, where the mindful subject is not oriented to anything, but to being present.

Equally problematic is the idea that mindfulness practice is within the direct compass of the will. For Ross (2013, 33) it is this intentional aspect of mindfulness that places it apart from beholding. I do not want to baldly assert the need to attend to attention in education, which would entail a contradiction. Rather I am drawn to the domain of attention and its significance, and hope to bear witness to that. It is this more gentle bearing witness to being (rather than an assertive demonstrative posturing) that entails the gathering of teacher, student, and world. The delicate event of education can, I have suggested, be distilled down to a moment of beholding, a moment that does not boil down to the ahistorical *now*. As part of the sacred liturgy of the Eastern Orthodox Church, icons reveal what might be called the *play of beholding*. To look upon an icon is to see oneself: it is not just that the worshipper looks upon the image of God, but that God looks upon the worshipper to the extent that the beholder, the beholding and the beheld become indistinct. This is not the reductive subjectification reminiscent of Sartre's look that makes of me an object for the other (*en soi*), but a dialectic of agency, an intimation of transcendence, that traces a liturgical pattern to be found in many religious traditions. A little more theological context will help to illustrate this dialectic.

In *De Magistro* St Augustine (1979, 40) says that the student "is taught not by words, but by the realities themselves made manifest to him directly by God revealing them to his inner self." Augustine's Platonic disposition seems evident in his conception of education as a form of bearing witness. The idea that teaching is bearing witness and learning is beholding would sit well with an Augustinian pedagogy. More broadly, the Christian mystical tradition associates silence and contemplation with a relinquishment of self that more widely relevant to education. This tradition has formulated stages of prayer that follow a roughly threefold pattern of recollection, quietude and union (Underhill 2012).[7] This pattern involves a transition from the activity and concentrated efforts of the religious subject in recollection, to a mode of relinquishing that activity and submitting the self to the darkness, or emptiness of God and the self in quietude. The final stage of union is to follow, though the less said about that, the better (see Chapter 7). Such a transition from the concentrated power of recollection to the submissive attention of quietude entails the relinquishment of the self as subjective agent. This tradition (or range of traditions) has often sought to educate the novice into the recognition of his ultimate impotence before God. Yet the subject must take that step along the path to relinquish the path. Christian theologians such as St Augustine, St Bernard of Clairvaux, Meister Eckhart, St Teresa of Avila, St John of the Cross and so on, all suggest something like a structure in which the religious subject comes to know God through a *via negativa*, a path of negation (Turner 1996). But while that negation might correlate in a certain sense with silence, it is a path fundamentally related to the affirmative mode as its dialectical partner. It is never only negation since negation follows affirmation. The negation is achieved through the rich polyvalence of the *via positiva* without which negation is groundless (Sells 1994, 1–4). In *On the Divine Names* the fifth-century theologian Pseudo Dionysius, cataphatically affirms God first in order for the negations within his text *Mystical Theology* to have substance. And it is not that we end with nothing, but rather that what is left in the contemplative desert of the mind is nothing human made: nothing but God who is, strictly speaking, nothing. In attention we become nothing. This seems true for a theological tradition that Denys Turner (1996) eloquently characterizes as developing an apophatic anthropology, evident particularly in St Augustine, Meister Eckhart, St Teresa of Avila, but also clearly evident in Simone Weil (1987, 30) who says, "[o]nce we have understood we are nothing, the object of all our efforts is to become nothing."

Weil and Murdoch on attention

Although a controversial figure in the history of Christian mysticism (McClellan 1990), Weil has something distinctive to contribute to the discussion of attention and education, encapsulating the tensions and paradoxes present in the foregoing discussion. Weil seems to understand that attention eludes efforts to become too directly attached to the will, and yet she wants to make attention a central focus of education, even the primary locus of instruction. As we will see, this tension is extremely fruitful for developing a nuanced conception of attention in education. Weil's ideas are also relevant insofar as they illuminate the sense in which education involves a negation of the self, an idea that seems to run counter to present educational culture which is more about self-development than self-negation (Roberts 2011).

For Weil attention is of primary significance for education, for life, and for faith. Running through much of her work is a view of attention as something that can be taught, but also that does not respond directly to the will. In some moments Weil (1959, 66) sees attention as the "real object and almost the sole interest of studies", and that with the right kind of discipline and effort, attention can be cultivated in students. "Teaching", says Weil (1959, 108), "should have no other aim but to prepare, by training the attention, for the possibility of such an act" namely to fully attend to something. On the other hand, she wants to maintain some separation of attention from will. Weil (1959, 106) says that "absolutely unmixed attention is prayer" and suggests that the personal will, with its concern to fix itself on a particular problem constitutes a dependency at odds with the purity of desire for which the infinite is the only pure object of desire. Grace is not far away in this account of our relation to attention. In her more Platonic moods it seems as though attention responds almost spontaneously as though a magnetic force of attraction commands it: "[a] divine inspiration operates infallibly, if we do not turn away our attention, if we do not refuse it. There is not a choice to be made in its favour, it is enough not to refuse to recognize that it exists" (1987, 107). Here exists a negative capability, akin perhaps to Socrates' daimon that spoke only negatively, in which the will can operate by its power to *not refuse*. The will is thereby operative without being autonomous, in the modern liberal sense.

While I have argued that attention is not within the direct purview of the will, I acknowledge the sense in which something like the right kind of effort can be employed to create conditions in which attention can flower. I would suggest that Weil might well offer some insight for this understanding, though most clearly through an indirect route. Iris Murdoch provides a wider context into which the mystical strain of Weil's thinking can be understood. It seems that Weil incorporates a complex theological anthropology but in somewhat terse and apparently contradictory terms, and so it is helpful that Murdoch provides an elaboration (albeit only implicit) so that the apparent contradiction in Weil can be maintained as a fruitful tension. Indeed the mystical tradition more widely is too often taken at face value, by which I mean as expressing an 'ineffable' or 'mystical' truth that rationalists are unable to appreciate. The sad consequence of this is a view of mystical thinking as irrational and purely affective. Such mystification does not serve our understanding of the mystical

Attention 117

traditions not does it help us in appreciating the complex relations of rationality to truth. So I believe that Murdoch provides a helpful bridge to this tradition.

In *The Idea of Perfection* Murdoch (1970) proceeds by problematizing the conceptions of identity, freedom, will, and decision that moral philosophy has expounded or assumed. Philosophical debate about the status of decision has tended, in Murdoch's account, to follow what she calls an existentialist-behaviourist philosophy of action. There is in this account a Cartesian and Kantian legacy in which the inescapable responsibility of an autonomous *cogito* must be affirmed. While this anthropology is unequivocal in assuring the agent has moral responsibility, its natural corollary turns out to be forms of determinism or fatalism. If this anthropology is denied or threatened in some fundamental way, then the self as such seems to be in danger. Analytical philosophy seems to be struggling to defend a locus of agency as neuroscientific research seems to encroach ever further upon the stages of human decision making, leaving scarcely any place for the still centre of decision (see, for example, Brassier 2010). The *ipseity* of Cartesian foundationalism has nowhere to hide. But Murdoch provides us here with some resources to escape this reductive bind, and to explore identity and agency without committing to the either/or of Kantian/Cartesian subjectivity: that we are either fully rational agents, or we are fully determined patients.

Murdoch elaborates her point by using an example of a mother (whom she calls M) and her daughter-in-law (called D). M feels that her son has married beneath him, a view that encourages certain perceptions/judgments M has/makes of D: unpolished, lacking in dignity and refinement, tiresomely juvenile and so on. This image M has of D may settle and harden with time, sedimenting M's intolerance. But there are other possibilities. Murdoch explores the possibility that M's view of D can soften and change even without any direct contact between the two women (for the sake of the argument Murdoch supposes that D is absent, thereby ensuring that M's perception is not altered by changed behaviour of D). "D is discovered to be not vulgar but refreshingly simple, not undignified but spontaneous . . . not tiresomely juvenile but delightfully youthful." (1970, 18) This shift in attitude is not arbitrary but can come from a reflective process that M goes through where she is able to attend to her self: "I am old-fashioned and conventional. I may be prejudiced and narrow-minded" (1970, 17) and so on.

Does M make a decision to change her view? Did she in the first place decide on the view of D she would take? For Murdoch it seems that decision exists within a flow of attitudes and experiences that draw our past, present and future together into a coherent narrative, or as Murdoch calls it, "the continuous fabric of our being" (1970, 22). It would be wrong to say that no decision is made to take a particular attitude. But it would be no less wrong to say that a decision is made to take a particular attitude, and so it seems better to speak of the mother's *orientation* to her daughter-in-law. A simplistic binary conception of agency or decision is inadequate to account for much that we might call human

118 Attention

action. Indeed Murdoch is not the first to point this out (Heidegger, Gadamer and Ricoeur make similar arguments though in rather different terms – e.g., Heidegger's conception of being-in-the-world speaks to very similar anthropological issues), but the connection between Murdoch and Weil makes the example worth developing.

Interestingly, it is attention that is key to Murdoch's employment of Weil. If M can attend to herself and the world, then she has opened a possibility for insight into her own conditioned existence. The way we see the world (our orientation to being) offers us a structure in which certain possibilities for action are conceivable (and similarly other possibilities fall outside of what is conceivable and become invisible to us). There is, then, a horizon within which attention operates. A view of attention as a singularity, a moment of radical purity where all conditioning is transcended could not, in Murdoch's account, fully appreciate the structural context of attention. A timeless and ahistorical view of attention means only a conception of attention that is unaware of itself and is rather inattentive to itself – it is, in some sense, a failure of attention. But the recognition of this historicality should not be interpreted as a negation of freedom since the conception of freedom is not to be identified with a pure unconditional voluntarism, of which Murdoch is highly critical (1970, 26–27).

There can, therefore, be some sense in saying that attention is both responsive to the world, but also available to us to develop, but only if we can avoid the tendency to regard human agency in absolutist terms. As Murdoch (1970, 43–44) says "we have to accept a darker, less fully conscious, less steadily rational image of the dynamics of the human personality." And if we do, we can appreciate the sense in which our historicality and our projections constitute our being-in-the-world without wholly negating our agency. We are given an orientation to being in which our values and perceptions emerge. This orientation is not, of course, a fixed feature of the self but an apprehension that constitutes our being here now. It is part of the effort of education to attend to this orientation that, paradoxically, is an important aspect of the power of attention. There are other more familiar examples of our orientation to reality offering us ways of being that similarly deconstruct the duality of freedom and determinism. Musical taste is a good example, being rarely the pure expression of aesthetic sensibility or arbitrary historicality, but formed both by historically formed 'taste', and personally expressed 'temperament'. In Chapter 3 I argued that religious beliefs, not being straightforwardly propositional in nature, cannot be simply chosen or inherited. I wonder also whether James Smith's conception of the formative power of liturgical practices could be usefully applied here as a way of opening out the horizon of possibilities open to us.

Despite the significance of Murdoch to this analysis, there is a problem with her account. The mother's shifting orientation to her daughter-in-law locates the truth of the situation too readily. M's perception of D as common and juvenile is regarded as false, a state of illusion (1970, 37). M is able, Murdoch

Attention 119

says (1970, 38), to directly break through to the "honest perception of what is really the case" through a moral process of patient and just discernment in which the daughter-in-law is perceived justly. It is not the morality of the process that is of concern here so much as the readiness with which Murdoch speaks of what is really the case. Murdoch is suggesting that the moment of attention can break apart the failures of attention (which really amounts to inattention), as though we can take a short route to an unmediated apprehension of the truth of being.

It is tempting to imagine that the relinquishment of self that attention entails involves putting aside the images and projections of the other so that we can truly meet them in their singularity. This is why relinquishment, or as Weil (1987) calls it 'decreation', can seem to be a return to the things as they are. But I want to emphasize that such singular contact cannot be regarded as utterly ahistorical. Therefore, I want to maintain the significance of attention that Weil and Murdoch develop while making explicit the hermeneutic dimension to their phenomenology of attention. I will agree then, that our ability to move towards a "more honest perception" is something desirable, both personally and educationally. But it would be better to understand these perceptions in their interpretive complexity: that they are ways of seeing (albeit *more* honest, and therefore better). This should indicate a move away from a binary false/ true perception itself redolent of the propositional understanding that we have hitherto questioned. This interpretation of Murdoch might be read as introducing an unhelpful relativism into her ontology. But I do not want to confuse pluralism and complexity with relativism. I reject the idea that hermeneutics is inherently relativist and it is for this reason that I prefer to use the metaphor of a hermeneutic spiral rather than a circle to describe an interpretive movement that is oriented towards something actual which acknowledging the interpretive structure of knowledge as such.

The freedom of seduction

In Chapter 3 I drew attention to Smith's account of the ways both secular and sacred liturgies shape desire. Both Smith and I share an interest in bringing the liberal conception of the autonomous human subject into question. But if agency is indeed more complex than Cartesian foundationalism supposes, then this raises delicate questions about our responsibilities in the formation, manipulation and seduction of desire. Talal Asad (2013) focuses on the question of seduction by comparing the liberal context in which subjects are presumed free to manage their desire and will, with contexts in which seduction is regarded as an offence because it is perceived as a constraint on natural liberty. Asad gives an example from ancient Greece, where seduction was regarded as a more serious crime than rape because it involved the capture of a person's attention, affection, and loyalty from the man to whom they belonged. The context of Asad's point is his desire to collapse the "liberal distinction between coercion and reasoned choice that underlies the notion of free speech" (Asad 2013, 31). The idea that those who manipulate desire (such as advertisers, politicians, clerics and so on) bear no responsibility, and those whose desire is so seduced are (being free autonomous subjects) entirely responsible, makes too much of the distinction between coercion and freedom of choice, and concedes too much to the autonomy of the liberal subject. Asad (2013 31) argues that in fact "both seduction and coercion are ambiguously present," a point that resonates with the complex and distributed conception of agency developed in this chapter. Restricting his discussion to the rights of the adult to "dispose of his or her body, affections and speech at will, so long as no harm is done to the property of others" (2013, 31), Asad does not discuss education in reference to the formation and manipulation of desire in young people. Nevertheless, his point becomes that much more potent in the context of education, where even modern liberal society would have to query the idea that the child is sovereign over his or her desires and so is free to resist or to acquiesce to the seductions of society, be they consumerist, political, religious or educational. But the argument also addresses the need to appreciate why some religious cultures are more concerned about the manipulation of desire through seduction than others:

> Muslim theologians and jurists assumed that seduction in all its forms was necessarily dangerous not only for the individual (because it indicated a loss of self-control) but for the social order too (it could lead to violence and civil discord). They were wrong, of course, because they didn't know about market democracy, a system that thrives on the consumer's loss of self-control and one in which politicians have learned to seduce their audiences while maintaining overall political stability
>
> (Asad 2013, 44).

This is obviously a dangerous idea, playing into the possible justification of violence and abuse against women in a Wahhabist state like Saudi Arabia where, under a certain interpretation of Sharia law, the victim's responsibility to *purdah* (laws around the seclusion of women that extend to dress) can result in harsher punishments against the victim than the assailant. I am not, of course, suggesting sympathy with such reasoning, but I am at least interested in where such ideas might be philosophically derived. Still, connecting this violation of human rights with the problem of the manipulation at attention through mass media (Lewin 2016) or, even more problematically, the ambiguous nature of agency and responsibility as I have framed it, might appear unjustified, and Asad seems careful not to make any similarly crude associations. Whether Asad is being ironic here when speaking of the fact that Western liberal democracies thrive on loss of self-control, the point for my argument is that the manipulation of desire offers an interesting example of the distributed nature of responsibility that has particular implications for education; for nowhere is this more potent than in the case of forming the desire of young people. With the attention economy seeking to manipulate the minds of the young (and old) through new media, for example, we cannot shrug our shoulders and assume that attention is within the purview and responsibility of the liberal subject to determine for him or herself. Nor can we suppose that mindfulness interventions in schools can offer meaningful resistance to the manipulations of media, advertising, politics or religion. It is legitimate to ask about the scope and limits of autonomy, agency and responsibility with respect to the seductions of modern society. But we must also critically consider the wider freedoms of the advertisers and consumerist industries (along with political, religious and other 'ideological' influences), to think more carefully about how desires are formed and manipulated. It should not be too controversial to point out that religious traditions are fairly unanimous in offering practices and teachings that entail an attenuation of agency and subjectivity. It is interesting to consider whether the individuating activities within education could or should draw on a similar recognition that subjectivity and agency is far more complex than is supposed by certain kinds of liberal politics.

Conclusion

An important aspect of effective education is that we are challenged and unsettled, that the assumptions and images that we carry with us are seen in the light of fresh attention to the world around us. Practices of silence might be helpful in creating the right space for this attention, though there are problems with this. Positive silence might be better understood as the affirmation of attention in which the noise of the self is lost in submission of the self to the other.

The task of educators is surely to call attention to the world, and thereby to attention itself. In essence attention involves looking at – or better, being with – the other, whether that other is the object of educational inquiry, or the student herself. From the theological perspective, the other is, of course, God. But in the context of pedagogy, the other is the world that calls to be known by the student. It has been tempting to speak of this attention as involving a self-emptying or self-negation. But too often such negations become the object of attention and lead, paradoxically, to inattention. Paying attention to our mode of attention is itself a historical exercise and so requires the constant effort of attending to what calls for attention.

The attenuation of subjectivity cuts across many ideas within this book: the criticisms of the propositional and voluntarist framing of religious life, cultural liturgies as the formation of desire, the Heideggerian conception of being-in-the-world, the idea that education involves a moment of submission, the idea that attention resists the culture of managerialism so universal within modern educational discourse. A more radical consummation of identity is considered in the next chapter where the idea of union, mystical and otherwise, is presented as educationally relevant.

122 Attention

Notes

1 All biblical quotations are taken from the Kings James Translation.
2 Silence has all sorts of significations within education. A phenomenology of silence within education would be a fascinating project: the silences of exam halls, detentions, or classes engaged in focused activities; the many awkward silences as tutors invite comments from seminar students upon a reading that few students may have read; there are those silenced by the political or social conventions and customs in societies; there are moments of mindfulness so popularly evoked in many schools around the country; occasional prayers and reflections where groups of students perform remembrance of, for example, the war dead; sponsored silences that students occasionally engage in. At a different level exist forms of silent teaching, or direct instruction, of the sort traditions in the Far East are more familiar with. I am thinking of particularly of Zen Buddhist traditions, though Indian religious culture has some similar processes with such figures as Sri Ramana Maharshi or Mother Mira, for whom the enlightened state could only be taught though silent transmission.
3 See, for example, Michael Sells, *Mystical Languages of Unsaying* (University of Chicago Press, 1994), Chapter 6; Joseph Milne, *The Ground of Being: Foundations of Christian Mysticism* (Temenos Academy, 2004).
4 I spent two years living and working at Brockwood Park School, the only Krishnamurti school in the UK. I have also visited a number of Krishnamurti schools in India, as well as Oak Grove the Krishnamurti school in California. For many years Brockwood Park school has committed all staff and students to a morning meeting which usually, though not always, would involve sitting quietly for 15 minutes.
5 "I do not know if you have ever examined how you listen, it doesn't matter to what, whether to a bird, to the wind in the leaves, to the rushing waters, or how you listen to a dialogue with yourself, to your conversation in various relationships with your intimate friends, your wife or husband. If we try to listen we find it extraordinarily difficult, because we are always projecting our opinions and ideas, our prejudices, our background, our inclinations, our impulses; when they dominate we hardly listen to what is being said. In that state there is no value at all. One listens and therefore learns, only in a state of attention, a state of silence in which this whole background is in abeyance, is quiet; then, it seems to me, it is possible to communicate" (Krishnamurti 1967).
6 One of the key ideas that Stiegler rests his discussion upon is that attention is not simply there, but it can be formed: to capture attention is to form it. This conception of attention formation would resist a foundationalist notion of attention: "The constitution of attention results from accumulation of both primary and secondary retentions, and the projection of protensions as anticipations" (2010, 18).
7 Underhill (2012, 310) explicitly relates the concern of prayer to pedagogy: "It is the object of contemplative prayer, as it is the object of all education, to discipline and develop certain growing faculties."

References

Asad, T. (2013). "Free Speech, Blasphemy, and Secular Criticism" in T. Asad, W. Brown, J. Butler, & S. Mahmood (eds.) *Is Critique Secular? Blasphemy, Injury, and Free Speech*. 2nd rev. ed. New York: Fordham University Press, 20–63.

Augustine. (1979). "On the Teacher" in *Augustine: Earlier Writings*. Philadelphia, PA: Westminster John Knox.

Brassier, R. (2010). *Nihil Unbound: Enlightenment and Extinction*. New York, NY: Palgrave Macmillan.

Caranfa, A. (2004). "Silence as the Foundation of Learning" *Educational Theory*, 54: 2, 210–230.

Carboni, J. A., Roach A. T., & Fredrick, L. D. (2013). "Impact of Mindfulness Training on the Behavior of Elementary Students with Attention-Deficit/Hyperactive Disorder" *Research in Human Development*, 10: 3, 234–251.

Davidson, R., Dunne, J., Eccles, J., Engle, A., Greenberg, M., Jennings, P., Jha, A., Jinpa, T., Lantieri, L., Meyer, D., Roeser, R., & Vago, D. (2012). "Contemplative Practices and Mental Training: Prospects for American Education" *Child Development Perspectives*, 6: 2, 146–153.

Davis, B. (2007). *Heidegger on the Will: On the Way to Gelassenheit*. Evanston IL, Northwestern University Press.

Dewey, J. (1915). *The School and Society*. Chicago: University of Chicago.

Ergas, O. (2015). "The Post-Secular Rhetoric of Contemplative Practice in the Curriculum" in P. Wexler and Y. Hotam (eds.) *New Social Foundations for Education: Education in Post-Secular Society*. New York: Peter Lang, 107–130.

Greenberg, M. T., & Harris A. R. (2012). "Nurturing Mindfulness in Children and Youth: Current State of Research." *Child Development Perspectives*, 6: 2, 161–166.

Heidegger, M. (1968). *What Is Called Thinking?* J. Gray, trans. New York: Harper and Row.

Heidegger, M. (1969). *Discourse on Thinking*, J. Anderson and E. Freund, trans. New York: Harper and Row.

Heidegger, M. (1977). *The Question Concerning Technology and Other Essays*, W. Lovitt, trans. New York: Harper and Row.

Heidegger, M. (1993). *Basic Writings: Second Edition, Revised and Expanded*. New York: Harper-Collins.

Heidegger, M. (1996). *Being and Time: A Translation of Sein and Zeit*, J. Stambaugh, trans. Albany, NY: SUNY Press.

Hyland, T. (2015). "On the Contemporary Applications of Mindfulness: Some Implications for Education" *Journal of Philosophy of Education*, 49: 2, 170–186.

James, W. (1890). *The Principles of Psychology: Volume One*. Dover Publications.

Jennings, P. A., Snowberg, K. E., Coccia, A., & Greenberg, M. T. (2011). "Improving Classroom Learning Environments by Cultivating Awareness and Resilience in Education (CARE): Results of Two Pilot Studies" *Journal of Classroom Interaction*, 46: 1, 37–48.

Krishnamurti, J. (1963) *Life Ahead: On Learning and the Search for Meaning*. Novata, CA: New World Library.

Krishnamurti, J. (1967). "Talk and Dialogues Saanen, 1st Public Talk 9th July 1967." Retrieved from http://www.jkrishnamurti.org/krishnamurti-teachings/view-text. php?tid=41&chid=l

Krishnamurti, J. (1985). *The Ending of Time*. New York: HarperCollins.

Krishnamurti, J. (1996). *Total Freedom*. New York: HarperCollins.

Lees, H. (2012). *Silence in Schools*. Stoke on Trent: Trentham Books.

Lewin, D. (2011). "The Middle Voice in Eckhart and Modern Continental Philosophy" *Medieval Mystical Theology*, 20: 1, 28–46.

Lewin, D. (2016). "The Pharmakon of Educational Technology: The Disruptive Power of Attention in Education" *Studies in Philosophy and Education*. Online First.

Lin, J., Oxford, R., & Brantmeier, S. (eds.). (2013). *Re-Envisioning Higher Education*. Charlotte: IAP.

Lotz, A., Slagter, H., Rawlings, N., Francis, A., Greischar, L., & Davidson, R. (2009). "Mental Training Enhances Attentional Stability: Neural and Behavioral Evidence" *The Journal of Neuroscience*, 29: 42, 13418–13427.

Masschelein, J. & Simons, M., (2013). *In Defence of School: A Public Issue*, Leuven: E-ducation, Culture & Society Publishers.

McClellan, D. (1990). *Utopian Pessimist: The Life and Thought of Simone Weil*. New York: Poseidon Press.

McGinn, B. (2001). *The Mystical Thought of Meister Eckhart*. New York: Crossroad Publishing.

Murdoch, I. (1970). *The Sovereignty of Good*. London: Ark.

Picard, M. (1972). *The World of Silence*. Washington, DC: Regnery Pub.

Roberts, P. (2011). "Attention, Asceticism and Grace: Simone Weil and Higher Education" *Arts and Humanities in Higher Education*, 10: 3, 315–328

Rojcewicz, R. (2006) *The Gods and Technology: A Reading of Heidegger*. Albany, NY: State University of New York Press.

Ross, M. (2013). "Behold Not the Cloud of Experience" in E. A. Jones (ed.) *The Medieval Mystical Tradition VIII*, Cambridge: DS. Brewer, 29–50.

Sells, M. (1994). *Mystical Languages of Unsaying*. Chicago: University of Chicago Press.

Shaw, M. (2010). *The Paradox of Intention: Reaching the Goal by Giving Up the Attempt to Reach It*. Oxford: Oxford University Press.

Stiegler, B. (2010). *Taking Care of Youth and the Generations*. Stanford, CA: Stanford University Press.

Turner, D. (1996). *The Darkness of God: Negativity in Christian Mysticism*. Cambridge: Cambridge University Press.

Underhill, E. (2012). *Mysticism: Third Edition*. Mineola, NY: Dover Publications.

Weil, S. (1959). *Waiting on God*. London: Fontana.

Weil, S. (1987). *Gravity and Grace*. London: Ark.

Chapter 7

Union

Introduction

Mystical experiences do not necessarily involve God. A phenomenology of mystical life recognizes mysticism as being both sacred and profane, natural and supernatural (Zaehner 1957; James 1985), where nature (e.g., a forest), science (e.g., an insight), art (e.g., a Mozart string quartet), sickness (e.g., a lesion on the brain), or drugs can give substance to the mystical experience. However, religions – and God – have often played an important role, and will provide the context for discussing mysticism and religious experience in what follows. Religious institutions have tended to give form and shape to mystical experiences, making of extraordinary events and interventions something more structured. Figuring the sacred through the institution helps the religious subject make sense of what might otherwise be compelling but overwhelming. The more structured paths of mysticism within different religions suggest a linear progression, reflected in traditional images of ascent, such as the ascent of Moses up Mount Sinai and the ascent in Plato's cave (Turner 1996, 11–19). These potent images become problematically articulated within Western and Eastern traditions as the denial of the body, the flesh and the world, with priority given to the mind, the spirit and the logos. These dualisms seem to arise when doctrines become reified. One way to avoid reification is to see the 'truth' of mysticism not as some profound insight that the mind can scarcely contain (but with considerable effort might just do so), but as a practice that can always and everywhere be undertaken. This unconventional idea of the immanence of mystical union is paralleled with an understanding of education in which knowledge is immanent to the student who can progress independently, not dependent upon a teacher. In this chapter I want to explore how, as a structural aspect of both religion and education, the concept of progression can stultify and create dependency.

In Chapter 3 I discussed James Smith's argument that liturgies form desires whether or not those liturgies are sacred or secular. As the discussion has developed, a more mystical horizon has opened up in which the relation to desire can be more radical than simply the training or straightening of the will. Why call

126   Union

this mystical? The proper orientation of desire, from Socrates' speeches on love in the *Symposium*, to the rules of Monastic life, to Buddhist practices oriented to the understanding of human craving, to Hindu insights into insubstantiality of human will and identity, is grounded here, in the developing argument of this book, in a (possibly paradoxical) statement of non-dualism. By this I mean that desire is not to be extinguished, but understood, and that education is the development of this understanding. The religious traditions in their mystical strains tend to recognize the unity and perfection of all dimensions of life, a vision that can be summed up in Julian of Norwich's (1966) modest affirmation that "All shall be well, and all shall be well, and all manner of thing shall be well" or more metaphysically in the Upanishads, "That is perfect, this is perfect. Perfect comes from perfect. Take perfect from perfect, the remainder is perfect. May peace and peace and peace be everywhere" (Shree Purohit Swami 2003, Eesha Upanishad).

Education is in tension with these visions of perfection principally because it presupposes a deficit, lack or absence. The student requires development, intellectually, morally, practically and also (though this is less often discussed) in the domain of desire (Leclercq 1982). Such a deficit view does, of course, find roots in the Western tradition through ideas of original fault or sin, a primordial condition that places human beings at some distance from a more original unity in God.[1] In his analysis of what he calls "the anthropology of need," Sahlins (1996) points out that it was both an ontological and epistemological obstacle that the origin of evil introduced into the West.[2] Education finds its theological heritage through the idea of a return to the perfected image of God through the influential concept of *Bildung* (Bruford 1975). Meister Eckhart introduced the concept of *Bildung* to contemplation of human development, a term picked up and elaborated by Hegel and Humboldt.

In contrast to these images of primordial lack and human finitude, there have been varied theological responses. Ideas of divine providence seem to lie behind philosophies of ultimate order, from Voltaire and Leibniz to Pope and Berkeley (Sahlins 1996), though these efforts to recognize totality shade into the more radically stated form of unity, even of mystical union, which tend to affirm that nothing requires anything, since everything is already perfected. Union might be said to embody this radical insight into the realization of perfection which, as I type it on the screen, seems absurdly conceptual and therefore some distance from anything genuinely mystical. I am tempted then, by a sense of diffidence, to suggest that I cannot possibly know this truth for myself and that my best hope is to have chanced upon (or been given by God?) correct opinion. But this, too, is dualistic since any such 'modest' claim – indeed modesty itself – seems to presuppose that I know that I do not know. On what basis do I know that I do not know? This Socratic reversal – what for Socrates was a recognition of absence is here posited as a failure to take responsibility for the world as it appears to me, since I vainly assume that I have not achieved the enlightened state and can speak only in the second-hand terms of ruinous academic discourse – might mirror the genuine modesty of Socrates with ironic false modesty. The point here, to be elaborated in different ways in what follows, is that education entails a spiritual paradox, or perhaps better, that mysticism entails an educational paradox encapsulated in words attributed to Lao Tzu: "Nature does not hurry, yet everything is accomplished." Everything is accomplished yet there is work to be done. Children will develop and yet we must consider their formation.

In previous chapters I showed that submission and attention have important roles to play in the effacement of subjectivity, and with that an attenuation of will and desire. But there is a more practical concern for educationalists about how we rightly form desire. How do we ensure that children and young people learn to want the right things? Plato's *Meno* opens with a similarly blunt inquiry.[3] The answers explored in the course of that dialogue seem unsatisfactory, as does the arguably ironic conclusion: that the love of virtue is a divinely bestowed true opinion that cannot be rationally justified. We find no ready answers here, just as we equivocate on the notion that we can straightforwardly install a moral compass within young people. That does not mean, of course, that there is nothing to consider with respect to the structuring and forming of character and desire. We expend a good deal of energy in the presentation and representation of living well. Still there is something problematic about conceiving desire as an instrument that is tuned in order to work correctly. I suspect that the problem is a perceived instrumentalization of the self. This concern goes to the heart of education and philosophy, a heart that recognizes the mysterious role of *love* in the formation of desire: being in love is, as Sam Rocha (2014, 50) eloquently puts it "where philosophy and education begin anew." We should not dismiss the idea of love born of arrangement (an arranged marriage) too readily. We can, I suppose, learn to love. And if we can't, then perhaps we already do love, we just do not love the right things, which means to not yet recognize the beloved. But confused or misdirected love is still love. As Augustine recounts in the *Confessions*, a misguided love of God is still a kind of love which remains restless and unfulfilled until it (re)turns to God. Clearly our conception of love – and of desire also – does not sit comfortably with a model of a faculty or skill to be learned or trained. Nevertheless, the formation of desire has a rich theological heritage within the West (Leclercq 1982) as well as being of great interest to other religious traditions (often in critical terms as an obstacle to enlightenment), most obviously Buddhism. Within the Christian tradition love is excessive, able to break through the procedural logic of equivalence by a transformative power which, Ricoeur (1996, 39) argues, governs the parables of the New Testament and which he names the "logic of super-abundance," a love that Christian theologians once problematically supposed can supersede the Jewish law. This is dramatically illustrated, for example, in Shakespeare's *A Merchant of Venice*, where the logic of superabundance is seen to countermand the logic of exchange. To understand the law, from this point of view is not the same as to love the good. Education is never fulfilled in such an understanding, but requires the development of the soul and the orientation of desire. The teacher might love their students or their subject, but that love is not a professional duty. It is the disruptive quality of the excess of love along with the paradoxical recognition that perfection is already present that disrupts and subverts the structural operation of educational progress and growth and undercuts the secularized discourse of managing education.

I have already sketched out some ideas that can be associated with a person seeking God or enlightenment (call it what you will), who may pass through stages of submission, quietude (or attention) and then, finally, union. This linear path of a set of stages is a device. It is inaccurate insofar as there is no curriculum or set of stages of love towards God. Most paths to God or enlightenment are self-subverting in one sense or another: e.g., heuristic, metaphorical or dialectical. The notion of linear paths, particularly where that linearity is suggestive of method, recipe or mapped curricula, is a constructive fiction that suits managerialist conceptions of education. But the idea that linear progression does not properly describe religious learning (or learning more generally) would need considerable justification. After all, the scholastic traditions or monastic orders, for example, feature a range of practices, stages and paths to God. A well-known monastic example is the Rule of St Benedict which has been in operation for fifteen centuries. Monastic life for Benedictines is known as the 'Benedictine way', involving Vespers and Compline (regular prayers), contemplative reading of Scripture (Lectio Divina), study and other structured meetings and activities.[4] The point is that monastic communities can be understood as places in which religious insight and closeness to God is possible through disciplined methods, a point that seems to contradict my sweeping denial of progression towards God. After all, why follow the Benedictine or any other 'way' when it leads nowhere in particular?

In fact I want to suggest that one can understand the idea of progress and preparation for God as images to be taken as heuristic devices to orient the spiritual life, but images that are, at least qualified, but will at some point be abandoned. Once the river has been crossed, to use the Buddhist metaphor, we leave the boat on the shore. Put another way, I am seeking to retain some of the imagery of progression and development while abandoning the ontological hierarchy that it seems to depend upon. I justify this move because, as Denys Turner (1996, 267) has shown so well in reference to Western mysticism, the apophatic and mystical traditions (Christian and Neo-Platonic) do just this: "while we have retained the discourse of the apophatic we have abandoned the dialectics; while we have retained the metaphors of ascent we have abandoned the ontological hierarchies." The emphasis here is less on the conceptual and propositional understanding of various positions, than on the processes of inquiry enabled through the movement of apophatics. Apophatics (as believing in general) is more a practice than a position. As performative metaphors, these ideas of progress, development and stages might be useful. But as descriptions of actual processes they are deeply damaging to education for reasons that, as we shall see, Jacques Rancière has also pointed to.

Education without how: Rancière, education and mysticism

To my knowledge Rancière has not discussed religion or more particularly mysticism to any substantial extent. This is a curious omission. When reading his critique of the dependency inherent to educational institutions, most famously developed in *The Ignorant Schoolmaster*, I have been struck – to put it bluntly – by the way mysticism and education (and, in the context of Rancière, capitalism too) share a structural tension: that *emancipation institutionalized becomes its opposite*. For Rancière the problem hinges upon the idea of the teacher as the mediator or master explicator who is there to help the student understand, a problem that pertains equally to religious life and practice. Let me *explain*.

Certain traditions within religion and education have in common a need to both utilize and deconstruct 'explanation'. In its positive valence, explanation can enable, facilitate or support us to see what is before us: it can bear witness, as long, so the sages warn us, as we do not confuse the moon with the finger that points. Explanation can be disabling not because it is not employed skillfully enough, but because it tends to install the very thing it seeks to overcome: dependency. We begin to believe that we depend on explanation in order to see anything at all, *and that belief becomes a practice* (a cultural liturgy). We wait to be taught or enlightened by those with superior insight, experience, charisma or knowledge, and thereby enact educational stratification through the liturgy of participation in educational institutions. Relationships with figures of religious authority, gurus, lamas, priests and so on, take many forms, from radical submission and unquestioning devotion, to more complex subversions of that authority where the goal of the guru is to help the student to achieve independence of the guru (e.g., in yoga, see Feuerstein 2011, 127–131). But the religious subject, submitting him or herself, might not fully undertake or practise that subversion or transcendence, preferring instead to remain at the feet of the guru. Krishnamurti (1929) is one figure who renounced any guru status and was highly critical of the dependency that such a feature of much Hindu spiritual culture, for instance, entailed. Although individual authorities or gurus might draw upon charismatic authority to engage devotion (not properly to them, but to truth itself), religious institutions can provide countervailing forces to the charismatic authority of the guru, through, for example, structured and communal religious practices. This does not need to be the bureaucratized displacement of an enchanted teaching encounter, but might just provide a corrective to potentially abusive or coercive educational practices. Not only do institutional communities provide a larger framework in which structural dependency can be moderated (and sometimes enforced), but also institutions have strategies for dealing with the problem of the dependency structured by explanation, through, for example, the negative theology of the Christian tradition, or the Zen Buddhist use of koans. It is perhaps ironic, then, that the final chapter of Rancière's celebrated account of Joseph Jacotot's experiments with 'universal teaching' (a kind of teaching that requires no expertise on the part of the teacher who is ideally ignorant of the subject matter ensuring that no intellectual authority is established) presents the institution as the enemy of genuinely emancipatory universal teaching since it is intrinsically method-based. Echoing Ivan Illich, Rancière (1991, 133) calls this "the integral peda-gogicization of society – the general infantilization of the individuals that make it up." The same skepticism towards institutions could be (and often is) directed against the Christian church – and other religious institutions – though at least here strategies of negation exist to mitigate the oppressive inertia of institu-tional processes, an argument I will develop later in this chapter. For Rancière, no strategy, still less any method, could justify an institutional role in universal teaching, because only personal relationships are capable of announcing real equality. Exactly how individual relationships escape the structures of depend-ency is not entirely clear.

Rancière is insistent that the structure of education in the present age cannot be emancipatory since the superstructure of emancipatory discourse obscures the real substructural relations of dependence. This promise of emancipation never needs to be broken, rather the fact that it is not yet fulfilled (and never will be) is what places students within its thrall. It remains indefinitely deferred. This echoes the concerns that Carol Black has about the *Education for All* agenda in which the presupposition of inferiority with respect to indigenous knowledge and culture is built into the relations of support, development and progress. The very conception of an international community which can, through educa-tional intervention into developing nations, bring those nations into the mod-ern world, enacts a particular notion of equality and form of dependency. For Rancière we can, if we are sufficiently attentive, see through this structure of dependency by perceiving that equality is not something absent, to be achieved through educational intervention or progress, but present, to be *realized*. The promise is already fulfilled; it just needs to be believed, which for Rancière means practised. To quote from the gospels, the Kingdom of God is at hand. There are many religious tropes to be explored here beyond the structure of dependency that is fundamental to both Rancière and the religious.

Consider the messianic structure of eschatology in which hope can be the glue that holds together the status quo in the face of structural injustice (the classic Marxist attack on religion). The putative future-oriented ontology of religions invites this critique, as does the future orientation within much edu-cational theory and practice.[5] Consider also the idea, not uncommon among Hindu cultures and traditions (e.g., Advaita Vedanta, Ramana Maharshi) as well as various Buddhist traditions (e.g., Madhyamika, Zen), that the true self is already enlightened, but the subject does not realize it. These traditions are often characterized as *non-dual*, a reference to the fact that the idea of separa-tion from the truth (one view of dualism) is itself illusory. Concepts of stages towards, or degrees of, enlightenment can serve to inhibit the non-dual insight of the religious devotee if he or she is unable to step beyond (or break out of) the performative requirements of rituals and practices. Andrew Rawlinson's taxonomy of religious teachings suggests a spectrum across structured and unstructured forms of religious practice. Here Rawlinson (1997, 98–99) defines unstructured traditions as follows: "there is no gap between the starting point and the finishing post. Method and goal are identical. We are not separate from reality/truth/God and so no map is required. Everything is available now and always has been." But the so-called 'unstructured' Hindu and Buddhist traditions are not straightforwardly denying any place for structure, practice and ritual. Rather the structure must not be depended upon in and of itself. That is why I have suggested that the religions often enact a self-subverting discourse and practice, most explicitly in the negative theological traditions (of apophatics in the West and forms of negation in Eastern thought: e.g., Advaita Vedanta, Dao de Ching, Buddhist Anatta and Sunyata).

These parallels between Rancière and religious traditions suggest a range of questions that point to the ground of human understanding and enlightenment: Can we be future-oriented (which education will surely be to some extent) without thereby doing violence to the present? Can we seek the wisdom of another without conferring authority, obstructing understanding and deferring emancipation? Can we acknowledge the fully enlightened state (or equality) without denying the work to be done or the paths to be explored? Is there any value in an institution (either in education or religion) if it inevitably structures the unstructured? The non-dual description of the situation again suggests that these questions are likely to be answered negatively, so to speak, that there is something aporetic about the relation between authority and freedom, between paths and insight, between truth and institutions. Furthermore, in drawing these parallels I am also conscious that comparison itself can be the bedfellow of explanation, in the Rancièrian sense, and often a meager representation of one can simply be conflated with a facile representation of another, in which neither is really encountered on its own terms and both are thereby obscured. From Rancière's perspective, what is the point of explaining one worldview in the terms of another? Does it not entail a kind of explanatory function, leading down the self-defeating path that Citton (2010, 25) warns us of when he says that "[f]ew endeavours could appear more self-contradictory (and self-defeating) than an attempt to explain the argument developed by Jacques Rancière in his 1987 book *The Ignorant Schoolmaster.*" This problem of comparison is an acute and long-discussed problem within comparative religious studies (Segal 1983), a danger I want to at least acknowledge (without assuming I have thereby avoided).

I want to come at this problem by examining the conception of 'how' that is taken for granted in the present age. In education more than religion we tend to assume that a change requires a planned strategy, procedure or method – in short, a how. This procedural mindset has become so normal that one might get the impression that only philosophers like Rancière have seen and commented on it. I want to also bring in Krishnamurti who in the previous chapter we saw resisted any methodology for managing attention. Both Rancière and Krishnamurti, alongside a generation of progressive and critical educators, such as Ivan Illich and Everett Reimer share a suspicion of educational institutions which form cultures in which effective procedures are irresistible. But relying upon the insights and expressions of these philosophers and social critics takes us back to dependency: that only certain elite members of society – those with leisure to undertake philosophy and social commentary, for example (often happening to be white males) – can perceive and explain this problem. In fact, I suggest that my argument is so straightforwardly self-evident that just to point it out is, in a sense, sufficient for any interested person. This is a model of philosophy as the act of engaging attention; if we must speak of philosophers doing anything then perhaps we can say they are drawing attention or bearing witness (as discussed in Chapter 6), to an act which requires no specialist knowledge or complex cognitive capacities. A procedural approach, dominant today, supposes that effective education entails not so much knowing why as knowing how. Gert Biesta (2010) has clearly shown that present educational theory provides little opportunity to discuss the why's of education, preferring to address itself to questions of procedure and process – questions of how. There might be other ways to approach this issue, and through exploring the dynamics of *how* in mysticism and in Rancière, I hope to show what lies beyond the how.

By way of summary and transition, I quote from the popular martial artist Bruce Lee (1971, 24) who published an article about the problem of dependency in martial arts pedagogy called "Liberate Yourself from Classical Karate":

> At this point you may ask, 'How do I gain this knowledge?' That you will have to find out all by yourself. You must accept the fact that there is no help but self-help. For the same reason I cannot tell you how to 'gain' freedom, since freedom exists within you. I cannot tell you what 'not' to do, I cannot tell you what you 'should' do, since that would be confining you to a particular approach. Formulas can only inhibit freedom, externally dictated prescriptions only squelch creativity and assure mediocrity. Bear in mind that the freedom that accrues from self-knowledge cannot be acquired through strict adherence to a formula; we do not suddenly 'become' free, we simply 'are' free.[6]

Of course the irony here of being told that one must find out for oneself plays out across all theorists across this chapter. This irony animates the 'dialectics of enlightenment' found in the apophatic theology of the Middle Ages where language is employed to explicitly subvert itself (Sells 1994). So we are already free, happy, enlightened beings, whose only challenge is to realize what already is. If this is not your own self-understanding, it raises the obvious problem of how we might realize what is.

How in religion

In his critique of theories of the unconscious Ricoeur (1966, 373) stated that "becoming aware of character is not the most serious crisis of freedom." More than most, educationalists are conscious of the fact that character is not a given, but a part of formation. Our formation is not wholly restricted by the religious (or irreligious) culture we are born into. On the contrary, there is a key role for agency, what Ricoeur (1992) called capability. The strength of Ricoeur's work is his conception of agency that accounts both for the determining forces that structure freedom, such as the physical constitution of the brain, the 'unconscious,' or 'fixed' aspects of character, and the capability to make choices within constrained aspects of identity. Freedom and dependency are less absolute and more dialectical for Ricoeur than for Rancière.

Yet much of the discussion of agency and capability in relation to religious life (particularly in philosophy of religious education) seems, as we have seen, to be framed by a one-sided voluntarism, the view that religious life hinges upon the propositions believed and decisions made by a religious agent. If religion is simply a matter of choice and decision, then we might understand why Paul Hirst (1974, 77) characterizes a 'Christian Education' as a kind of nonsense, why Richard Dawkins (2006, 406) calls raising children within a particular religious context 'abusive,' and why religious commitments are often regarded as private to be left out of public education.

The question of the capability (or agency) of the religious subject is complex where religious acts are not simply confined to the affirmation or denial of propositions. In seeking 'God', 'enlightenment', or indeed the good life, one might well wonder *how* to act. What should I do to become enlightened or know God? Should I find a teacher or guru who can guide me to the truth, or do teachers get in the way of the purity of ultimate questions? Should I join a monastic order and follow something like the Benedictine way, or perhaps study religion at university, or study religious texts on my own? As I have suggested, the subjectivity of the religious individual is not simply taken for granted within these religious paths since the movement of submission and attention entails an attenuation of that subject. We need to work with the middle realm between the activity and passivity which suggests a dialectical movement between the truth as it appears to us, and a recognition that any appearance is relative to the structural limitations of our present form of life. In other words, we find ourselves within a hermeneutical circle, where we are already delivered over to a holistic interpretation of our world despite the fact that we have glimpses of the contingency of our view. This places us in an awkward position with respect to revelation which, by definition, seems to be something that exceeds our structures and breaks the hermeneutical circle. I am uncomfortable with the idea that a book about educational philosophy can argue the case that revelation is always already structured by the horizon of possible experience, but that is, I think, the consequence of the general argument.

134 Union

My justification for this is that the argument is really calling for a *process and practice* of education and religion rather than advancing a more or less convincing position. This will become clearer when we return again to Rancière and his account of the presupposition and practice of equality.

For many religious practitioners, the guru, priest, text or institution, does offer some confidence that a structure or path holds meaning. As important as those structures can be, many traditions simultaneously and paradoxically complicate or subvert what they set out. A subversive or dialectical logic is an important feature in religious traditions, illustrating the hermeneutical context, perhaps even the interruptive power of revelation. For example, children may learn to pray 'outwardly' for certain concrete outcomes of benefit to themselves, those around them and wider society, a conception of prayer which, in due course, becomes problematized within many parts of the church. The Catholic tradition identifies various states or stages or prayer, sometimes referred to in threefold terms as purgation, illumination and union (Devine 1912). These stages cannot be structured in a conventional sense because they involve a complex interaction between human agency and divine grace that deconstructs any overly structural analysis that is seeking the aims and outcomes of engaging in prayer. Nor is explicit prayer 'transcended' since it is retained as an important dimension of the most elevated spiritual life, as in the Lord's Prayer. The dialectic of theology which draws together reason and faith is not a logical and linear progression or ascent from human reason to revelation – or if it is, it is only so metaphorically. Its path is indirect, circuitous, even spontaneous and interruptive of structure and progression. The dialectic between human agency and divine grace is further evident in the fact that the goals of religious life do not directly align with religious practices. In other words, religious practices cannot be said to lead directly to significant religious insights, experiences or progression. There is no clear causal link between religious practice and enlightenment. Enlightenment cannot be contained within a particular set of practices: if it could be, we could just engage in a certain practice, become enlightened and live happily ever after. For Christian theologians a spiritual recipe would leave little room for dialectic since grace would thereby be supplanted by the hubris of reason. To speak in the biblical symbolism of the encounter of Moses with Yahweh, "Thou canst not see my face: for there shall no man see me, and live" (Exodus 33:20).

A straightforward method for an encounter with God or enlightenment seems theologically, empirically and intuitively wrong. Of course this does not mean that spiritual practices and spiritual experiences are totally unrelated. People practise for a *reason*, even if that reason can withdraw within the practice itself, leaving the practitioner either to practise 'without why' or to wonder why they bother with their practice. Moreover, many religious traditions speak of the possibility of certain kinds of experience (of visions of angels or devils, for example). But on the whole, the more extreme experiences associated with practices such as deep prayer or meditation are regarded with caution or suspicion.

One is bound to ask what, then, is the point of religious practice if it does not bring about enlightenment or insight? Clearly it is problematic to frame religious practice only in terms of the insights to be gained, as though devotion cannot be free of subjective will. Nevertheless, one common answer is to regard religious practices as the 'necessary but not sufficient' ground of enlightenment. We meditate in order to empty the soul. God may enter an empty soul, but the meditation does not force God to enter. The meditation creates the conditions for the possibility of an encounter with the divine. The American Zen master Richard Baker once put it this way, that *satori*, or enlightenment, is an accident, and that meditation makes one more accident-prone (Storey 2012). This logic allows for the significance of religious practice to be affirmed without circumscribing God within the agency of the religious subject. It seeks to undercut the notion that enlightenment or encounter with the divine can be managed or produced. It remains a spontaneous gift that cannot be coerced or schematized. There is an important difference between, for example, a heavy-handed expectation that forms of mindfulness will result in increased productivity and better mental health, and an invitation to 'sit quietly' with any strong sense of an outcome being effaced (Hyland 2015).

Here we meet an important idea: that we can engage in a practice that involves a range of aims that are conflicted, inconsistent and porous. Meditation is simultaneously intrinsically and extrinsically oriented. There is no contradiction here, although some reasons for practice will come under pressure and will, in the end, evaporate, leaving perhaps the only ground for religious practice, which, as it happens is also the only ground for love: that there is no ground. This might be called a dialectic of intention: that the aims are articulated only to be eroded in the practice itself, an idea that many teachers will recognize from their own efforts to plan classes while allowing for spontaneity and contingency, secretly hoping that the class will revolt against the structures that frame it. The case of spiritual practices is often more radical, leading to a total deconstruction of all intention where meditation is undertaken 'without why' (i.e., for the love of God) at a normative level, whilst simultaneously, and perhaps less consciously, fulfilling other less elevated aims (such as social pressures or hopes for an attenuation of insecurity and fear).

Much of my discussion so far seems unable to fully expel the deficit model, the idea that the religious subject lacks something and is seeking what they lack: the religious subject is not enlightened or does not know God and therefore seeks enlightenment or God. We have already noted that this framing of religion in terms of subjective will is problematic. But it raises another question: how is it that the religious subject knows that they are lacking some profound truth or experience? We opened this chapter with passing reference to Plato's *Meno* and Augustine's *Confessions*, both of which are animated by this central question of Neo-Platonism. The conventional Socratic answer to this question is *maieutics*: the process of midwifery by which the truth within the student is given birth by the labour of the student, an answer that seems broadly

136 Union

consistent with Augustine's Neo-Platonism. As we saw earlier, many religious traditions (particularly Hindu and Buddhist, but also Christian) express something akin to the idea that the truth of God or enlightenment is already within us and only needs to be recognized or realized. As Christ puts it, "the kingdom of God is at hand: repent ye, and believe the gospel" (Mark 1:15). A form of Japanese Tendai Buddhism particularly expresses the common theme within Buddhism, that Buddha nature is intrinsic and only in need of realization. The twentieth-century Hindu guru Ramana Maharshi (2002) taught a similar idea: "Realization consists of getting rid of the false idea that one is not realized." Not only is the truth already present, but the intentions of the religious subject to find the truth can be a barrier to realization. There is a concern that the practitioner can become attached to the religious practices at the risk that they forget the reference point of the practices. Consequently many of the more 'mystical' elements of religious traditions express ambivalence about religious practice and we come back to the dialectical logic of religious life. Meister Eckhart's (1981, 292) sermon "On Detachment" provides a clear statement of this dialectic:

> But now I ask: "What is the prayer of a heart that has detachment?" And to answer it I say that purity in detachment does not know how to pray, because if someone prays he asks God to get something for him, or he asks God to take something away from him. But a heart in detachment asks for nothing, nor has it anything of which it would gladly be free. So it is free of all prayer, and its prayer is nothing else than for uniformity with God.

Eckhart does not abandon prayer, rather prayer is transformed through detachment. Even more heretically Eckhart calls us to be free of 'God' in the pursuit of God. Eckhart is, of course, not alone is deconstructing the primary sources of our reverence as apophatic theological traditions engage in just this kind of deconstruction. My argument entails an invocation of certain authorities in the pursuit of emancipation from authority: it is a call to be free of Eckhart, Augustine or Rancière and so on insofar as they become new idols around which scholars congregate. So having returned to Rancière, I will now draw attention to what is quite obvious in reference to Rancière and religion.

The mysticism of Rancière

Rancière has challenged a number of prevailing assumptions about the nature and role of teaching, progression and explanation in pedagogy. He rejects the transmission model of education since it entails a structural inequality and contradiction whereby in order to become independent, the student must give up their independence. This contradiction can only be overcome, argues Rancière, if we regard the educational relationship as one of present equality to be verified and practised.

Explanation for Rancière is a mediation that inhibits the autonomy of the student and introduces a gap that in reality does not need to be there. As Rancière (2010, 3) says: "[i]f explanation is in principle infinite, it is because its primary function is to infinitize the very distance it proposes to reduce." The concept of progress built into our conceptions of pedagogy likewise serves to install the infinite distance between the student and their emancipation. We see students placed along a linear continuum of development in which the tutor's intellectual authority authorizes domination: "Scholarly progression is the art of limiting the transmission of knowledge, of organizing delay, of deferring equality" (2010, 8). It is this deferral of equality that is actually for Rancière a failure to recognize its presence. Stages and levels are the means by which a fictional distance is installed: "there are no stages to equality, that equality is a complete act or is not at all." Thus the presence of equality is to be realized, not sought: "equality . . . is not an end to be attained. It is a point of departure, a presupposition to be verified" (2010, 9).

The correspondences between the structure of mystical and pedagogical practices are striking: 1) truth is present and yet unfulfilled, needing only to be realized or verified; 2) there are no methods or paths to fulfill or realize the truth (there is no causal relation between preparation and realization); 3) no teacher can ultimately bring about realization/emancipation (though they may bring about an orientation of the will and support practices that prepare the ground);[7] 4) the concept of progression in both religious and pedagogical contexts serve to install the very distance it pretends to overcome (if you see the Buddha on the road, kill him).

This suggests that the non-dual insight of the mystical life contains an imminent critique of conventional educational practices and processes, a critique that Rancière seemed also to have come very close to in his own challenge to educational institutions and structures. Rancière's critique of dependency is powerful, but a recovery of the institutions of religion and education is something that religions, could bring to Rancière's analysis. With Rancière and Krishnamurti we see a thoroughgoing suspicion of institutions, a suspicion that can also be read into the relations between mysticism and mainstream religion, since mystics are often characterized as being institutional outliers. It is true that many Christian mystics like Meister Eckhart and Marguerite Porete had difficult relationships with the mainstream church, being condemned as heretics for their radical teachings. Similarly, the Sufi mystics of Islam have had a tense relationship with mainstream religious Islam. However, I will argue that, in fact, the mystical element of religion is by no means fringe, providing a powerful corrective against the inertia of institutionalization. This argument is also metaphorically deployed to show that Rancière goes too far in his critique of the institution, failing to recognize that institutions, like language itself, can be self-subverting. Just as negative theology is not a failure of language, the 'mystical fringes' reveal not a failing institution, but the opposite.

138 Union

The institution: Discarding the boat and forgetting the finger

In his essay on liberation from classical Karate, Bruce Lee (1971, 24) refers to two well-known images, particularly common among martial artists: 1) the boat is to be discarded once the river is crossed; 2) the finger should not be confused with the moon. These metaphors engage with the tension between institutional structure and mystical insight, referring quite directly to the problem of dependency in teaching and learning. But they seem to acknowledge different *times* or *moments*. There is a time for using the boat, and a moment for following the finger. This temporality is not exactly the linear and progressive time of the standard curricula, though does fold into it rather too easily, as it suggests preliminary phases of taking up the boat or the finger followed by leaving them behind. But the reminder not to mistake the finger might be repeatedly used at different times and in different ways, as new, more refined forms of pointing are perceived. The capacity to behold the moon directly is both implied and also negated by this continued refinement. For Rancière this is the problem: the refinement of perception becomes the installation of an infinite distance. This structure holds across so much learning. The pianist must master techniques in order to realize creativity beyond technique. The cook must internalize the recipe before they can disregard it. There is an obvious difference between the idiot who ignores technique and method to *go with the flow*, and the master who ignores technique and method. We could employ Ken Wilber's (1999, Introduction) typology of religious insight here where he uses the phrase "pre trans fallacy" to describe mistaking pre-rational states of awareness with spiritually realized trans-rational states of awareness. Put rather crudely, the idiot is pre-understanding and pre-technique, while the master, trans-understanding and trans-technique. These examples illustrate the formative and timely nature of a certain kind of learning of technique and method. This is not a blanket process for equipping someone with skills because of the great sensitivity needed to know how and when to apply or attenuate the techniques and methods. For this reason, leaving the boat on the shore is not a general pedagogical statement or principle, but a particular utterance that *performs* an insight (when used appropriately). In other words, the statement "do not confuse the moon ..." is a practice, not a proposition, requiring, if I may throw in yet another concept this time from the ancient Greek thinking of Aristotle, *phronesis* (practical wisdom). To put these statements into practice requires a sensitivity to the timeliness, rather than being placed on an objective curricula or scheme of work. This is not the *chronic* time of objective measurement by the clock, but *kairotic* time, the interruptive time of the gods. If the institution is only there to enframe learning within a progressive scheme of work, then Rancière's suspicion is well founded. If, on the other hand, institutions can operate through self-subversion to bring about reappropriations of learning, being sensitive to the interruptions of kairotic time, then perhaps we do not need to oppose insight and institution, as has been done time again by reformers and radicals.

Institutions might be said to stand between two poles: between the short route to creativity without energy and commitment, a kind of pre-technique; and the interminable march through stages, levels and unending progress, ending only in the endless stultification that so concerned Rancière. Either pole of this dualism is to be avoided, which, it might be argued, is one capacity of the institution. This institutional role is context-dependent, reflecting the manner in which the institution is instantiated and exists. Beyond the truism that the institution is really the people that form it, I propose that the institutional tension provides sufficient form and structure to enable agency without the structure extinguishing agency. But this is a fluid relationship, which requires constant structural deliberation and challenge. The student might need rigid structure at certain points and total absence of structure at other moments. The Zen master *performs* this knowledge. This sensitivity might be enacted through a changing relationship to relatively fixed institutions of tradition. This institutional mediation is well known among readers of the hermeneutic philosophy of figures such as Gadamer and Ricoeur, for whom the poles of history and truth provide not a choice but a creative and ongoing dialectic. Let's briefly revisit this hermeneutic arc but now with reference to the institution.

The student begins with some interest that is perhaps vague and ill informed, but sufficient to engage with the institution. Upon encountering first-hand the power of the religious institution, the student may become engaged, even enamored, displaying a deep, perhaps uncritical appreciation of the structure. In other words, the student falls in love with the truth she perceives in the institution, as a first naïveté (though for Ricoeur the first naïveté implied the unconscious absorption of a culture from early childhood, whereas my narrative here suggests a slightly more conscious appropriation). Over the passage of time, that love and enthusiasm might wane as the power of ritual is less effective in capturing the attention of the student who performs sometimes through habit as much as passion. More problematically the structures can begin to look more like expressions of power or perhaps conservatism. As anomalies in the narrative build-up, a crisis may befall the student, at which point the institution must be able to subvert itself.[8] Where subversion or reappropriation is possible, through, for example, the original narratives being re-read as metaphorical rather than historical, then the tradition can be said to live. Indeed, the institution must be capable of this flexibility no matter how infallible its ground is said to be.

Mystical union does not negate the religious institution. The institution is renewed by the practices of those that make it up. That the ultimate realization requires no institution does not render the institution worthless, since it can redirect the student when either pole proves to be too magnetic. The institution can steer the course between inertia and charisma, between history and truth, between tradition and transcendence. Although educational institutions may not be necessary, and may often enact a damaging inequality through the conception of stages and levels and so forth, they still have the power to draw attention to this very problem, and to thereby enact a different mode of being.

Conclusion

In this chapter I have sketched some of the paradoxes and dialectics of spiritual and educational intervention. I suggest that these dialectics provide illuminating analogies, enriching and extending Rancière's account of the paradox of educational interventions. There is no straightforward *how* in religious or pedagogical practice. Just as in religious life, the dynamics of education require a commitment of attention that cannot be confined within a formal process. But what is the institutional role within this confinement within practice?

Educational institutions enact many things. It is too easy, particularly these days, to assume that institutions enact stultification. It is a related suspicion of conservatism that leads many today to identify as *spiritual but not religious*. Since the middle of the twentieth century it has been fashionable to denounce Western institutional religions and seek an authentic spirituality freed from the inertia of history and tradition. That this quest practices a kind of individualism informed by the cultural liturgies of the marketplace should encourage a revaluation of other institutions, religious, social, political, etc. The political institutions, for example, filled with the political classes, can seem more concerned with career than the common good. Thus many people feel disengaged from politics and religion in this (post-) secular age. But a wider (and more urgent) critique of the conditions of capitalist consumer culture (which is easily identified with a neutral secularism) is forgotten when we vilify the political classes and religious institutions.

Rancière's and Krishnamurti's rejection of pedagogical *hows* seems altogether too sweeping, unable to account for what could, and must, be drawn from within our own traditions and the institutions that enact them. That does not entail an uncritical commitment to the religion of our parents, but a reinterpretation of tradition for the post-secular age. I take mystical union to entail just such an appreciation for tradition and transcendence. Whereof this is not real mystical union, thereof one must be silent.

Notes

1 Paul Ricoeur's *The Symbolism of Evil* (1967) provides probably the best phenomenology of Western conceptions of evil and 'disproportion' between the human and divine worlds.
2 My thanks to Anna Strhan for drawing attention to this connection with Sahlins' work.
3 "Can you tell me, Socrates, whether virtue is acquired by teaching or by practice; or if neither by teaching nor practice, then whether it comes to man by nature, or in what other way?" (Plato 2016)
4 It is not obvious that such monastic precepts and activities as those of St Benedict's rule need to be understood as exclusively 'religious' since they are designed not only for the development of 'religious' understanding, but for the practical organization of communities in which the relational challenges of human communities could be understood quite generally. But such a statement might be rejected as anachronistic: projecting the present-day conception of 'religion' onto medieval life in which the separations between secular and sacred realms are not so clear-cut.

5 Hence Dewey's critique that education is not preparation for the future, but is a form of life with intrinsic value (Dewey 1916).
6 Paul Bowman (2013) has skillfully shown the context of Lee's pedagogy, and has drawn attention to the parallels between Rancière's and Lee's emancipatory pedagogies.
7 This raises a range of parallel questions about the emancipation or infantilisation of the will. It is not clear to me that the structure of dependency enacted in educational institutions can be overcome by removing any intellectual authority but by replacing that by an authority of the will. Does this not represent an equally corrosive form of dependency?
8 The reader may detect echoes of Thomas Kuhn's *The Structure of Scientific Revolutions* in this brief narrative. What might be called 'normal religion' – instead of Kuhn's normal science – is not overturned by the few anomalies. Only when the anomalies pile up does the religious subject feel a mounting crisis in faith. A new spiritual paradigm is possible when the tradition is re-appropriated in symbolic terms, or perhaps when a different religion or worldview is adopted.

References

Biesta, G. (2010). *Good Education in an Age of Measurement.* Colorado: Paradigm Publishers.
Bowman, P. (2013). 'Bruce Lee Beyond Pedagogy' in *Beyond Bruce Lee: Chasing the Dragon through Film, Philosophy and Popular Culture,* Columbia: Columbia University Press, 65–99.
Bruford, W. (1975). *The German Tradition of Self-Cultivation: Bildung from Humboldt to Thomas Mann.* London: Cambridge University Press.
Citton, Y. (2010). "'The Ignorant Schoolmaster': Knowledge and Authority" in J. Deranty (ed.) *Jacques Rancière: Key Concepts.* London: Routledge, 25–37.
Dawkins, R. (2006). *The God Delusion.* Boston: Houghton Mifflin.
Devine, A. (1912). "State or Way (Purgative, Illuminative, Unitive)" in *The Catholic Encyclopedia.* New York: Robert Appleton Company. Retrieved August 24, 2015 from New Advent: http://www.newadvent.org/cathen/14254a.htm
Dewey, J. (1916). *Democracy and Education: An Introduction to the Philosophy of Education.* London: Macmillan.
Eckhart, M. (1981). *Meister Eckhart: The Essential Sermons, Commentaries, Treatises and Defense,* E. Colledge and B. McGinn, trans. Mahwah, NJ: Paulist Press.
Feuerstein, G. (2011). *The Deeper Dimension of Yoga: Theory and Practice.* Colorado: Shambhala Publications.
Hirst, P. (1974). *Moral Education in a Secular Society.* London: University of London Press.
Hyland, T. (2015). "On the Contemporary Applications of Mindfulness: Some Implications for Education" *Journal of Philosophy of Education,* 49: 2, 170–186.
James, W. (1985). *The Varieties of Religious Experience: A Study in Human Nature.* London: Penguin.
Julian of Norwich. (1966). *Revelations of Divine Love,* Clifton Wolters, trans. London: Penguin.
Krishnamurti, J. (1929). *The Dissolution of the Order of the Star, A Statement by J Krishnamurti.* Retrieved from http://www.jkrishnamurti.org/about-krishnamurti/dissolution-speech.php
Leclercq, J. (1982). *The Love of Learning and the Desire for God: A Study of Monastic Culture.* New York: Fordham University Press.
Lee, B. (1971). "Liberate Yourself from Classical Karate" *Blackbelt Magazine.* Retrieved from http://www.blackbeltmag.com/daily/traditional-martial-arts-training/jeet-kune-do/liberate-yourself-from-classical-karate/
Maharshi, R. (2002). *The Essential Teachings of Ramana Maharshi: A Visual Journey.* Carlsbad, CA: Inner Directions.

Plato. (2016). *Meno*, B. Jowett, trans. Retrieved from http://classics.mit.edu/Plato/meno.html

Rancière, J. (1991). *The Ignorant Schoolmaster: Five Lessons in Intellectual Emancipation*. Palo Alto, CA: Stanford University Press.

Rancière, J. (2010). "On Ignorant Schoolmasters" in G. Biesta and C. Bingham (eds.) *Jacques Rancière: Education, Truth, Emancipation*. London: Continuum, 1–24.

Rawlinson, A. (1997). *The Book of Enlightened Masters: Western Teachers in Eastern Traditions*. Chicago: Open Court.

Ricoeur, P. (1966). *Freedom and Nature: The Voluntary and the Involuntary*, trans. Erazim Kohak. Evanston: Northwestern University Press.

Ricoeur, P. (1967). *The Symbolism of Evil*, E. Buchanan, trans. Boston: Beacon Press.

Ricoeur, P. (1992). *Oneself as Another*, Kathleen Blamey, trans. Chicago: University of Chicago Press.

Ricoeur, P. (1996). "Love and Justice" in R. Kearney (ed.) *Paul Ricoeur: The Hermeneutics of Action*, London: Sage, 23–40.

Rocha, S. (2014). *A Primer for Philosophy and Education*, Eugene: Cascade Books.

Sahlins, M. (1996). "The Sweetness of Sadness: The Native Anthropology of Western Cosmology" *Cultural Anthropology*, 37: 3, 395–428.

Segal, R. (1983). "In Defense of Reductionism" *Journal of the American Academy of Religion*, 51: 1, 97–124.

Sells, M. (1994). *Mystical Languages of Unsaying*. Chicago: University of Chicago Press.

Shree Purohit Swami. (2003). *The Ten Principal Upanishads*, Shree Purohit Swami and W.B. Yeats, trans. New Delhi: Rupa.

Storey, D. (2012). "Zen in Heidegger's Way" *Journal of East-West Thought*, 2: 4, 113–137.

Turner, D. (1996). *The Darkness of God: Negativity in Christian Mysticism*. Cambridge: Cambridge University Press.

Wilber, K. (1999). *The Collected Works of Ken Wilber: Volume 1*. London: Shambhala.

Zaehner, R. (1957). *Mysticism Sacred and Profane: An Inquiry into Some Varieties of Praeternatural Experience*. Oxford: Oxford University Press.

Chapter 8

Deliberative religious cultures

Introduction

A guiding supposition of this book is the urgent need for religious literacy. I have suggested that this urgency increases the more religion is viewed in opposition to criticality, as though religion entails an irrational and inviolable commitment. This view, I argued, involves a largely secular propositional framing of religion, requiring it to be placed in the private sphere, detached from any intervention from, or upon, public life. Such a view does not support religious literacy, but tends to generate polarized and fractured debates about the place of religion in society. In contrast to the attitude that seeks to privatize religion, I have claimed that religions are fundamentally public-facing not least because they act as social institutions binding communities together.

In this chapter, I return to the philosophical hermeneutics of Ricoeur to indicate the possibilities that exist for interesting and rich interpretive traditions and insights for and from religion. This is in contrast to the reductive views of what it means to be religious often associated with more fundamentalist religious orientations which tend to boil down to competing and irreconcilable truth claims. The *post-secular* age presents an opportunity to reinstate the significance of more nuanced interpretive traditions and thereby gives religious perspectives opportunities to demonstrate creative relationships with modernity that are not predicated on the assumption that religion is an uncritical commitment to be separated from public life. I argue, in fact, that religious commitments must be opened up to deliberative culture if either religions or public life are to flourish.

There are several important implications for education. First, the problem of indoctrination which characterizes much educational theory presupposes the kind of non-deliberative and hermeneutically naïve religiosity that I am keen to denounce. Second, religious education can operate as a space in which deliberative culture can be nourished. By this I mean that religious educators need to take seriously that the different views of students are not simply private preferences of a plural world, but bear upon the lived experience of meaning. To disregard the claims to 'truth' as some phenomenological approaches do,

144 Deliberative religious cultures

is not, in fact a mark of tolerance and inclusion. Third, faith schools demonstrate just how much distance there is between the propositional conception of religion where orthodoxy is expected, and a more embedded religiosity in which religious identity is as much orthopraxy than orthodoxy. Finally, the post-secular indicates a relation between religion and education that rejects any lingering progressivism in which secularization, disenchantment and criticality are aligned with good modern education.

The hermeneutics of religious understanding

Ricoeur (1986, 15) summarized his hermeneutical relation to understanding as follows: "there is no self-understanding that is not mediated through signs, symbols and texts; in the last resort understanding coincides with the interpretation given to these mediating terms." Ricoeur calls the mediation towards any understanding a *long route* to the self, and to interpretation in general, in contrast to what he considers to be Heidegger's short route to ontology via Dasein. It is important that this long route entails an acknowledgement of a constructed moment in (self) understanding. This is an ancient paradox: we need the self to see the self. For Ricoeur, there is no direct route to understanding, no unmediated experience of the self or world, an idea with devastating implications for certain views of religion. This might be read as an outrageous denial of religious insight by a philosopher who sailed too close to the theological wind but who also emphatically wished to remain a philosopher rather than a theologian. A central claim of most religious traditions and practitioners would, at first sight, be opposed to Ricoeur's mediation. Revelation, so the 'believers' assume, is the unmediated experience of God, rendering mediation not a universal phenomenon, but a problem to be overcome by contact with the unalloyed truth. The idea that religious experience is constructed gave lethal ammunition to many of the great atheists, who, like Feuerbach, claimed that God is *nothing more* than a construction, or projection, of human nature. How can a philosopher like Ricoeur justify such an apparently postmodern reduction of religion to experiences mediated through signs, symbols and texts?

In response to atheist confrontations, but also as a consequence of larger shifts within modernity, many philosophers of religion have come to terms with the projected nature of religious encounter – that Christians *encounter* the sacred through Christian symbols, Buddhists through Buddhist symbols, and so forth – without thereby denying the significance, even the revelatory possibility, of those encounters (Dupré 1998). One can, indeed today one must, acknowledge the projected aspects of human experience without thereby asserting that (religious) experience is *only* a human projection. Ricoeur's hermeneutic phenomenology allows for a mediation between the projected and the revealed, or, as Ricoeur (1995) frames it, between the manifestation of truth and the historical proclamation that follows. Sharing Ricoeur's recognition of and commitment

Deliberative religious cultures 145

to mediation, Henri Duméry has effectively disarmed the atheists of their greatest weapon:

> Consciousness is projective, because it is expressive, because its objective intentionality cannot fail to express itself, to project itself on various levels of representation. This does not mean that these representations themselves become projected upon the objective essence, or upon the reality which this essence constitutes. When contemporary phenomenologists write that the thing itself becomes invested with anthropological predicates and becomes known through those predicates, they merely allude to the need to represent the object in order to grasp its intrinsic meaning with all the faculties of the incarnated consciousness. But they do not deny that the object, the objective meaning, the "thing itself," orders, directs, rules the course of these representations
>
> (Quoted in Dupré 1998, 10–11).

Still, non-negotiable commitments to supposedly unmediated religious experience have not gone away. On the contrary some kind of retreat into more extreme assertions appears to be fueled by a fear of the secular among fundamentalist religious groups. Indeed the renewed interest in religion announced as the post-secular seems to arise from a reaction against more militant and fundamentalist religious ideologies (Schaafsma 2015). The idea that God is revealed in the particular historical moment, which appears to be non-negotiable among certain religious traditions – notably but not exclusively the three Abrahamic faiths (Judaism, Christianity and Islam) – entails a complex history of its own, rendering a simple literalist (unmediated) reading of Scripture highly suspect. In general, the idea of non-negotiable principles is problematic, particularly with respect to religion. Although (as argued in Chapter 5) the notion of an apprehension or intuition of totality is, in one sense, non-negotiable, it is also the basis for the claim that a given religion (as 'true') should be the universal institution embodied in the Ecclesia, the Caliphate or some other state-sanctioned or established religion. My argument is about the relationship that practitioners have with belief: religious traditions or individuals within them are not best understood as standing for inviolable obligations and beliefs (which tend to be fixed and reified), but committing to, or practising, a particular tradition. Still, secular culture frames religions as though they stand for reified beliefs or worldviews. Some secularists believe that religion should be placed in the private sphere for precisely this reason: that religion entails an inviolable commitment and therefore cannot be communitarian. The context in which religion is public, so this secularized reasoning goes, is a religious state, like the Wahhabi state of Saudi Arabia where Islamic orthodoxy is not genuinely valorized, but imposed. This incapacity to think of religion more deliberatively is less a result of the nature of religion than a particular – and relatively recent – way of framing religion (discussed in Chapter 3). It is a product of a particular reification that reduces religion to the propositional or doctrinal, a framing of religion that many philosophers of religion have recognized as particularly Western (Smith 1987; I'Anson and Jasper 2011). Interestingly, science itself it often reified in very similar ways, presented less as an approach to the world than as an object or set of secure statements about reality. Such reifications of putatively objective facts have led to the popular mind to mistake, for example, the outcomes of intelligence quotient tests with the intelligence of people, with ongoing implications for educationalists (Gould 1981).

Among the many associations and connotations of the post-secular, it is plausible to suggest a view of religions in which their own deliberative practices are acknowledged, through, in particular, a recovery of the interpretive traditions at their core. This might begin with recognizing that religions can inspire criticism of authority (Panjwani 2008). There are different ways to develop this post-secular reappropriation of what might be called *deliberative religiosity*.[1] Recent work within semiotics, for example, suggests that Western theological traditions contain a great store of symbolic capital which might inform present-day understandings of both of religion as well as education (Stables 2005; Stables and Semetsky 2015). But, as we have noted in Chapter 2, *the post-secular age* is an awkward concept to describe this since it can sometimes be conflated with a general postmodern skepticism towards a singular unifying narrative, and so those symbols often do not speak or are not heard. Forms of relativism that precipitated the failure of enlightenment reason have seemed unsatisfying. Postmodern incredulity towards grand narratives seemed to give way to a range of more pluralist and porous positions in which the phenomena of experience could be saved. This saving of appearances was possible either through allowing phenomena to be interpreted on their own terms (phenomenology) or by understanding the constructed nature of our experience (constructivism). These days, efforts to maintain contact with the possibility of ontological claims in this postmodern condition extend across forms of thin fundamentalism (across both science and religion), through Bhaskar's critical realism, to thicker hermeneutical accounts of history and truth, as in Gadamer, Ricoeur and Heidegger. So the postmodern denouncement of pure reason has led *both* to a revisionist reduction of religious traditions to forms of literalism, fideism and fundamentalism *and* a recovery of more hermeneutically informed and spiritually inclined forms of religiosity that lie somewhere between the secular and the confessional.

To give a concrete and educational instance of these processes, I turn to religious education as a curriculum subject within England. Historically we have seen religious instruction being used to form a buttress against the perceived relativist decline in the shared religious culture after the Second World War. As secularization took hold and plural religious traditions became an undeniable reality of England (less so, but to some extent also within other nations of the UK), and *confessionalism* became a term of abuse across the education community, 'religious instruction' gave way to a more phenomenologically informed 'religious education', which took a variety of beliefs and worldviews at face value. However, teaching about different religions in descriptive terms, as though the question of 'ultimate truth' could be bracketed out of an understanding of religion, led to a different kind of reductivism which provoked a further reaction. Critical realists like Andrew Wright (2004; 2013) have attempted to find a middle ground between naïve realism and forms of critical relativism by distinguishing between the ontological ground and epistemological claims: that acknowledging elements of critical divergence should not distract us from the ontological unity that grounds any religious debate. Critical realism has, however, seemed to some recent writers to reinforce other problematic framings of the religion and education debate, not least the propositional framing of religion (Strhan 2011; Aldridge 2015). What both phenomenological and critical realist positions also fail to fully acknowledge is the significance of 'meaning' to religious life, since phenomenologists consider the descriptive level of beliefs and practices, and critical realists see truth claims, to be the site of creative tension. The phenomena of meaning seems marginal within religious education today (at least at the theoretical level), though the instinct of critical realists to insist that truth is at stake arises from a recognition of the meaning of meaning. But if meaning is interpreted solely in propositional terms, as critical realism tends to do, then it does not take us into the lived meaning of religious experience. Perhaps a semiotic reorientation towards meaning will offer a corrective to this trajectory. This historical dialectic towards the authentic experience of meaning is, I think, only one way of conceiving of a more affirmative postsecular and post-confessional reappropriation of religious life.[2] This may entail the post-critical possibility of religious life – which Ricoeur (1967, 351) calls a second naïveté – that is hermeneutically informed but acknowledges the absolute claim made upon the subject by life itself.

The sacred need not be *sacred*

Many secularists, atheists and religious people understand divergent religious commitments to be both inviolable and irreconcilable (Barnes 2009). The sacred is marked off from the secular or profane by virtue of its sanctity. That sanctity cannot be determined by the religious subject but imposes itself, or makes a claim, upon that subject. As revelation, the religious subject has no choice but to receive religious insight which interrupts his or her own projective practices and capacities. This makes the insight or revelation of religion inviolable, opposes revelation and human reason, and thereby seals off revelation from the deliberative practices of discussion, debate and dialogue. If religious views and practices are inviolable in this way, then the only logical possibility seems to be the separation of private and public whereby the public is free of any religious influence. Anything else seems to entail conflict and division. But this separation is unsatisfying, not least because it reinforces the tendency to reduce education to schooling, since 'private' forms of upbringing (home, informal education, etc.) tend to be left out of the debates about public education which too easily become synonymous with schooling.

So if the straightforward secularist division between private and public is unsatisfying, what are our options? Whatever forms of secularism/post-secularism seem reasonable, the requirements of political life press upon us the need for some kind of shared understanding. So I suggest a need for some practical, if not fully theoretical (or theological), consensus. In this respect I share Ricoeur's preference for philosophical rather than theological analysis, because theology, where it reacts against the rise of secularism is too prone to being defensive and can resist the deliberative culture that I am describing. This consensus acknowledges something of the historical dialectic of the post-secular that I have just outlined. It cannot be denied that something meaningful is at stake in how we bring children and young people into the world: a set of commitments of values is implied that cannot be bracketed out. This calls not for the choice between indoctrination into an inviolable worldview versus a neutral education where value-laden formation is excluded. Rather it calls first for the recognition that something profound is at stake, and an understanding that our formative context will always already be imbued with a 'decision' or orientation concerning what matters. So rather than see the educator as taking a position, it is better to recognize that an orientation to the world is already *undertaken* in the processes of education. This is the key insight of hermeneutics: that we are always already within an interpretive structure before we begin teaching or even developing a curriculum (Aldridge 2015).

I am tempted to draw again upon Rowan Williams' account of procedural secularism in which religious views are taken up alongside other non-religious perspectives (humanist, atheist) to inform a properly deliberative culture while rejecting the programmatic secularism of a pure French Republic in which no reference to religion can enter the public domain.[3] Williams' account does not presuppose that the deliberative culture of procedural secularism necessarily entails framing religions propositionally. Although Williams seems to move in the direction of a Habermasian communicative rationality in support of pluralism, his account seems not fully deliberative in the sense that he does not give attention to the important process of finding the theological and practical limitations of 'given' religious views. We must, in other words, be able to open discursive channels to aspects of religions that might appear beyond the realms of public debate. The framing of inviolability and irreconcilability with its singular logical secular outcome encourages us to look past the possibility that religious views need not be antagonistic to deliberative culture. Faith positions and religious lives need not be treated as 'sacred' and unquestionable, outside the realm of deliberative debate. Indeed, respect for religious views must entail a capacity for deliberation. If someone simply grants me my private religious view on the basis that it is my personal religious right and nothing to do with them, then the actual message is not one of respect, but that there is nothing really at stake; that religion is a personal preference, a lifestyle choice. Of course for many religious believers (as well as atheists) 'truth' is certainly at stake. Philip Barnes is concerned about the educational relativism that fails to take commitment seriously, arguing that many adherents of religion feel that

> ... their religious beliefs and values are misrepresented by educational aims and methods that imply the equal truth of all religions. They conclude that there is no true respect for religious difference, for true respect acknowledges the right of religious believers and traditions to define themselves and not to have imposed on them the kind of fluid relativist identities that follow from liberal theological commitments.
>
> (Barnes 2009, 13)

While I appreciate Barnes' commitment to the depth of belief that goes beyond preference, it is still caught within the propositional frame. Part of my argument for a deliberative encounter within education is to challenge the believer about the nature of belief, or should I say, to draw attention to the fact that the propositional framing of beliefs and worldviews has already structured conventional debates about religious pluralism. It is not enough to retain the liberal notion that belief should not be imposed upon, as Barnes does. We must go further to develop the case for deliberative encounter that places those commitments in a creative tension that can (sometimes) produce fruitful dialogue by showing the shape and limits of belief itself. It is true that I would rather have my own attitude and orientation scrutinized and challenged so as to better understand its grounding in reality, but this does not just entail challenging the truth content of my beliefs but also the kind of framings that are presupposed by them. Indeed, deliberative practices and dialogue help us to recognize these framings. This entails an encounter with other people that does not bracket out the most important aspect of human identity: the meaning of things, what matters. This kind of deliberative attitude does not require us to import alien ideas and practices to traditions that are defensive, conservative or resistant to dialogue. This is because in fact, many histories of religious interpretation and practice reveal a living tradition in dialogue with itself, as the rich and largely hidden history of semiotics shows (Stables and Semetsky 2015). The Christian church, for example, entails a complex history between schism, reform, tradition and transformation. Islam, often framed as particularly antithetical to modernity and committed to the propositional frame, has similar deliberative and interpretive histories and possibilities (Volpi 2011; Radwan 2015). None of this is to deny the tensions and violence that often attend tradition, change, reform and revolution within religious institutions, or that there are tensions here between religion and modernity. But tension and violence are general dimensions of social, political and religious change. It is too easy to attribute violence solely or primarily to religious histories, especially where the story is one of heroic reason bravely battling against dogmatic faith (the putative conflict between religion and science being the paradigmatic example).

As a former schoolteacher of philosophy and religion, I recognize that this account might appear to underestimate the complexities of managing dialogue between conflicted, even opposed, positions within the classroom. My experience of teaching suggests in fact that the theoretical accounts of religious education within the literature construct sharper tensions and less reconcilable polarities than do students engaged in debate. Nevertheless, the argument, that hermeneutical subtlety and deconstructing the propositional nature of religion will facilitate a better appreciation of the interpretive context of the student is not, of course, intended as the final word, but as progressing a complex theoretical case that is largely absent, as well as addressing a culture in which religions and secularisms often talk past one another. My argument should suggest, though, that the very idea of people standing for faith positions that may or may not be opposed already concedes so much to an unhelpful framing of the debate.

So if religion cannot be pressed out of public life, are we authorized to question the inviolability of particular religious positions? More specifically, who is authorized to do so? Who am I to suggest to any religious person that their view may be partial – partially constructed by the projecting subject? Is it not a public responsibility to do just this? No doubt there are more and less sensitive ways of engaging in such public deliberation around religious identity. But generally speaking, those with some religious literacy (and they may or may not be religious themselves) will understand that capacity for deliberation is not just a possibility, but is a vital necessity, now more than ever. This will be aided by an appreciation of the fact that acknowledging projection in religious experience does not require rejection of that experience. At its best, religious education in schools can provide not just an affirmation of different traditions or irreconcilable positions, or a reinforcing cultural narrative that binds a community to its past and future, but spaces for reflection on one's own and each other's religious upbringing and assumptions that give rise to some recognition also of the interpretive frame in which things are seen. This is why Aldridge (2015) calls for a hermeneutics of religious education. Students might expect less to "justify their belief in the existence of God" than to explain the meaning of religion and to explore the significance of symbols. Dialogue within and beyond the classroom should then not be about justifying answers, as examination questions will inevitably require (Strhan 2010, 23–25), but coming to a mutual understanding which explores the scope and limits of the symbolic and metaphorical aspects of tradition. One could say, with Ricoeur (1990), that one's self understanding is only really possible in encounter with another, that the self is constituted through and by the other. Thus religious education must be cosmopolitan.

Deliberative religious education

To illustrate the deliberative model I will briefly draw upon Gert Biesta's analysis of democratic processes in education.[4] For Biesta, educational theory and practice does not generally reflect a deliberative democratic culture but is increasingly under the sway of a representative democratic model.[5] The representative model takes each individual's view into account through an aggregating process, typically in democracies, through a system of voting, with the majority view forming the general will. This common sense view of democracy has some problematic features.

Representative democracy 'respects' the individual preferences of its citizens by leaving them intact, and aggregates those preferences to form a general will. This process assumes that each citizen's preferences are inviolable and inalienable. A problem with this model is that politicians develop policies and ideas in accordance with majority preferences, caricatured as policy derived through focus group.[6] The political role is then conceived not as one of forming and leading public opinion, but rather of following the majority view. There are, no doubt, many problems with supposing that politicians should lead and form public opinion, rather than respond to it, not least the implied paternalism. But it is generally unproblematic to presume that some views are more considered than others, and that some authority is legitimately conferred upon those with more considered and principled views. More importantly, leadership entails establishing, engaging and modelling deliberative practices. Moreover, it is easy and tempting to overdraw the binary: in reality politics cannot exist without principles any more than it can entirely ignore public opinion. Admittedly this view of democratic representation is restricted and simplified, but Biesta's application of it to education theory is illuminating.

Along with many educational philosophers, Biesta expresses a concern about the increasingly economistic relationship between teachers and students across formal education (Biesta 2006). In the context of his critique of the learning culture, learners are framed as customers, educators as providers and education the consumable. Put simply, the economistic model places the educator in service of the inviolable preferences of the student as consumer. This market model is problematic, argues Biesta, because it fails to distinguish between market approaches and professions. By contrast to the 'student as consumer' model, the professional model (e.g., law, medicine, education) requires the producer to inform and refine the preferences of the consumer. The doctor does not respond to the whims of the patient through prescribing what is requested without question, but informs the patient of their needs following professional consultation and judgment. A profession does not leave the preferences of the consumer intact, but informs and refines them through an educational process. It is obvious that the infant who wants only to eat chocolate and watch cartoons should not have those desires met without hesitation. Parents and teachers seek to educate those desires. But the commodification of education structures the educational transaction in such a way that it encourages providers not to challenge or refine consumer preferences, but to leave them intact, as inviolable and given desires to be satisfied by the market.

It is easy to see that this market model is inappropriate for framing educational relationships. Teachers have a kind of authority that salespeople seldom do. They are there to guide students, not just to satisfy preferences. It is widely understood that the culture of student satisfaction in higher education in the UK is in danger of enacting this transactional framing of education and is considered a dangerous development since it is corrosive of the properly educational relationship that ought to exist between students and teachers (White 2013). So Biesta argues for the deliberative culture of education to be recognized in which desire satisfaction is not as important as desire formation. Can a deliberative culture be developed within discussions around the place of religion in public life? If we accept that some religious activities and ideas are intrinsically public-facing, we must also accept that those ideas and activities, and the forms that they take, are not given and inviolable. When we recognize the capacity of religious interpretations to vary and change with time and context, then we open up the possibility that religious ideas are indeed not inviolable. When we acknowledge that the projecting 'subject' does not entail a rejection of the 'object', then we will give confidence to religious communities to acknowledge the scope and complexities of their interpretations.

That capacity to change does not mean, of course, that we must privilege a 'neutral' secular authority which can demand that religions reinterpret their own tradition in heteronomous terms. In other words, drawing out the deliberative structures within religious traditions is a very different proposition to requiring religions to conform to a putatively neutral secular state. This is because religions have, on the whole, the capacity for deliberative practices within them, and where resistance to that deliberation exists (such as the flat fundamentalisms of modern religious discourse, notably but not exclusively in forms of Christianity and Islam), there are particular and peculiar historical, social, political and economic circumstances that go beyond (while still inclusive of) 'religion' per se. In sum, religions are not homogenous fixed points whose tenets are simply revealed and therefore unquestionable.

Some problems with deliberative culture

On the face of it, a culture that seeks some kind of practical consensus through what I have termed 'deliberative religiosity' seems to involve the kind of rational agreement that invites a propositional framing of religion. Religious dialogue does not need to be framed in these terms, but can be seen, for example, as engaging different religious sensibilities, such as the aesthetic or the experiential. Even if such a sensibility allows for a meaningful pluralism that acknowledges that varied figurations of the sacred, one might still detect a danger here that the conception of deliberative culture described above enacts a kind of neocolonialism, suggesting an intolerance of what I have loosely referred to as fundamentalist, literalist and fideist orientations to religion. This intolerance of commitment is clearly a danger that must be taken seriously. That all religions are historical and hermeneutical might not be tolerable among some religions or cultures. We have already noted, for instance, that the rise of less tolerant forms of literalist and revisionist religiosity suggests that a significant number of people are impatient with the kind of equivocation of interpretation that frustrates simple one-dimensional interpretive paradigms. Specifically, acknowledging the projective nature of religious encounter will be perceived as a threat to certain fundamental positions (without the connotation of 'fundamentalism' in a more reductive sense). The historical Christ, for example, is not for many Christians an optional element that can be as easily demythologized as my account might seem to suggest. On the other hand, religions are not monolithic worldviews, but stretch across a great variety of forms and practices from the exclusive, literal and reductive, towards more inclusive, symbolically charged and hermeneutically rich traditions. Concerns about holding on to the true interpretation of tradition can sometimes entail both reification and historical naiveté, both of which disconnect people from the interpretive traditions. To some extent extremism and fundamentalism arise not from the institutions and traditions of religion, but from a separation from them: where *the truth* is fed through online channels accessed in private and examined alone. Thus public debate of difficult apparently irreconcilable views should be recognized as an essential aspect of deliberative culture. This should encourage us to reconnect with public-facing religious and cultural traditions rather than argue for them to be placed in the private sphere. Complex scriptural traditions exist in all great religions, from Jewish Midrash to Christian and Islamic hermeneutical schools. Indeed, the differing sects or traditions within religions express precisely that layering. So the danger of imposing a pluralist/relativist view of religion is not as pressing as the dangers of allowing these concerns to stall deliberation and privatize religious debate. Deliberative culture is not an option for the world, but is a political, theological and existential necessity. The pursuit of shared transcendence, which seems so absurd in the present geopolitical climate, requires us to discover the deliberative heart of our religious and cultural traditions. So while we should be alert to the danger of imposing what might appear a rather insecure set of interpretive processes on traditions, there are ways, I think, of drawing out inherent interpretive subtleties that already exist.

The reader might also perceive a tension in this chapter between the idea of encouraging a deliberative culture on the one hand, and challenging the reduction of religion to propositional doctrines and truth claims on the other. It may seem that the construction of debate and dialogue characteristic of deliberative culture as I have briefly outlined it here would tend to presuppose debate undertaken within the propositional frame. Does deliberative discourse not presuppose the propositional, even if we are then invited to engage in debate? Doesn't something like UK parliamentary debate, for example, epitomize the rather reductive framing of different ideas as competing and irreconcilable views to be settled less through participative consensus than through the imposition of the general will which cannot be fully inclusive? My point throughout

154 Deliberative religious cultures

has been to suggest that deliberative religiosity does require some significant examination of religious practices. But this begins with deconstructing our tendency to reify religion: religions are not things or objects but instantiations and practices shaped by the traditions of the past and oriented towards transcendence. They are people and practices interwoven with tradition and inspiration. Religions are more readings than books, more teachings than truths.

Conclusion

Many questions have been left unexplored in this exposition of the importance of deliberation for religion and education. I have not been able to explain how this deliberative culture would operate within different communities and how exactly those communities would be engaged in public debate and dialogue. Nor have I been able to extricate those religious interests from a range of other political and social problems that make doctrinal identity and distinctiveness attractive to communities. No doubt I have loosened the bond between the religious and the historical too much for many readers. Nevertheless, in the present geopolitical context, some cultures no doubt regard Western culture and education as aligned to a kind of critical and groundless secularism, and so the adoption of extreme religious identity appears to be a reaction to that. Attempts to understand what is religious here, in relation to what is social, economic or cultural requires a mammoth and global deliberative effort. There appears to be little appetite for this at present, but nevertheless I remain optimistic.

I have tried simply to draw attention to a few problems that should be more widely addressed: first, the alignment of education and criticality, which is too often regarded in opposition to religion and credulity; second, the reduction of religious life to doctrinal positions or propositional truth claims; third, the notion that religious claims are, by their very logic, necessarily irreconcilable; and finally, that therefore religious views are inviolable and should be insulated from deliberative culture. If we can demonstrate that religions do not operate fundamentally as worldviews, then a key constraint on consensus building might be removed. If we can show that projection does not falsify religion but opens us to greater interpretive contexts, then religious people may be more content to draw upon the hermeneutical traditions within their own religions. Fundamentalist revisionist religiosity disregards the hermeneutical complexity that informs religious traditions, and this trend must be examined critically if we are to create a more deliberative culture in which religious literacy can be taken seriously.

Notes

1 I appreciate that this phrase might grate against certain prevailing cultural assumptions. The standard view that religious thinking is more intuitive than deliberative is certainly plausible and has been recently attested to by psychologists (Shenhav et al. 2012). I would

Deliberative religious cultures 155

suggest that our conceptions of intuition and deliberation require more careful theorization. As I argue in Chapter 5, the faculty of intuition cannot be simply separated from reasoning, but depends upon it. But a more important concern might be that the concept of deliberation evokes ideas of a Habermasian rationalist account of understanding which seems at odds with my argument that religions are not fundamentally propositional in character. As will become clear, deliberation does not need be interpreted purely as a process of developing rational consensus, but can be seen as a process of dialogue in which the scope and limits of the propositions and practices of religion can be explored.

2 It should be kept in mind that the existentialist philosophical school and its characteristic form of atheism would generally find any suggestion that meaning is a universal grounding concept deeply problematic especially where meaning is not something self-generated. For Nietzsche, for example, meaning is just a post-Kantian anthropological crutch that is a failure to stand independently of theological consolations.

3 While understandable given contemporary media representation, this picture of the French republic as entirely hostile to any public forms of religious expression is as misleading as it is commonplace. For a clear account of the ways in which French public life does not exclude religious influence, see Arthur, Gearon & Sears (2010, Chapter 1).

4 For a summary, see Biesta (2006, 19–21). This project is at the heart of Biesta's theory of education (2006; 2010; 2013).

5 I have resisted wider discussions of democratic education and examination of forms of democracy undertaken by political philosophers. For educationalists, such debates often entail wider discussions of the role of citizenship education, which, in England at least, is often thrown into the smorgasbord of topics to be covered in religious education classes. Here I restrict my discussion to the possibility of a deliberative culture for religious education and for the treatment of religion in public life more broadly, and discuss democracy only as far as is necessary to make quite a limited argument about religion and education.

6 Although a focus group discussion might, in itself, be supportive of deliberation, policies based on them are designed to reflect the majority, not shape it.

References

Aldridge, D. (2015). *A Hermeneutics of Religious Education*. London: Bloomsbury.

Arthur, J., Gearon L., & Sears, A. (eds.). (2010). *Education, Politics and Religion: Reconciling the Civil and the Sacred in Education*. London: Routledge.

Barnes, P. (2009). Religious Education: Taking Religious Differences Seriously. *IMPACT*, No 17. Philosophy of Education Society of Great Britain.

Biesta, G. (2006). *Beyond Learning: Democratic Education for a Human Future*. Colorado: Paradigm Publishers.

Biesta, G. (2010). *Good Education in an Age of Measurement*. Colorado: Paradigm Publishers.

Biesta, G. (2013). *The Beautiful Risk of Education*. Colorado: Paradigm Publishers.

Dupré, L. (1998). *Religious Mystery and Rational Reflection*. Michigan: Eerdmans.

Gould, S. J. (1981). *The Mismeasure of Man*. New York: W. W. Norton & Company.

I'Anson, J., & Jasper, A. (2011). "'Religion' in Educational Spaces: Knowing, Knowing Well, and Knowing Differently" *Arts & Humanities in Higher Education*, 10: 295–313.

Panjwani, F. (2008). "Religion, Citizenship and Hope: Civic Virtues and Education about Muslim Tradition" in J. Arthur, I. Davies, & C. Hahn (eds.), *The SAGE Handbook of Education for Citizenship and Democracy*,. Los Angeles, CA: Sage, 292–304.

Radwan, H. (2015). 'Muslims Can Reinterpret Their Faith: It's the Best Answer to Isis' *The Guardian*. Retrieved from http://www.theguardian.com/commentisfree/2015/dec/16/muslims-faith-isis-religion-islam

Ricoeur, P. (1967). *The Symbolism of Evil*, E. Buchanan, trans. Boston: Beacon Press.

Ricoeur, P. (1986). *From Text to Action*, K. Blamey & J. Thompson, trans. Evanston: Northwestern University Press.

Ricoeur, P. (1990). *Oneself as Another*, K. Blamey, trans. Chicago: University of Chicago Press.

Ricoeur, P. (1995). "Manifestation and Proclamation" in *Figuring the Sacred*, D. Pellauer & M. Wallace, trans. Minneapolis: Fortress Press, 48–67.

Schaafsma, P. (2015). "Evil and Religion: Ricoeurian Impulses for Theology in a Postsecular Climate" *International Journal of Philosophy and Theology*, 76: 2, 129–148.

Shenhav, A., Rand, D., & Greene, J. (2012). "Divine Intuition: Cognitive Style Influences Belief in God" *Journal of Experimental Psychology*, 141: 3, 423–428.

Smith, W. (1987). *Faith and Belief*. Princeton: Princeton University Press.

Stables, A. (2005). *Living and Learning as Semiotic Engagement: A New Theory of Education*. Lewiston, NY: Lampeter: Edwin Mellen Press.

Stables, A., & Semetsky, I. (2015). *Edusemiotics: Semiotic Philosophy as Educational Foundation*. London, New York: Routledge.

Strhan, A. (2010). "A Religious Education Otherwise? An Examination and Proposed Interruption of Current British Practice" *Journal of Philosophy of Education*, 44: 1, 23–44.

Volpi, F. (ed.). (2011). *Political Islam: A Critical Reader*. London: Routledge.

White, M. (2013). "Higher Education and Problems of Citizenship Formation." *Journal of Philosophy of Education*, 47: 112–127.

Wright, A. (2004). *Religion, Education and Post-modernity*, London: RoutledgeFalmer.

Wright, A. (2013). *Christianity and Critical Realism: Ambiguity, Truth and Theological Literacy*. London: Routledge.

Chapter 9

Conclusion

The aim of this book has been to explore the significance of the *post-secular* for educational philosophy and theory. Short of direct practical recommendations, I have tried to indicate that the framing of debates in religion and education is tied to a range of social, political and educational tensions. Those tensions are hard to ignore as every day brings news reports of terrorist activities and of splintering alliances and coalitions. Of course religious literacy is no panacea: the first lesson of education studies is that education cannot compensate for wider social and political problems. But this does suggest that a centralization and consolidation of prevailing structures of power and process (that might be perceived in the one-dimensional culture of UNESCO, the World Bank and the International Community) is not the only or best way to deal with such problems.

From the outset, the concept of the post-secular has played a conflicted role. The connotations of the term have seemed almost hopelessly wide-ranging, reflecting not only (I hope) my own ill-discipline in the conceptual development of the argument, but also our strained political and philosophical condition. While this is more than post-9/11 soul-searching, that context cannot be ignored. No doubt the desire to impose order upon the multifaceted panorama of the post-secular has led to generalization, omission and overstatement, and, in the end, I wonder whether the discourse of the post-secular reinstates the kinds of grand sociological theorizing that have been called into question. It might be better, then, to speak of a post-secular *moment* rather than a post-secular age, a moment that will remain dynamic, that will transform itself into as yet unimagined possibilities.[1]

I began by questioning the alignment between education, critique and secularism, challenging the idea that to be secular means to be critical, and therefore by implication, to be religious means to be not yet fully critical. The ongoing presence of religion in the present age makes any such alignment problematic, even dangerous. Social theories of historical and educational progress and development also seemed tied a certain view of secularization as general disenchantment, associations that have led to a suspicion that Western education is inherently antithetical to religion. In some contexts the fear of the secular

158 Conclusion

becomes aligned with anxieties around certain forms of education. These associations are not simply wrong, but speak of a geopolitical context that cannot be ignored. Religious literacy can help us understand these cross-pressures without engaging in apologetics.

I went on to examine religion and belief, particularly as those terms and their associations frame debates within current educational theory. The idea of cultural liturgies seemed to both move us away from propositional framing, but also oriented the discussion very explicitly in terms of educational formation, specifically the formation of desire. The propositional frame became a central concept here because of its subtle influence on educational discourses. I took Heidegger's critical analysis of Western metaphysics to be an interesting way of interrupting the propositional frame. One cannot engage with Heidegger's critique of the West without recognizing the critique of rationalism and cognitivism that underpins it. And so the problem that religion is too rationally and propositionally framed is implicitly challenged by Heidegger's deconstruction of Cartesian and Kantian foundationalism.

The experiments in re-framing religion that formed the second part of the book were really interruptions, educational illustrations of questions intended to reveal the cracks in the secular and overly rationalized discourses of modernity. The idea that submission, attention and union are concepts generally foreign to educational theory was an impetus to explore them in ways that brought out the attenuation of subjectivity expressed within many religious traditions. One might identify the negative capability of the *apophatic* as the golden thread here, since the argument has presented an apophatic anthropology in which education concerns not the development of a stable self, but as much a recognition of the self's insubstantiality. The self is something to be practiced or verified and sometimes undone. Ricoeur describes the construction of the narrative self, a concept that resonates with the critique of the propositional frame and Heidegger's related deconstruction of Western metaphysics. These experiments in re-framing could all be considered as forms of Heidegger's question of being: What indeed does it mean for a thing to be? Object or practice? Noun or verb?

The trinity of submission, attention and union culminated in an idea, borrowed from Rancière and mystical theology, that metaphors of progress and ascent can only take us so far, and that practices of undoing these kinds of discourse are essential to the health of institutions. In order to live, institutions must be dynamic. Despite wide critiques of schooling and of religion, institutions are not in principle antithetical to the insight of a genuine educational or religious experience, although in practice schools and churches often feel like it. Again it is the apophatic practice of deconstructing all that is constructed that makes being into a practice as much as an object or thing.

A political consideration has been simmering throughout the argument, surfacing from time to time and somewhat developed in the discussion around deliberative democracy in Chapter 8. First of all the postcolonial affirmation that history has not ended with secular liberal democratic systems led me to point out that the idea that other cultures are not on their way to being us (Anglo-European consumer capitalists) is important for educationalists. This is important not just in acknowledging the many and varied answers that exist to the great questions of existence, but also, and more importantly, that the secular liberal neutral reply, neatly summarized in a favourite scene from a favourite movie, *This is Spinal Tap*, as "Have . . . a good time . . . all the time" is at best incomplete though certainly unsustainable and ultimately quite depressing.[2] Secondly, Ricoeur's post-critical second naïveté describes a moment in which we are able to reinterpret our own religious traditions in light of the critical phase of modernity and secularization. The argument that religions are open to deliberative culture is vital for a post-critical appreciation of them. In summary, we can see the possibility of a renewed, post-critical appreciation of other ways of being-in-the-world, forms of life that intrinsically and inescapably bear witness to the fullness of being.

An undercurrent of rationalism has been a target for critique: the propositional framing of religion, the deconstruction of Cartesian and Kantian foundationalism, the dialectics of mystical and apophatic theology, the wider challenge to the hegemony of Western philosophical and educational discourses. This rationalism is hard to evade, however, since it is framed within (and as) the form of the rational/philosophical discourse of the book itself. Where does the reader (or author) draw the line between mythos and logos? Does the postsecular moment offer a reassessment of poetic, literary and religious orderings of the world, as forms of life and discourse richer than the tame logic of belief systems or worldviews? Ricoeur invites a receptivity to the resonances between literature, philosophy and religion, exemplifying a mediation between mythos and logos (Ricoeur 2004; Lewin 2012). I have also drawn attention to the Christian mystical theological tradition and referred to comparative religion to suggest opportunities for encountering other modes of being in the world. I have certainly struggled to remain faithful to my own account of education as bearing witness, an account that tries to show more than say. Poetry and myth speak the world in ways that I seem bound to describe, represent and therefore deform. It seems, to some extent, inevitable that in the shadow of the idols of modernity (disinterest and objectivity), the practice of philosophy too easily falls into the object of an argued position. But that mediation between the literary, the philosophical and the religious, that fusion between mythos and logos which defies the kinds of reductive views of religion I have argued against, can be found within contemporary educational theory today.

Efforts within philosophy of education to crack open the rationalist framings of education are varied and ongoing. Feminist critiques have much to contribute here since they demonstrate how the framings of religion and education have reflected the prevailing patriarchal hegemonies in ways that are rarely considered. Graham (2013) argues that in fact the post-secular revivals and returns of religion are in danger of reinstating some patriarchal discourses that we could well do without. These insights are relevant to educational theory

160 Conclusion

since the political nature of education reminds us that people are embodied. So we must take care not to simply call for a return to some reputed tradition without critical questions about how that tradition was founded and how it will be appropriated. Like radical orthodox theology, the recent interest in the theological and philosophical liberal traditions of education (O'Hear and Sidwell 2009; Tubbs 2014) seem rather too conservative, at risk of attempting to recover a post-secular without fully learning the lessons of critique. Recent work in edusemiotics appears to move in the direction of a more inclusive and radical recovery of alternative discourses not yet suffused with the rationalism and subjectivism of modernity (Stables and Semetsky 2015), but one wonders whether its attachment to American pragmatism (Peirce and Dewey) renders edusemiotics still too rationally framed.

The interest in Cavell's more transcendental American philosophy is suggestive of a more radical deconstruction of some of the rationalist idols of modernity. Saito and Standish (2012) are leading the charge in this innovative area, though there is wide interest here. As Mahon (2014) shows, the literary, poetic and intuitive use of, and appreciation for, language in Cavell marks his philosophy out. Standish's (2014) recovery of the virtue of impudent practices in language is another example, where explicit clarity is shown to betray language. This interest in disruptive discursive forms and the relations between more rational and literary devices stands in marked contrast to the orientation behind some of the debates I have entertained in this book, as, for example, between Cooling and Hand. These emerging *practices of language* suggest that educational theory is broadly engaged in the kinds of debate that have occupied this book, even where explicit references to religion and secularism are absent. The philosophical enclosures and practices of late modernity have shown their limitations, even if there is wide divergence about what might come after the post-secular (Paul-Smith and Whistler 2011). The emergent and fluid practices of Cavell's ordinary language philosophy indicate an appetite for something at least post-rationalist (and perhaps post-metaphysical, in a Heideggerian sense). The devices and practices of language within mystical theology and continental philosophy seem to be addressed in the literary turn in philosophy of education that Cavell brings. Indeed the possibility of being authentically religious is surely at stake here. Understanding religion through this literary turn is one alternative expression for the hermeneutic tradition that I have employed. In this context, and alongside Heidegger, being among the most widely discussed figures in twentieth-century philosophy, Wittgenstein deserves more discussion than I have been able to offer.

Secularism is not over. But perhaps the idea or concept of it has become questionable. As representational, the concept stands and dies. The idea that we can understand a range of historical and social forces and phenomena in narrative terms is appropriate as long as we recognize that we are telling stories that are dynamic and incomplete: the story never ends. Can we take the metaphors of ascent, of progress and of truth and enlightenment as ideas to practice

Conclusion 161

without taking them as endpoints or positions we inhabit, defend or oppose? Is this what is meant by *the meaning of life*, that it is an ongoing practice? We don't, then, live in the security of a correct representational world any more than we live *happily ever after*. This is not the movies – but then, neither are the movies.

Notes

1 I acknowledge David Wolken here who presented this idea of a *post-secular moment* in contrast to a post-secular age at the North American Philosophy of Education conference in Toronto, 2016. It was my pleasure to respond to this paper at the conference. Both Wolken's presentation and my response is to be published in the Philosophy of Education Yearbook.
2 This is surely an unfair characterization of the secular, but one that I will let stand given the context of the concluding thoughts. Reversing this trite characterization, Sahlins (1996, 415) shows how, in fact, the Western tradition has often affirmed the virtue of pain and unhappiness: "anyone who defines life as the pursuit of happiness has to be chronically unhappy."

References

Graham, E. (2013). *Between a Rock and a Hard Place: Public Theology in a Post-Secular Age*. London: SCM Press.
Lewin, D. (2012). "Ricoeur and the Capability of Modern Technology" in T. Mei and D. Lewin (eds.) *From Ricoeur to Action: The Socio-Political Significance of Ricoeur's Thinking*. London: Continuum, 54–74.
Mahon, A. (2014). *The Ironist and the Romantic: Reading Richard Rorty and Stanley Cavell*. London: Bloomsbury.
O'Hear, A., & Sidwell, M. (2009). *The School of Freedom: A Liberal Education Reader from Plato to the Present Day*. Exeter: Imprint Academic.
Paul-Smith, A., & Whistler, D. (2011). *After the Postsecular and the Postmodern: New Essays in Continental Philosophy of Religion*. Newcastle Upon Tyne: Cambridge Scholars Publishing.
Ricoeur, P. (2004). "Myth as the Bearer of Possible Worlds," in R. Kearney (ed.) *On Paul Ricoeur: The Owl of Minerva*. Aldershot: Ashgate, 117–126.
Sahlins, M. (1996). "The Sweetness of Sadness: The Native Anthropology of Western Cosmology" *Cultural Anthropology*, 37: 3, 395–428.
Saito, N., & Standish, P. (2012). *Stanley Cavell and the Education of Grownups*. New York: Fordham University Press.
Stables A., & Semetsky I. (2015). *Edusemiotics: Semiotic Philosophy as Educational Foundation*. London, New York: Routledge.
Standish, P. (2014). "Impudent Practices," *Ethics and Education*, 9: 3, 251–263.
Tubbs, N. (2014). *Philosophy and Modern Liberal Arts Education: Freedom Is to Learn*. Basingstoke: Palgrave Macmillan.

Index

Adam and Eve 107
aesthetic imagination 7
Africa 20
agency 56–7, 79, 110, 117
"The Age of the World Picture"
   (Heidegger) 71
'aggressive secularism' 22
Aldridge, David 57–8, 147
aletheia 72
allegiance 95
American civil religion 15
Americanization 27–8
American pragmatism 160
analytical philosophy 117
ancient Greece 119
ancient Greeks 66
Arendt, H. 3
Aristotle 47, 138
Arnold, Matthew 20
art 47
Arthur, James 3, 42, 47
Asad, Talal 18, 19–20, 119
atheism 1, 18
attention: awareness 68; beholding 107–8;
   coercion and 9, 119; contemplation
   68; etiology of 5; freedom of seduction
   119–21; intended attention 114–15;
   paradox of intention 110–14; paying
   attention 108–10; spiritual culmination in
   union 9; Weil and Murdoch on 115–19
attention economy 101
Augustine of Hippo, Saint 47, 98, 115, 127, 136
Austin, John L. 50
autonomy 46–7
Ayer, Alfred J. 50

Barnes, L. Philip 149
Barth, Karl 22

beholding 107–8
belief: Christian and cultural liturgies
   43–6; criticality versus credulity 38–40;
   deliberative attitude 149; privileging
   of worldviews and 36–8; propositional
   truth claims and 50–1; and religion in
   post-secular age 7, 36–59
'belief systems' 48
believing 49–51
Bellah, Robert 15, 42
Benedictine way 128, 133
Berkeley, George 126
Berlin, Isaiah 47
Bernard of Clairvaux, Saint 115
Bhakti tradition 42, 95
Bhaskar, Roy 146
Bible 54, 107
Biemel, Walter 74
Biesta, G. 98, 132, 150–2
Bildung 126
Black, Carol 28, 48, 130
Blair, Tony 3
blind faith 38
Bloom, Allan 2
boundless present 107
Bowman, Paul 91
Bronowski, Jacob 23
Brown, Wendy 17, 24
Bruce, Steve 16–17
Buddhism 76–7, 130–1, 136
Bultmann, Rudolf 22, 40

Campbell, Alastair 3
Caputo, John D. 69, 76
Cartesian cogito 78
Casanova, José 17
Catholic schools 3
Catholic tradition 133

Index   163

Cavell, Stanley 160
A Charlie Brown Christmas 15
China 20, 21, 41
Chinese martial arts 91–3, 94
choice 24, 37, 55
Christian church 149
'Christian Education' 133
Christianity 20–1, 42–3
Christian liturgies 43–6, 114
Christian mystical tradition 115, 159
Christian schools 29
Christmas 15
citizenship education 42
civic identity 42
civic liberty 47
civil religion 42
coercion 9, 119
coincidence 52
colonialism 29
colonialist education 29
common good 46–7
Confessions (Augustine) 98, 127
Connolly, William 17, 18
consumer capitalism 8, 29
consumerist liturgies 43–4
contemplation 108
Cooling, Trevor 27, 37, 57, 59, 160
'counter-liturgies' 47
Craver S. 95
creation 113
creationism 54
crisis of technological enframing 66
critical realism 146

Dalai Lama 68
Daoism 76–7
The Darkness of God (Turner) 97
Davie, Grace 21
Davis, Wade 29
Dawkins, Richard 22, 133
deliberative democratic processes 10
deliberative religiosity 146
deliberative religious cultures: deliberative
    religious education 150–2; hermeneutics
    of religious understanding 144–7;
    sacred need not be *sacred* 147–50; some
    problems with deliberative culture 152–4
De Magistro (Augustine) 115
Dennett, Daniel 22
Der Ister (Hölderlin) 73
Derrida, Jacques 24–5
Der Spiegel 66, 67

Descartes, René 65, 75, 99, 117
desire 127
"On Detachment" (Meister Eckhart) 136
Dewey, John 42, 108, 109
dharma 42
dialectical approach 27
Diamond, Jared 23
Dinham, A. 2
"direct doxastic voluntarism" 55
Discourse on Thinking (Heidegger) 68, 69,
    79, 110
disenchantment 24
distanciation 89
On the Divine Names (Pseudo
    Dionysius) 115
divine providence 126
doctrines 42
"Dover Beach" (Arnold) 20
Duméry, Henri 145
Durkheim, Émile 8, 16, 27, 42

Eastern collectivism 99
Eastern Orthodox Church 114
education: Americanization of 27–8;
    curricular interventions for mindfulness
    114; deliberative democratic processes
    in 10; etiology of attention in 5; federal
    laws protecting educational institutions
    from religious interference 15; liturgical
    practices 45–6; marginalization of
    religion within 37; models of learning
    26–7; religious education 2–4; role
    of religion in 18, 57–8; separation of
    religion and 26; significance of attention
    in 112–13; visions of perfection and 126
educational theory and practice 150–2
'Education for all' agenda 21, 28, 48,
    67, 130
Education Reform Act 27
edusemiotics 58
elenchus 27
enframing 29
England 2, 27
enlightened secularism 51
enlightenment 48–9, 130–1, 133
épistème 49
Equality Act (UK) 3
Ergas, Oren 24
eschatology 130
'European exception' 21
evangelical Christian movements 53–4
evolution 40

164 Index

'exotic other' 29
exploitation 95

fact/value distinction 39–40
faith 39, 50–1, 89, 148
faith schools 3, 37, 144
fear 17
federal laws 15
feminist critiques 159
Fichte, Johann Gottlieb 75
Formations of the Secular (Asad) 17, 18
Foucault, Michel 49
France 3, 20, 21
Francis, M. 2
Frazer, James 23
freedom 46–9
freedom of seduction 119–21
French Enlightenment 48–9
French Revolution 48

Gadamer, Hans-Georg 100, 113, 139, 146
Galileo affair 53
Garden, Mary 95
German idealism 66
God 97–8, 125, 128, 133–6, 145
good life 46
Graham, E. 159

Habermas, Jürgen 25
halten 107
Hand, Michael 37, 42, 56, 57, 59, 160
Harris, Sam 22
Hebrew Bible 41
Hegel, Georg W.F. 126
Heidegger, Martin: "The Age of the
  World Picture" 71; approach to doing
  philosophy 8–9; contribution to
  hermeneutic project 110, 111, 113,
  160; deconstruction of the willful self
  75–9; *Discourse on Thinking* 68, 69, 79,
  110; enigmatic claim 29; hermeneutical
  account of history and truth 146;
  hermeneutic phenomenology 107;
  influence of 44; ontotheology 24, 67,
  69; overcoming Western metaphysics
  65–8; *Parmenides* 72; philosophical
  hermeneutics of 100; poetry and
  73–5; *The Principle of Reason* 69;
  representational/correspondence theory
  of truth 59; thinking as releasement
  68–70; understanding of agency 110;
  way of thinking 70–3; *What Is Called
  Thinking?* 70; work on language 47, 58

Heraclitus of Ephesus 74
hermeneutic phenomenology 107
Herrigel, Eugen 96
heteronomy 47
Hindus 42, 130–1
Hirst, Paul 133
history 23
Hobbes, Thomas 99
Hölderlin, Friedrich 69, 73
human condition 47
human rights violations 120
Humboldt, Alexander von 126
Husserl, Edmund 75, 107

icons 114
The Idea of Perfection (Murdoch) 117
idolatry 44
Idou 107
The Ignorant Schoolmaster (Rancière)
  74, 129
Illich, Ivan 4, 130
immanent frame 51–2
India 20, 21, 29, 41
Indian *gurukula* tradition 95
indigenous education 28
individual autonomy 47
indoctrination 37–8, 41, 55, 143
'inquiry-based' approach 27
institutional religion 2
intelligent design 40
intended attention 114–15
intention 110–14
intentionality 58
international community 25, 28, 157
Islam 54, 137

James, William 39, 68, 108–9
Japanese Tendai Buddhism 136
Jesus Christ 136
Jewish Midrash tradition 54
John of the Cross, Saint 98, 115
Journal of Philosophy of Education 36
Julian of Norwich 126

Kant, Immanuel 47, 75, 117
Kantian autonomous will 78
Keane, Webb 53
Keats, John 5
Kentucky 15
Kierkegaard, Søren 89, 94
Krishnamurti, Jiddu 9, 101–2, 112, 129,
  132, 137
Kuhn, Thomas S. 49

Index 165

The Ladder of Creation (Bronowski) 23
laïcité 48
Lao Tzu 127
Latin Christianity 49
leap of learning 100
learnification 98
Lee, Bruce 132, 138
Lees, Helen 108
Leibniz, Gottfried Wilhelm von 126
liberal democracy 29
liberal theology 22
"Liberate Yourself from Classical Karate"
    (Lee) 132
literacy 2
liturgical practices 43–6, 114, 125–6
logical positivism 39, 50

Mahmood, Saba 17
Mahon, A. 160
martial arts 91–3, 94, 96
Marx, Karl 8, 16, 27, 111
Masschelein, J. 109
meditation 135
Meister Eckhart 68, 76, 111, 115, 126,
    136, 137
Meno (Plato) 127
A Merchant of Venice (Shakespeare) 127
Merton, Thomas 68
metaphysics 65–8, 71
Milbank, John 6
mindfulness 114
modernity 8, 21, 23, 27, 28–9, 46, 51
moral law 47
Moses 125
Murdoch, Iris 116–19
Muslim madrasas 3
mystical experiences 125
mystical life 136–7
mystical theology 97, 115, 125–6, 128
Mystical Theology (Pseudo Dionysius) 115
mystical union 139
myth 159

Nagarjuna 75
neo-Hegelian narrative of *Geistesgeschichte* 22
neoliberalism 5, 8
New Testament 40, 127
Nietzsche, Friedrich Wilhelm 66, 71, 112
Nigeria 20
non-belief 1
non-dual tradition 130
non-religious 20, 30
non-secular 7, 27

Norway 20
"Notes on a Post-Secular Society"
    (Habermas) 25
numeracy 2

ontotheology 24, 67, 69
'Osho' Bhagwan Shree Rajneesh 95
"over-belief" 39
Ozmon, H. 95

paradigm 49
paradigm of submission 93
paradox of intention 110–14
Parmenides (Heidegger) 72
Parmenides of Elea 67, 74
paying attention 108–10
Peanuts 15
Pelagian controversy 47
Peters, Michael 71
Phaedrus (Plato) 74
phenomenology 66, 69, 107
philosophical hermeneutics 87–91
phronesis 138
Plato 71, 74, 94, 97, 125, 127
plurality 95
poetry 73–5, 159
Polkinghorne, John 39
Pope, Alexander 126
Porete, Marguerite 137
positivism 39, 49
positivist philosophy 8
post-critical second naïveté 88
post-critical understanding 88–9
Postman, Neil 5–6
post-secular: conceptual core 27–30; as
    'crisis of faith' within secularism 24;
    defining 18–21; disenchantment and
    24; end of progress and 21–4; end of
    secularization and 16–18; formations of
    2; refining 24–7
post-secular education 2–4
post-secular *forms of negation* 5
practicing doctrine 45
prayer 9, 133–6
pre-critical first naïveté 88, 159
primary affirmation 88, 93–7
The Principle of Reason (Heidegger) 69
procedural secularism 7, 20, 26, 30,
    100, 148
programmatic secularism 7, 20
programmatic secularism 17
progress 21–4
progressive messianism 22

166 Index

propositional frame: educational implications of 55–8; immanent frame and 51–4; of religion 8, 49–51, 147
propositional truth claims 50–1
Protestant voluntarism 8
Pseudo-Dionysius the Areopagite 115
public/private distinction 3, 8, 10, 18, 20, 25, 48
puja rituals 41–2

Qur'an 54

radical orthodox theology 160
radical revisionist theology 22
Ramana Maharshi 96, 136
Rancière, Jacques 9–10, 28, 74, 128–30, 136–7, 158
rationalism 23
Rawlinson, Andrew 131
Readings, Bill 27
Reimer, Everett 4, 132
releasement 68–70
religion: and belief in post-secular age 7, 36–59; as 'belief systems' 48; decline in Britain 18, 20; dimensions of 40–1; growth of Christianity 20–1; marginalization within education 37; as matter of individual choice 24; phases of Habermas' engagement with 25–6; presence in modern life 10; propositional frame of 8, 49–51, 147; putative post-secular return of 18; reductive view of 8–9; role in public education 18; role in the social organisation of public educational institutions 26; role of aesthetic imagination 7; science and religion debates 40; separation of education and 26
"Religion and Education" (Strhan) 36
religious choice 24, 37, 55, 148–9
religious education 2–4, 27, 143, 146–7, 150–2
religious encounter 144
religious experience 133–6, 144
religious expression 4
religious history 2
religious identity 38, 42, 55
religious institutions 25
'Religious Instruction' 27
religious interference 15
religious life: dimensions of 40–3; exhibition at St Mungo's Museum

58; post-secular education and 2–4; voluntarist conception of 44
religious literacy 2, 18, 143
religious practices 41, 133–6
religious traditions 54, 129–31
religious truth claims 38
religious understanding 144–7
representational/correspondence theory of truth 59
representative democracy model 151
Republic (Plato) 94
Republicanism 42
"restorationist religiousity" 18
revelation 144
Richardson, William J. 72
Ricoeur, Paul 9, 40, 88, 100, 102, 111, 127, 133, 139, 143, 146, 147, 159
rights 37–8
Rilke, Rainer Maria 69
ritual practices 45
rituals 42
Rocha, Sam 127
Rorty, Richard 22
Ross, Maggie 107
Rousseau, Jean-Jacques 42
Rule of St Benedict 128
Russia 21
Russian Orthodox Church 21

sacred need not be *sacred* 147–50
saeculum 6
Sahlins, M. 126
St Mungo's Museum 58
Saito, N. 160
Sartre, Jean-Paul 47, 114
Sathya Sai Baba 95
Saudi Arabia 120, 145
scholastic theological tradition 66
Schooling the World (Black) 28
science 23, 39–40, 90
secular 8
A Secular Age (Taylor) 25
secular culture 5
secular education systems 21
secularism 6–7, 8, 18, 20, 25
secularization 8, 16–18, 25, 27, 30, 97
secular liturgies 43–6
secular nations 21
seduction 119–21
separationism 3
Shakespeare, William 127
Shankara 68

Index   167

Sharia law 120
Shaw, Marvin 110
silence 108, 121
Simons, M. 109
Smart, Ninian 40–1
Smith, James 30, 43–4, 47–8, 49, 119, 125
Smith, Wilfred Cantwell 49–50
social contract 99
"social imaginary" 51
Socrates 74, 116, 126
Socratic conception of being 66
South Sudan 20
speech 110
Spencer Foundation 37
spiritual pedagogy 95
Standish, P. 160
Stiegler, Bernard 113
Strhan, Anna 36, 43
'strong silence' 108
'student-centred' paradigm 99
subjective freedom 47
subjectivity 110, 117, 121
submission: appreciating 100–2;
    philosophical hermeneutics 87–91;
    primary affirmation as 93–7; role of 9;
    spiritual culmination in union 9; Tai Chi
    Chuan 91–3; theological affirmation and
    97–100
Sufi mystics 137
The Symbolism of Evil (Ricoeur) 89
symbols 42, 144
Symposium (Plato) 125

Tai Chi Chuan 91–3, 94, 96, 101
Taylor, Charles 25, 30, 45, 51–2
Teilhard de Chardin, Pierre 4
Teresa of Avila, Saint 115
theological affirmation 97–100
therapy 109
thinking 68–70
"threefold mimesis" 89
Through Phenomenology to Thought
    (Richardson) 72
Tillich, Paul 22, 44, 48
timeliness 138
Tocqueville, Alexis de 15, 42
Trakl, Georg 69
transcendence 4, 5
truth 58, 72

truth claims 23, 38, 143
Turkey 21
Turner, Denys 69, 97, 101, 115, 128

understanding 144–7
union: how in religion 133–6; institutional
    structures and 138–9; mystical
    experiences 125; mysticism of Rancière
    136–7; prayer and 9; visions of perfection
    and 126
United Kingdom (UK) 3, 18
United Nations Educational, Scientific and
    Cultural Organization (UNESCO) 21,
    28, 67, 78, 157
United States (US) 3, 21
universal institutional public
    education 4
U.S. Supreme Court 15

Vattimo, Gianni 16, 23
Vienna circle 39
Voltaire 126
voluntarism 55–6

Wales 27
Weber, Max 8, 16, 24, 27, 51
Weil, Simone 68, 108, 115–16
Western bias 23
Western individualism 99
Western liberalism 28
Western metaphysics 8
What Is Called Thinking? (Heidegger) 70
White, John 18
Wilber, Ken 138
Wile, Douglas 91
will 56–7
willful self 75–9
Williams, Rowan, Archbishop of
    Canterbury 6, 7, 18, 26, 27, 30, 47, 56,
    100, 148
will to power 66, 112
Wittgenstein, Ludwig 69, 160
Woolf Report 3, 18, 55
World Bank 28, 157
worldviews 36–8, 57–8
Wright, Andrew 58, 147

Zen Buddhism 66, 76, 80, 96, 139
Zen in the Art of Archery (Herrigel) 96